CALL OF THE SOUL

Answers to the big questions we ask about our lives

NIGEL BRETT

Swift Publishing Ltd,
145-157, St John Street,
London,
EC1V 4PW

© Nigel Brett.
All rights reserved.

No part of this book may be reproduced, stored in a retrieval system,
or transmitted by any means without the written permission of the author.

First published by Swift Publishing in 2016
ISBN: 978-1-911032-02-1
E-book ISBN: 978-1-911032-03-8

Contents

Foreword   5

Definitions   7

Introduction   9

Part 1: Mindfulness   11

Who am I? • Why am I alive? • What is the meaning of life? • What is happiness?
Life is against me • I wish my life was different • It's no good, I always fail
I just want to be myself • Your mind; and it matters • Keep things in perspective
Think for yourself • Count to ten • Don't worry it may never happen • Less is more
You are too impulsive • It's a habit, I can't change now • I always expect the worst
There is nothing negative about realism • Love yourself • If he/she can do it, so can I
I don't like change but change is the only constant • Be neither judge nor jury
Visualise your future • We are made up of many parts

Part 2: Mind/True Path   61

You can't be happy all of the while • I am not good enough, I have nothing to offer
Feel the fear and do it anyway • Life is a game • I feel it in my soul
Who said life was easy? • I've got it all but am still unhappy
Talent isn't rare, persistence is • Stop the world, I want to get off!
I don't know who I am anymore

Part 3: True Purpose   85

Don't flog a dead horse • Follow your dreams • There must be more to it than this
Men will be men • It's the same old story • Don't follow the crowd
Don't go with the flow, go with your flow • I am an individual, not a number
I don't know why I'm here • I never have time • Smell the roses
They are the same as us, only different

FOREWORD

I appeal to young people considering a first career, older people thinking about a change of life or even school students deciding upon A level subjects or a university degree to look first at what you love. If the love word is a bit strong for you then at the very least, please genuinely like your choices. Do your utmost to choose a direction for yourself that represents an overriding passion, an instinctive, ever-intriguing interest; something you would still do even if you had all the money or success you needed. This is the pathway that will bring happiness into your life. This is the solution to life you should be focusing your mind upon.

Do not blindly follow the well-trodden road you think leads to money, status or possessions in the belief these things will guarantee inner contentment and happiness. Many have mistakenly taken this path before only to be 'rich' and miserable or to crash down bewildered and beaten en-route.

Seek what you love doing and true happiness and success will follow. You already know in your heart and soul when doing something you love that you become absorbed with it. You persevere with it and find meaning even when overcoming obstacles or set-backs.

With this effortless level of commitment you become excellent at such an activity and it follows that by being excellent, you will be successful. What logically follows success and excellence, especially unique success and excellence, is worldly reward.

This is as natural a law of our world as night following day.

DEFINITIONS

The Universe: 'The whole system of things, comprising all people, all that is.'

Nature: 'The power that creates and regulates the world, the established order of things.'

Spiritual: 'Of the mind, the higher faculties, the soul, highly refined in thought and feeling.'

Soul: 'Innermost being or nature, that what thinks, feels, desires, the essential part of something.'

Meditate: 'To consider deeply, to reflect upon, to revolve in the mind, to intend.'

Divinity: 'The nature and essence of a god, a god-head, a celestial being.'

Purpose: 'A useful function, a definite intention.'

Meaningful: 'Of the mind and thoughts, full of significance, valid.'

Belief: 'Conviction of the truth of anything, faith.'

Affirmation: 'A solemn declaration, statement.'

INTRODUCTION

The aim of all transformation writing is to bring about a change in your life in order you may find happiness and fulfill your true potential. These are the key objectives whether the writings are philosophical, religious, spiritual, mythological, scientific, self-help or derived from psychiatric study. These key objectives remain the same whether the text is 2500 years old or written only last week.

Mankind has remained fascinated with this subject across millennia so, understandably, there is a vast amount of literature available. So much, in fact, it can be daunting and difficult to know where to begin. My research may have made only a small dent in this vast library but I did discover something significant. From among the millions of words, emerge two central and recurring themes as the twin keys to unlocking happiness. One is controlling your mind and the second is finding your true purpose. These core principles surface and overlap constantly and are explicitly linked and interdependent. Of course, the various authors, depending on their points of view or beliefs - religious or otherwise - differ in the emphasis they place on the methods employed but none of them stray far from the core principles of mindfulness and true purpose.

We read these books because as a species we need, in varying measure and at differing times; reassurance, guidance, purpose and hope in our lives. I would add belief to this list because it helps to believe. To believe there is a reason you are here, a purpose you have to fulfill, a meaning to your existence and a contentment and happiness you can achieve. All this starts with the most important belief of all which is belief in your unique self.

You will derive greater benefit from life transformation literature of any type if you believe or are prepared to. It doesn't matter where this belief comes from. It can be held on a personal spiritual level, based on a divine being or religious faith, on a scientific or philosophical conviction or just a deep-rooted gut feeling. This belief will reinforce your hope and hope is your best friend, your last refuge, the air, food and water of your mind. So, I would ask you to read this book with belief, if you are unable to commit to that at least approach it with an open mind and be prepared to believe.

As you flick through the pages I hope you will find the title phrases and emotions familiar. I also hope you will consider most of it common sense because I believe it is. However, I soon realized that although it was sense it wasn't common. People could use or hear these phrases everyday but still do nothing about them. The simple conclusion drawn was that most people didn't think deeply enough about their lives. Whether from too much rushing around, a sense of helplessness, or just unthinking inertia; it was plain most people instinctively knew the message but didn't listen to it. I hope this book will give you some pause for thought, a breather where you might stop and listen to these messages you already know.

In writing this book I have realized that hope and optimism are crucial to our existence. What we must all avoid is being trapped in small, windowless rooms without aspiration or expectation. Even if your true purpose continues to prove elusive, you must ensure you retain your positivity and freedom of mind to consider all of your opportunities. If you are already in that small room I hope this book can help with your escape.

Mindfulness

Who am I?

Why am I alive?

What is the meaning of life?

What is happiness?

Life is against me

I wish my life was different

It's no good, I always fail

I just want to be myself

Your mind; and it matters

Keep things in perspective

Think for yourself

Count to ten

Don't worry it may never happen

Less is more

You are too impulsive

It's a habit, I can't change now

I always expect the worst

There is nothing negative about realism

Love yourself

If he/she can do it, so can I

I don't like change but change is the only constant

Be neither judge nor jury

Visualise your future

We are made up of many parts

WHO AM I?

Good question, what definition or definitions can we attach to you?

We define people in lots of ways and we cannot help ourselves. We make instant assessments based upon education, upbringing, speech, age, address, job title, wealth and status, gender, race, religion and, of course, looks and appearance. We have an endless list of criteria for classifying people. Believe me when I say; if you do not know who you are there will be plenty of people ready to tell you, in fact they will fall over themselves to attach a label to you. The danger for you lies in believing it.

Another definition of you could depend on who you are in contact with at any point in time. You can be all things to all people or different things to different people it probably means the same; you are adapting who you are in response to other people. You could be an employee, employer, mother, wife, sister, daughter, aunt etc. All these titles call for a different you and carry a corresponding definition. Then, of course, there is the passage of time. Who you are now might not be who you are when you are older. Events and circumstances may change who you are on a regular basis, you will tell people that you are not the same person - you have moved on. So, we will have to keep redefining you.

It seems the question really is a good one in that there appears to be no definitive answer.
So, let me provide one.

You are the unique product of your own mind and soul. You may have a physical resemblance to your parents or greater family, you may even share some characteristics, but your soul and subconscious is singular to you. There is no other copy in the world. You will have different expectations, priorities and emotional reactions to other people whether related or not. I am a triplet who shared the same household, upbringing, education and external influences of my two sisters but, although close, we remain different people. We may have shared the same birth but our souls and subconscious remain unique and that is what defines us individually.

So, you are not a product of indoctrination derived from your culture, environment, parents, teachers, employers or anybody else although you may allow yourself, in varying degrees, to become one. The essence of you rests within your soul and subconscious and is only available to you. It is this essence or inner spirit that makes you inimitable and, if you choose to use it, is the power to enable you to think and exist independently of all else. It is your unchanging definition of yourself, your deepest meaning of what it is to be you.
It is your first and last freedom.

'We are not human beings having a spiritual experience; we are spiritual beings having a human experience.' Teilhard de Chardin.

Action: Drill down into your subconscious or soul to really know who you are. Do not be defined by changing events, circumstances or other people.

WHY AM I ALIVE?

You could never be a mistake, a surprise or unexpected. You are not the unwanted result of a casual, fleeting union or a scarcity of contraception. In your highest sense, you are not even here as a product of loving parents. You are here because you are needed.

You are alive because you have a particular purpose in life. A reason for being, a contribution to make to mankind and the universe that only you can make.

You are alive to move humankind forward if only in a miniscule way. Small steps are fine; they define the history of human achievement and the evolution of the universe. All discoveries or advancements owe their emergence to previous work, to incremental additions or improvements to what has gone before.

You have a responsibility to yourself to forge your own special destiny, the true purpose you were brought into this world for. This calls for single-mindedness and maybe some selfishness but remains the reason you are alive and where, for you, happiness and success await.

Don't question why you are alive, but rather what are you going to do to justify being alive. Dare to think, dare to be different and create something unique to you as that is why you are here. Don't feel you have to create something so new it has never been conceived of before, an addition or improvement to what is already known will do.

Musicians have used all the musical notes known to mankind in all their possible sequences millions of times but still move us forward with new music by adding their own unique interpretations and adaptations.

Before philosophy began in around 600 BC, the Greeks held a theory about the universe. According to this theory, every person and everything had their or its appointed place and appointed function. This even applied to the Olympian gods. Even then, this theory was connected to necessity, i.e. we are all necessary.

Action: Do not accept mediocrity in whatever you do, that level of achievement will never move us forward. Be courageous and find the special work in this world that is your destiny alone. The reason you are alive.

WHAT IS THE MEANING OF LIFE?

For many this remains the only question worth answering. The trouble we have with squaring a definitive answer in our minds is that the question comprises many different interpretations each with a different answer.

Does it mean what is the purpose of all of the universe and nature and why is it here? Or, are we looking for an explanation of every physical or conceptual thing that exists? Another interpretation could be what significance we attach to all of life as we know it including our own. Then we could go down the road of asking why we always feel the need to ask this question at times of personal depression or disenchantment or when we are anxious and frightened about horrific events in the wider world. That could lead us to question why there is evil in the world and what possible constructive meaning could be attached to that. The list is endless so let's concentrate on the meaning of one life; yours.

In the simplest terms, the meaning of life is what you, as a unique individual, decide to give it. The meaning of *your* life is deciding upon and then doing what is meaningful to you. The source of this meaning can be creating a life purpose that provides fulfillment and inner contentment or by experiencing something of special resonance that creates the same well-being. It can be, in part, falling in love at one end of the happiness spectrum or how you rationalise and find meaning in times of difficulty at the other.

Our sense of meaning is one our greatest gifts. You will know yourself when undertaking a task without meaning for you how difficult it is to accomplish successfully. Life without meaning is just the same. Our sense of meaning is as vital to our mental function as sight, sound, smell, touch and taste is to our physical one. Finding our individual or true meaning in life, our true course; is the foundation stone of our emotional well-being.

'Only the unfulfilment of potential is meaningless, not life itself.' Victor Frankl.

Action: Search for meaning in your life whatever your circumstances. Seek personal meaning in realizing your full potential and true purpose. If meaning remains elusive in your current work or purpose, seriously question whether it is right for you.

WHAT IS HAPPINESS?

The definition of happiness is difficult to pin down. There is no rule of thumb or general answer that fits all.

A dictionary will describe it as well-being but it not generic well-being as, individually, we can be happy at some activity or during an event when others are not. Another dictionary definition is pleasure but as we will see later in this book mere pleasure can be a destructive substitute for the lack of real happiness. As it is so difficult to establish a common blueprint for happiness we are led to the conclusion that the concept of happiness is personal and individual. Happiness is a state of mind, a state of your mind.

It is not what you are doing or who you are with. It is not how much or little you have, it is not your circumstances or events or external forces, and it is not the pursuit of transitory stimuli or pleasure. Real, lasting happiness comes from within, from your soul and subconscious. It is the control and awareness of your thinking and belief systems that will give you that permanent feeling of happiness which you wish you could bottle when you fall in love or finish your exams or successfully overcome a major challenge.

A calm and absorbed mind engaged in a meaningful (to you) purpose equates to happiness.

Nor is real happiness a hostage to events; by practising positive thinking and meaningful thought and action you can retain inner peace and contentment despite your circumstances.

Do not make the mistake of confusing happiness with pleasure. Pleasure is a temporary heightening of the senses, a generally passive or uninvolving experience. It is highs and lows, peaks and troughs. Happiness is a persistent and stable raised sense of mind and self.

'To the western world, happiness is largely a mystery. We think the most we can reasonably achieve is to avoid misery' Dalai Lama.

Action: Cultivate the habit of positive thinking for yourself and compassion for others. Seek a purpose in life that has real meaning for you as that is where you find inner happiness.

LIFE IS AGAINST ME

Do the phrases: 'It's alright for some, it's not fair, it's not my fault, I am a victim of circumstance,' sound familiar? Even if you have never uttered them at some point in your life I would wager you have heard others say them. What you are hearing is an instinctive reaction to an external reference point, an immediate and negative default emotion of allocating blame. Mindfulness is about controlling these default and negative emotions derived from external reference points and instead concentrating on your own internal strength and beliefs.

Please understand that your mind is yours to control, it is your choice how you react to events or circumstances. It always remains your choice or decision to be angry, sullen, envious, embittered and everything else that is negative and unproductive. Life may be difficult but it isn't against you, it is your own mindset that is your adversary. If you feel you are always losing in life then please consider that by thinking negatively and always being influenced by external reference points you may be defeating yourself. If you constantly drip-feed into your subconscious thoughts of your own inadequacy, you will feel inadequate and other people will perceive you as so. The subconscious mind responds to habit and habitual thinking. If you repeatedly think you are useless, that you have no chance of getting a fair deal in life or somehow there is a conspiracy against you personally, that is what your subconscious, the essence of you, will believe.

Think deeply and question your beliefs about yourself and others. Control the thoughts and images you have of yourself and allow only positive ones. Understand that we do not attract what we want, but what we are.

'Circumstances do not make a person, they reveal him' James Allen.

'A person is what he thinks about all day.' Ralph Waldo Emerson.

Action: Don't ever countenance negative thinking. Avoid blaming others when the responsibility for you lies with you. By deep reflection and meditation, focus positively on the life you want, how you view others, and the person you want to be. Write down positive affirmations and repeat them daily until they are imprinted on to your subconscious mind.

I WISH MY LIFE WAS DIFFERENT

Everyone thinks like this at some time in their lives. It could be a different job that is desired, a different place to live or even a different partner. Most times it will be a temporary doubt that will disappear as your mood lightens or as your worries come to nothing or your circumstances change. However, if it is a permanent emotion you must heed it, your subconscious is nagging at you to change something.

The good news is it's within your own power to change your life and to achieve that change quickly. However, you must be prepared to retreat into deep introspection. This will mean clearing your mind of all your usual anxieties and meditating on your core values and beliefs. You will need to drill down to who you really are and how you want to change. By doing this, you will discover the beliefs you hold about yourself, the place you believe you occupy in the world and the external influences upon you. These will be the beliefs that have got you to where you are now and these are the neural pathways of your brain that must change - if you and your life are to change.

When your mind is quiet and you are still and settled into your subconscious, question your beliefs and values. Are they really yours? Where do they come from? Are they based on any true foundation or knowledge? Why do you think they are true and do they remain so? Do they still have any relevance for you or have things changed? Can you move on? Are they right? Are they good? Are they healthy? Do they contribute? If they are negative views and beliefs about yourself and others banish them instantly and replace them with positive intentions and an open mind. Repeat these positive thoughts to yourself constantly and have real faith this change of mindset will change your life.

Do not be discouraged by where you are now and disregard short-termism. Look at your big picture, your long-term plan to change and work towards it every day if only moving forward by inches. If you want to change, think deeply about what's really important and meaningful to you. Include in this internal discussion your beliefs, standards and values in life.

All beliefs can be improved and made more positive, some may need to be discarded. Search for meaning, there is no point being efficient at something that is meaningless to you.

'Thought is best. When the mind is gathered into itself and not troubled by sights and sounds or pain and pleasure, but takes leave of the body and aspires after true being.' Socrates (attributed by Plato)

Action: Please understand the only real limitations you have in life are those you place on yourself. Your subconscious responds to habitual thinking just as your muscles respond to habitual exercise. Change your mental habits and belief systems and affirm these changes to yourself every day.

IT'S NO GOOD, I ALWAYS FAIL

Accept as a fact of life that everyone fails at something, sometime. Some of the most successful people you know will be no strangers to failure; they fail more times than many of us until they achieve what they want. The important thing is they do not view failure as an ending and they do not give up. So, failure is not personal to you but is tediously common and thank goodness it is because it is how we learn. We attempt, we fail, we reassess, we learn, and we advance. However, ensure that you don't learn to make new mistakes from old ones. It is said that one definition of insanity is to do the same thing repeatedly and expect a different result. So failure isn't the problem, it's more about your personal perception of it. Look on it as necessary and normal not as defeating and singular to you.

If you don't know what to do with your life the first step is to realize that you are here to do something, to contribute in some way to the evolution of the planet and universe. The second step is to realize that your true purpose is not only your obligation to your fellow man but to yourself in order to achieve a happy and successful life. There is no joy to be found in aimlessness, only despair.

The third step is to seek quiet and solitude and really think about what you love doing. What feels natural to you, what brings instinctive, inner satisfaction and contentment together with an effortless lifting of your spirit where you are happy without even thinking about it. While in this deep thought, write down a list of all activities or experiences which activate these feelings. Don't worry about whether you think they have anything to do with careers or paid work. Then write down the recurring thoughts or beliefs in your life that you feel define you. These will be things like the following: It is better to be kind than nasty, I want to help people, I prefer to travel light, material things do not really interest me, I prefer nature to the city, I enjoy solitude rather than crowds, quiet rather than bustle, inner contentment rather than status, to walk unnoticed rather than be famous or a million other variations or opposites. Now compare the two lists; one listing where you are naturally happy and the other listing which defines the essential you. You will discover some synergy and relationship, somewhere in these lists will be a pointer to the purpose in life which is right for you. Think deeply about it.

'...............if you can meet with triumph and disaster and treat these two imposters just the same...........' Rudyard Kipling.

Action: Don't beat yourself up about failing. Failure is as normal as success and merely a precursor to it. Continue to seek your true purpose, as when you find it you will also discover that neither success or failure will affect you.

I JUST WANT TO BE MYSELF

If you have said this to yourself, you have made a good start in understanding why you are here and what you should do with your life. You are not alone in thinking this way, mankind and the universe wants you to be yourself as well in order you can move us all forward in a constructive way. When saying I want to be myself, you are voicing you are unique, have a distinct purpose in life and you have something special to offer us all.

All humans have three basic needs, all beginning with P.
Physiological: air, water and food.
Psychological: security, love, self-esteem, acceptance.
Purpose: personal development or true design.
Once the first two are achieved, humankind turns to the third for their reason for being.

Most of us strive throughout our lives, most of the time at tasks we do not like, to achieve power, position or possessions at levels far in excess of our basic needs. I call these three P's the anti-needs. In the process, we not only risk unhappiness, stress, ill-health, dissatisfaction or a, *'what's it all about?'* disillusionment but we lose sight of who we really are. In our misguided rush to have we forget to be. We completely lose sight of the third basic need of true purpose.

The person who is true to themselves, who really wants to find and act as their true self does not strive and want all the time but raises their thinking above the common aspirations of man. They become absorbed with and mentally free to develop their own purpose.

'Why do we set our standard of sanity so low? Can we imagine no better model than the dutiful consumer or the well-adjusted breadwinner? Why not the saint, the sage, the artist? Why not all that is finest in our species?' Abraham Maslow.

Action: Rise above the everyday. Glory in your uniqueness. Don't be taken in by society's material enticements but see them for the anti-needs they are. Ignore perceived restrictions of culture and environment. Free your mind, raise your expectations of life, raise your own standards and believe in your individual purpose.

IT'S YOUR MIND, AND IT MATTERS

How many times have you heard: 'I can't help it, it's just the way I am' or 'I'd like to do that but I'm scared .....'

All your emotions, behaviours, beliefs, moods, actions or non-actions, pessimism or optimism originate from your own thoughts. Of course, external events may play a part but as you retain the ultimate choice of how to respond to anything that happens to you, your emotions remain stubbornly self-generated. They originate with you.

So, if your emotions and subsequent actions are negative or destructive it is because you allow the thoughts dripping into your subconscious to be. You inadvertently become your own self-fulfilling, doomsday prophecy. If you believe nothing else in this book I urge you to believe this.

Because we can help ourselves and eliminate the fear of changing our beliefs and we can achieve this because we are capable of exercising mind over matter. We can banish negative and destructive thoughts from our subconscious or essence and replace them with positive, constructive ones. Our choices and decisions in life are based on our myriad experiences to-date. These are stored in our subconscious and our belief systems are established. Whatever interpretation (or belief) we have placed upon our experience will be treated by our subconscious as real and accurate, whether it is or not, and it is these belief systems that will dictate our decisions in life.

The basic motivating thought in the human mind is the movement toward pleasure or the movement away from pain. Our thought processes and decisions are based on these two opposing drivers and we interpret our experiences based on the pull between them. This is why we refuse to put our hands in boiling water but avoid quitting smoking even though intellectually we know both represent harm or pain to us. It is the belief system we place upon either pain or pleasure that dictates what we think about them not intelligent reasoning. Hence we correctly associate our hands and boiling water with pain and move away from it but as committed smokers we associate more fear or pain with the withdrawal symptoms of quitting so consider it more pleasurable to continue, contrary to any rational, intelligent analysis.

The same, of course, could be said of any addiction or negative thought – we have the wrong association with it. These associations between pain and pleasure are enacted by the brain. The more the association is employed or reinforced the more the brain accepts it as real and more neural pathways are opened up or existing ones widened so the brain can process these associations effortlessly. The brain does not compute whether what it is doing is right or wrong it simply carries out your instructions. It won't help you unless you help it.

It follows, therefore, that we must change our belief systems to change our lives. We must change those associations we have with pain and pleasure. If you are an addict this will mean associating more pain with continuing with your addiction than stopping it. You must close the neural pathways in your brain that accept your addiction as pleasure and replace them with new ones that associate it with pain. If you constantly think like this and reaffirm it by writing down or voicing these new thoughts your brain will eventually go into automatic mode just as it does with the boiling water.

'The unexamined life is not worth living.' Plato.

Action: Know that you can change your thoughts and beliefs. You can introduce all kinds of new possibilities into your mind. Both the subconscious and brain are yours to command. Question your existing beliefs and, if necessary, change them by repeated affirmations of your new way of thinking, the new meanings you allocate between pain and pleasure.

KEEP THINGS IN PERSPECTIVE

This simple phrase is of critical importance to your mental well-being and can be achieved by observing a few basic rules. Try to avoid cluttering your mind with things that do not matter and don't elevate insignificant events into great dramas. Accept people as they are not as you want them to be and look upon events as happening because they are predestined among the greater scheme of things. If you do not, you are simply clogging up your thought processes with froth and turbulence when you should be clearing them to consider your bigger picture.

This is not a phenomenon new to our multi-faceted, fast-paced society. In 300BC the Greek Stoicism school of thought extolled, among other things, acceptance of events and avoidance of pettiness and trivia to be able to concentrate on the things that matter in life.

Try to avoid judging and analyzing everything you come across. Avoid a running commentary in your mind about whether things are good or bad. Stop constantly evaluating whether things are right or wrong. If you mind is constantly cataloguing, classifying, categorizing and judging it will always be crammed full of stuff most of which is unimportant to you. This mental turbulence not only wastes your life energy but also never allows your mind to achieve the stillness it requires for truly creative and constructive thought.

Imagine your mind as a mountain lake on a windless day when the surface of the lake is still like reflective glass. If you place an idea or intention into this stillness it will ripple and grow outwards with ease like a small stone tossed into the placid waters. If the wind is howling and churning up wavelets on the lake or if torrential rain is punching holes into its surface you could throw a boulder into it and see nothing.

'Sometimes we just don't know. It is the West's way to always try and find the causes and reasons for things – which can lead to a type of agony when you cannot find an answer.' Dalai Lama.

Action: Free your mind from froth and turbulence. Only think deeply about things that are meaningful to you. Accept that sometimes the meaning of something will not be evident. Don't worry about it, not everything in life can be explained or analysed immediately. Sometimes, life just is.

THINK FOR YOURSELF

No matter what happens to you in life you still have the capacity of freedom of mind. The freedom to interpret and react to an event or set of circumstances in the way that you, and only you, choose. If you are in a situation where all is stripped away from you only a deep understanding of yourself together with the capacity to find some meaning for your life, even in the most difficult times, will help you. Material possessions will be revealed as the transient, unimportant things they are.

Those of us who appreciate stillness and deep thought live in greater accord with their true selves and their link with the deeper intelligence of nature and the universe. Of course, it is easier to let others think for you. That is why most people choose this option.

Let your employers tell you when to work and when to relax, advertisers tell you what to buy, supermarkets tell you what to eat, society and culture to instruct you on how to conform to their idea of living and thinking and the list could go on. But if you can achieve a true independence of mind, if you can really know yourself and your link or oneness with all that has been created then you will achieve peace of mind whatever life throws at you.

'Do not fear the ocean storms, dark forests or high mountains, nor try to conquer them. You are as one, you are siblings – you share your birth.' Author.

Action: By silence, solitude and reflection; think deeply about what constitutes the essence of you. Open your mind to the collective intelligence of the universe, nature and creation and, at your deepest level, your inherent oneness with it.

COUNT TO TEN

How many times have you reacted in a way you later regretted? How many times, after a period of reflection, have you said to yourself I could have handled that situation better?

When questioning yourself in this way you have realized that you must not allow your negative emotions to define you and the way you react.

All emotions drain your life force. All personal emotions are energy that is mixed and distributed with all energy in the universe. All this energy is recycled, given and received, in constant movement and shared around. What goes around comes around.

The sharing of good or constructive energy is what makes the universe and all of creation work. It makes the universe flow to the benefit of all those who can tap into it. Conversely, destructive or negative energy will not only be of little benefit to the universe or yourself, it will flow back to you. What you give out you will receive by return.

Negative energy is the result of wrong thinking. Cognitive psychologists believe depression or acute anxiety is the product of wrong thinking. What is agreed by all is that debilitating and negative thought is both draining and self-fulfilling.

Default-mode, instant thoughts create our anger not actual events. If you can be in control of your mind you can chose your response to any situation. If you rein in your emotions of anger and retain your self-esteem, you will avoid releasing negative energy into the universe. Next time you confront a situation where your instant reaction is anger; stop and consider if that emotion is going to change or improve the situation. Understanding and compassion might be much more effective.

'Anyone can become angry – that is easy. But to be angry with the right person, to the right degree, at the right time, for the right purpose and in the right way – that is not easy.' Aristotle.

Action: Don't waste your own energy and contaminate the energy flow of the universe on negative emotions. Think before allowing frustration and anger to be your automatic response to trying situations.

DON'T WORRY, IT MAY NEVER HAPPEN

People worry all of the time, every hour, every day, week in–week out. Deprived of personal worries, they will worry for other people. If they have no major worries, they will worry over insignificant things or illogically on things over which they have no control such as the weather. If the present doesn't offer enough worries they will turn their attention to worrying over an imaginary future.

Let me tell you now, ninety percent of what we worry about doesn't happen. Therefore, the vast proportion of our time we spend worrying is an exercise in futility.

In the nine times out of ten the fearful, frantic, negative emotion we call worry invades our consciousness, to the exclusion of more positive or creative thinking, it is on a wholly unsubstantiated premise and with no productive purpose. The great wonder of the future is that it is unknown, uncharted and unidentifiable. It is filled with endless opportunities and potential if only you would clear your mind of worrying about it and concentrate instead on creating the life you want within it.

If you can picture this life that is right for you and see your true purpose, you will be absorbed and contented in your task. You will not worry about specific outcomes or destinations, to be on the right journey will be enough. If you are on your true path and in accord with the greater intelligence of the universe you can let tomorrow sort itself out.

This eastern spiritual philosophy of detachment from outcomes does not preclude having goals or plans. It merely means that you should not stake your own self-esteem on achieving them. Ask yourself, does it really need the shock of death or disaster before we stop and say, 'That puts things in perspective doesn't it? We've got nothing to worry about.' The answer is it shouldn't, this mindset should be with us constantly.

'The circumstances of men's lives do much to determine their philosophy but, conversely, their philosophy does much to determine their circumstances.' Bertrand Russell.

Action: Relax and live for the moment, not what might be. Clear your mind of futile, negative thinking and concentrate instead on your life vision.

LESS IS MORE

There is a clear logic to the reasoning that the more possessions we accumulate the more stuff we have to concern ourselves with, the more we have to worry about, and the more our minds become as cluttered as our lives. These worries are not just about our attachment to these possessions and the attendant fear of loss we create, but also about earning yet more money to maintain them or replace them with the latest must-have.

This kind of thinking not only lacks depth but can be self-defeating. It can lead to a vicious circle of wanting, worrying, working, wanting more, worrying more and working more. Most of us give scant regard to the actual usefulness or worth of these possessions and no thought at all about the accumulation of worry they represent. After the initial high, our main emotion is a weary acceptance that we must work all hours God sends in employment that may drain and enslave our soul just to pay for them.

We no longer make decisions based on need but on want. We are devoid of self-knowledge. We define ourselves by what we own not who we are. The motor car has long ceased to be a mode of transport for people rather it has become a social statement, a substitute identity. It says, look at me, this car will tell you who I am because I cannot.

Worst of all, when we realize we have sold our soul, we also realize we are trapped in the spiral, we are signed-up members, we are contracted, we have made our Faustian pacts. So what do we do? We buy more and better 'things' to compensate ourselves for having no escape and the spiral accelerates. We continually purchase fleeting pleasure in compensation for life-long discontent. I hope you will agree this is not a great deal – we seem hooked on the sales pitch of the snake-oil salesman.

When living like this, our lives are not based upon any idea we might have of a purpose that offers contentment and stable happiness but purely on the temporary, ephemeral highs of ownership of 'things'. Even when we own them it is not enough. We then strive for bigger, faster, more modern, more high-tech, more luxurious, more status-laden 'things'. We have lost sight of who we are. We have abdicated responsibility and transferred the definition and essence of ourselves on to what we possess.

Sorrow, fear and worry arise from what is dear to us. While these negative, debilitating emotions are understandable (if controllable) in regard to family and loved ones, they are inexcusable in regard to the accumulation of 'things'.

Fundamentally, if you have not acquired profound self-knowledge or possess a meaningful direction for your life, then you own nothing of worth.

'It is hard to fight one's heart's desire. Whatever it wishes to get, it purchases at the cost of soul.' Heraclitus.

'Possessions and all things we think we need only serve to distract us.' Diogenes.

Action: Practise the philosophy of non-attachment and wanting less. Understand that constantly wanting simply illustrates inner dissatisfaction, lack of true direction and the absence of knowledge of your own real self. De-clutter, see these anti-needs for what they really are, and divert your thoughts to finding the purpose that will give you true happiness and success.

YOU ARE TOO IMPULSIVE

You need emotional intelligence or quotient to be successful in the world of today. EQ is as important, if not more so, than IQ. Intelligence alone will not get you far if you cannot control your emotions and the way you communicate with those around you.

Immediate or impulsive emotions are formed by our habitual thinking and beliefs and like various habits they can be destructive. By unlearning some emotions and creating new ones we can gain control of our lives and interact more successfully with others. Unless you are a wandering mystic or a hermit in a cave, the key to your success in this life is not intelligence in varying degrees but lies in your ability to interact productively with the people you come into contact with.

Intelligence quotient alone is not a good predictor of achievement. If you lack emotional intelligence, if you act and speak impulsively without thinking, if you alienate others when you should be empathizing and influencing them, if you default to anger just because you are faced with anger, if you prefer to shout instead of listen, if you feel compassion is for losers, if you pre-judge people without knowing them or if you automatically fight fire with fire; then you will never move our world forward or achieve true happiness and a sense of well-being and achievement.

'Hate is not conquered by hate, hate is conquered by love. This is law eternal. '

'Overcome anger by non-anger, overcome evil by good, overcome the miser by giving and overcome the liar by truth.' The Dhammapada (teachings of Buddha)

Action: Raise your standard of thinking. Think carefully before you speak and act and appreciate what others may be genuinely thinking and feeling. Empathy, listening and compassion will move people forward and influence them, not instinctive criticism or condemnation.

IT'S A HABIT, I CAN'T CHANGE NOW

Just because you have always thought in a particular way it doesn't mean you cannot change it, un-think it. You can change the way you look at life by challenging and releasing yourself from unconsciously accepted mental habits and norms. For instance, instead of instinctively saying, 'I better not do it' try changing it to, 'how can I do it better.'

Have a spring clean of your mind. Question your ingrained beliefs and perceptions. Look at things differently, in a new light, from a new perspective as an artist would trying to capture a subject by imagining they were looking at it for the first time. By this positive act you are creating mindfulness within yourself. By doing nothing, by never questioning, never looking at things anew, never considering there may be different viewpoints, possibilities and answers; you are being mindless not mindful.

Listen to your intuition, to the quiet but persistent voices or nagging thoughts in your head. These provide a good route to mindfulness because by their very nature they are outside of your normal thoughts and beliefs. They go against convention which is always a positive mental step. Their employment requires you to ignore previous interpretations of your experience and consider something different to your normal beliefs.

Thinking differently and questioning how you view things is highly valued by our world as thinking outside of the box. It is valuable as it's not only an expression of uniqueness but it also offers a rarity - a non-habitual vision aka an original thought. It offers the world something different and sets you apart from the mass of sameness.

'Genius…..means little more than the faculty of perceiving in a non-habitual way.' William James.

Action: Escape the blinkered, mindless striving of most modern lives. Do not permanently categorize yourself, others or things as unchanging and immutable. Ask yourself, where is the progress in unthinkingly accepting parameters just because, at this moment in time, they appear to be the norm.

I ALWAYS EXPECT THE WORST

As already discussed, there is no logic, scientific reasoning or natural law to suggest that pessimism is somehow more realistic than optimism. We know that 90% of what we worry about never happens so we must really start to question the validity of worrying. It is not foresight because that indicates some level of accuracy and it is not pre-planning which is merely reasoned anticipation and preparation. To arbitrarily expect the worst is not anything, it is aimless, negative conjecture which offers nothing of value. In fact, it offers the reverse - debilitating and frantic thinking, de-motivation and inertia.

When you next question positive thinking as some pie-in-the-sky, utopian, cure-all please consider how illogical the alternative is.

To expect the worst is a defence people employ against expectation and hope. A barrier erected against possible disappointment and disillusionment, a limiter which will confine them to spending their lives in small rooms. Ask yourself, why you would want to stifle hope? It is the most vital belief in life, the thought that keeps us going, and your last friend standing when all else has been stripped away.

Why would you want to commence a journey with the mindset the destination is going to be unsatisfactory or impossible to reach? The answer is you wouldn't - the result is you don't. People who always think the worst seriously limit their journeys and opportunities in life.

Change your outlook and really have faith that you can fulfill your potential. Consider dreams, journeys and pathways in your mind that you will love, do not concern yourself with ever reaching a specific destination or objective. Believe in yourself and you will master the fear of taking the first step. Have faith that you have a unique purpose which is why you are part of this world. Believe your individual destiny is part of the universe's destiny; that you are not on your own, there is a higher power we are all linked with. Have real faith there is something greater than our individual minds, a unifying intelligence that will help us once we start to help ourselves.

'Doubt closes the power flow (of God or the universe), faith opens it.' Norman Vincent Peale.

Action: Start your individual journey, do not worry about outcomes and have faith that when you are on your true path it will be made easy for you. As this is the path you have been allotted, the road you were meant to travel.

THERE IS NOTHING NEGATIVE ABOUT REALISM

Your true purpose will not be something impossible or unobtainable. It will not be beyond your natural talent, physical capabilities or mental faculties. Your purpose among the great scheme of things will only require you to contribute to the evolution of our intelligence, compassion and understanding in small steps, in achievable ways. So, remain open and optimistic to all the possibilities and potential you have but realize you are not going to fly to Saturn powered by your own rocket boots in your lifetime.

While positive thinking should always be employed, realism is important when considering your true purpose in life. If you were born with a disability which limits your movement then you are not going to break the world mile record but you could smash the para-olympic time. If you are tone-deaf you are unlikely to compose haunting, evocative music but you could still write beautiful lyrics or poetry. If you couldn't understand elementary mathematics at school, in all probability you will not have a career as a nuclear physicist or cosmologist but that wouldn't stop you discovering a new star.

Like good and bad human cholesterol, we can consider good and bad pessimism. Bad is ill-considered, unenlightened, doom-ridden conjecture created by belief systems which are paralysed by an habitual drip-feed of negative thought. Good pessimism is more like realism, it accepts the habit of optimism brings confidence and success but guards against unachievable expectation. It perceives present reality accurately while at the same time allowing the visualization of a compelling future.

It is also useful in assessing failure and mistakes. While bad pessimism would see them as insurmountable obstacles, the good will be realistic enough to see them as temporary problems that offer opportunities of readjustment and advancement. It recognizes set-backs as a means to step forward; it sees problems as temporary, external and specific and not a reflection on you as a person.

'What we want is not blind optimism, but flexible optimism – optimism with our eyes open. We must be able to see pessimism's keen sense of reality when needed but without dwelling in its dark shadows.' Martin Seligman.

Action: Do not discount pessimism in its realistic sense. Used in a sensible way it is our guide to keeping our feet on the ground and our dreams achievable.

LOVE YOURSELF

This is a prerequisite of enjoying a happy and contented life.

It is the foundation stone from which the rest of your life is built, the spectrum through which you view the world and how the world views you. If you do not know and love yourself, you will be unable to give love to anyone else, your view of life will be opaque and your decision-making confused.

This does not mean loving yourself in a narcissistic way. That is, finding sensual gratification in your own body or excessive admiration of your own beauty. That is inward looking, shallow, lacks benefit or meaning and is ultimately destructive. Loving yourself in the right way involves seeking the best person you can be. Your thoughts and standards are at a high level, you have compassion and empathy for your fellow man, you don't covet or envy and you seek to know your true self and your true purpose. You question yourself in order to improve but do not run yourself down by endless self-criticism. You realize that whatever you concentrate on increases so you do not dwell on negative things. You think positively, with daily affirmations if necessary, to improve your well-being and the well-being of those you come into contact with.

When you love yourself in the right way it will be easier to find a purpose in life that you love. You will deal with your life difficulties before they appear insurmountable and you focus on your possibilities not your problems as the latter incubates despair while the former provides hope and motivation. If you can love yourself you will be able to love and understand other people.

They will love you in return as you will be able to offer them what they need which is attention, acceptance, reassurance, guidance and purpose. You know this to be true as when you feel really good about yourself you want others to feel just as good.

'A good man should love himself, but nobly.' Aristotle.

'I cannot make my days any longer, so I will strive to make them better.' Henry David Thoreau.

Action: You need to be happy in your own skin before you can move forward. Change your mindset from what you are to the person you really feel you can be. Raise your standards and be the best you are able but don't constantly beat yourself up about it. If you are genuinely trying you are winning.

IF HE/SHE CAN DO IT, SO CAN I

On the basis we are all equally capable of achieving our true, individual potential the above page heading is true. However, if you believe that just because someone else has written a best-selling novel, climbed all eight Himalayan peaks over 8000' or built up a multi-million pound business empire; you will be able to do exactly the same; that is untrue.

Of course, that might not stop you trying and good luck to you. However, be aware your true potential and purpose is individual, it will not be the same as the next person. You will achieve something different. But what someone else has achieved in whatever field, what obstacles of upbringing, culture or environment they have overcome, the mistakes and failures they have encountered, the external pressures they have resisted to be successful - together with the inspiration all these things provide - will be very relevant to you in achieving your own true purpose and potential.

So, in the sense that individuals are constantly achieving a myriad of amazing things and with the realization that, whatever the chosen pathway, the mindset required and the obstacles encountered are very similar, it is a natural rule that if he/she can do it, you can too.

To share the experience and learning of others is not only what our universe is really about - a linked, collective intelligence - but also saves time and forearms you on your own journey. To model the actions and behaviours of successful people and be aware of their failures en-route to that success is an excellent springboard to achieving the same fulfilling lives as them.

Although you can aim high it is also important to maintain a sense of realism. Empedocles was a fifth century BC Greek politician, scientist and philosopher who also thought he was a god. It was said he leapt into a volcano to prove his immortality. A contemporary poet wrote:
'Great Empedocles, that ardent soul
Leapt into Etna, and was roasted whole.'

Action: Know that you can change the set of your mind if you constantly instruct your brain to do so. You can put your mind to anything you naturally love doing. To study and learn from others is the natural way of things but modeling does not mean copying. Your life purpose will be individual to you.

I DON'T LIKE CHANGE, BUT CHANGE IS THE ONLY CONSTANT

Please accept that things will not remain the same during our lives. Accept we will not be the same people doing the same things or thinking the same thoughts throughout our mortal span. Our lives are not static or stuck in time. We are part of an evolutionary universe, a constantly moving and changing entity. In this sense, all external stability will be temporary, change will be constant.

Luckily, change is usually incremental; we have time to adjust to it. That is why the sudden death of a young and healthy person is more shocking than the death of one who is old and ill. The premature death was beyond our expectation and, therefore, more unnerving as it gave us no time to mentally adjust.

We also have our own inner mental stability to help us with change and part of that is acknowledging the transitory nature of the universe and how we are going to deal with that movement. Endings and new beginnings, death and rebirth, stability then change, advancement and progression are part of the natural order of things and we have to have the internal mental strength to cope; as to go on as a species is what we do. To manage this, we must accept, recognize and embrace the stages of transition.

The first stage to a new beginning is to acknowledge an ending. Do not think of endings or the death of a loved one as a final destroying conclusion or, despairingly, that all that was has now gone. All things are recycled into the energy of our universe.

All things that were, still are; otherwise, among other things, we would not have memories. Greek philosopher Parmenides argued this case in circa 475 BC by stating that when you think you must think of something, when you speak a name it must be the name of something. So, whatever can be thought of or spoken about must exist at all times. I think this is a better way to view the loss of a loved one.

The second stage is the feeling of void or loss left behind. Here we must ensure we take time to retreat into quiet seclusion and thought. We must allow our mind time to adjust and reconcile with losing what was, to accepting what now is. Conversely, if we have left a job or relationship that clearly wasn't right for us we might feel elation. However, we still need to temper that delicious sense of freedom with quiet reflection on our new opportunities and direction. We want to avoid the frying pan and fire syndrome.

Out of stage two will emerge stage three. It may not be immediately obvious, may only be appreciated in retrospect; but new realisations, beginnings, opportunities and new hope and optimism will be the nature of stage three.

The search for something permanent is one of the deepest instincts of man hence that lure of religion which offers God and immortality. However, the idea of perpetual flux or change has also been around a long time. 500 years before Christ was born it was accepted by Heraclitus and other Greek philosophers.

'You cannot step twice into the same river, as fresh waters are ever flowing in upon you.' Plato.

Action: Do not crave unending external stability because that is against the evolutionary nature of the universe. Accept transition as a progression forward, do not fear or fight it. Remain internally strong and grow as a person from it. Remember that evolution or change is only the movement of learning more.

BE NEITHER JUDGE NOR JURY

People who are genuinely influential are so because they understand the core human needs of acceptance and self-esteem. They understand that if you are trying to influence people, criticism and condemnation are invariably counter-productive. They know that an appreciation of a point of view, the acknowledgement of the right to voice it and the ability to listen and really try to understand will be much more productive.

Criticism of people generally makes them feel worse about themselves so they become defensive, withdrawn, incommunicative and further entrenched in their own views. Although your purpose may be to encourage them forward the result will be that you have kicked them back. Their heels will be firmly dug in or they will be in full retreat. You will have hurt them and where before there was a basis for constructive dialogue - a meeting of minds - you now face a siege mentality or outright hostility.

The way to influence people, whether toward a point of view or to gain their appreciation and respect, is to listen intently and try to understand them. If you really listen and really try to understand, people will reciprocate in kind.

It is a law of human nature that people are much more interested in their own needs, desires and problems than they are in ours or the problems of the rest of mankind. Their recent pay cut or hernia operation is of far more importance to them than your triple heart bypass or devastating civil war and widespread famine in a far-off land. If you want to influence them let them speak. It isn't your role to judge their priorities or to judge them as a person; in many cases you will not know them well enough to even attempt an informed opinion. It's your role to make them feel better about themselves, to move them forward. Shouting them down, talking over them, or trying to impress them or onlookers with what you believe to be your greater intellect will not achieve this advancement. If you listen to people and try to understand them, they will warm to you and be more likely to view you as a friend or wise counsel, more likely to consider your opinion valuable.

We humans are too quick to pigeon-hole, rank, grade, and pass judgement on our fellow beings. This is often done on sight, in complete ignorance, in an attempt to bolster low personal self-esteem, and with no regard for the feelings of the judged. If you think about this, it says a lot more about the inadequacies of the judge than the judged.

Those who suffer most with personal insecurity and lack of self-knowledge justify themselves by condemning others. Instead of seeking personal enlightenment, they prefer to denigrate other people in order to make themselves appear better. They fail others and they fail themselves.

In the game of life, you will be constantly interacting with other people and you must, therefore, know the rules of human nature. You will need to employ emotional intelligence as, although your true purpose will be an individual one, it will require the involvement of others to achieve it. If you want influence, if you want to make friends, if you want your mind to be open and positive then don't arbitrarily judge others but try to understand and help them.

'Instead of condemning people, let's try to understand why they do what they do. That's a lot more profitable and intriguing than criticism; and it breeds sympathy, tolerance and kindness.' Dale Carnegie.

Action: You will not be popular if you treat life as a competitive power game of one-upmanship. Improve your own mental state in order to empathise with the people you meet and move them forward. If you cannot say anything constructive, then seriously consider saying nothing at all.

VISUALISE YOUR FUTURE

If you cannot see it, no-one else will. If you do not have a clear image within your mind of what you want to be and where you want to go, other people, who could help, will not be able to see your purpose clearly either.

Understand that your life tends to enact itself on the basis of the mental images you have of it. In the same way as how we think about ourselves, it is not relevant to our brain or subconscious how we picture ourselves. Whether these images are good, bad or indifferent they will be processed and reinforced as the truth in our brain. They will be the images we believe of ourselves.

Accepting this premise, why not imagine a future you really want? Plant positive images into your brain not negative ones. To visualize the future you want and to picture a positive action or purpose is a proven mental technique toward achieving that goal. Just like positive thought processes you are opening up new neural pathways in your brain; you are giving your brain and subconscious new and exciting, high-definition opportunities to work with.

Quiet your mind, banish everyday worries and trivia, seek solitude and deep thought and concentrate on things that really matter to you. Put pictures into your mind of what you want, put more pictures into your mind of doing what you want… effortlessly. Repeat this mental relaxation every day until the pictures become automatic to you, become your visual default setting.

Your brain will then be alerted to the fact it needs to enact them for you and it will work constantly towards that end. Have you noticed in your dreams that you can achieve any task effortlessly? It is the same if you feed and have faith in the power of your subconscious and brain.

In the physical world everything, including humankind, is made up of particles of energy moving and contributing within the universe. The image or thought energy of our imaginations is no less real and is no less at one with the universe. If you can believe your own true purpose is also at one with the greater intelligence and abundant energy of the universe, you will harness its unlimited power to fulfill your destiny.

If you find this belief difficult, consider for a moment what is constantly being created and maintained by our universe; what has already been created since the Big Bang, what will be created in the future, what was once nothing but is now actual, what was once dust and gas but is now solid or what was once uncreated but is now created. Everything we can see, hear, smell, touch and taste in this world has evolved from the unmade to the made. There is indisputably a power, purpose and intelligence to this.

'Creative visualization is magic in the truest and highest meaning of the word. It involves understanding and aligning yourself with the natural principles that govern the workings of our universe.' Shakti Gawain.

Action: We all use our imaginations so use yours to picture the future you want for yourself. Believe that when you walk your true path, in the direction meant for you; you walk in step with a greater intelligence and purpose.

WE ARE MADE UP OF MANY PARTS

Like the universe; our lives are a progression, a movement, an evolution. What defines us, what provides meaning to us, will change. We are all made up of different characteristics, traits or idiosyncrasies that shape how we act and think. These could be viewed as archetypes or models and they inform our behaviour and needs. These models represent aspects of ourselves that are apparent in the different situations we face or they can change as we develop through the different stages of our lives. This is why you will hear people saying, 'That used to be important to me, but now my priorities have changed.'

We need to recognize and understand these archetypes in order to know where we are in our lives and to decide if we need to change to a different model or, at least, merge with aspects of another model to refine our thinking.

The Orphan model is one of feeling victimized and dependant, so orphans seek safety. The Wanderer model is when we feel lost and alienated, where there is a call to the road or a new life. The Warrior personality is less about fighting others but more about harnessing the strength in ourselves to push forward, vanquish doubt and limitations and go for what we want.

The Altruist stage of life is perhaps when we want to give something back to the world, when we are looking beyond money and lifestyle success and looking for higher meaning for our actions. The Innocent archetype feels a yearning to return to the innocence of their youth when everything held possibility and we had an innate faith our lives would work out. Finally, the Magician personality will, like the Innocent want to trust in the universe to provide but will also be willing to make a stand, to change the world, to transform themselves and humankind.

It is important to know these different patterns of the human psyche to be able to recognize where you fit into them in any given situation or at any given stage of life. Only this recognition will allow you make informed decisions about changing or refining the person you are and then only action will achieve it.

Socrates agreed with fellow Greek philosophers Protagorus and Heraclitus that everything is always changing. In a quote attributed to him by Plato he says:

'All the things we are pleased to say are; really are in the process of becoming.'

Action: All these archetypes are within us and come to the fore in different situations and stages in our lives. Question which one is paramount within you and then decide what you need to change. If you take action to change your archetype you will find that your perception of the world will change with it.

Mind/True Path

You can't be happy all of the while

I am not good enough, I have nothing to offer

Feel the fear and do it anyway

Life is a game

I feel it in my soul

Who said life was easy?

I've got it all but am still unhappy

Talent isn't rare, persistence is

Stop the world, I want to get off!

I don't know who I am anymore

YOU CAN'T BE HAPPY ALL OF THE WHILE

Do not be surprised or disheartened by suffering and misery in life. It is a part of living that has always been, is now, and will always be. You are not a robot so accept it as one defining aspect of being human. But be a wise sufferer. See the logic in how you are feeling and understand your emotions will die down, that you will move forward having learned something about yourself.

Do not rely on others for your happiness. If you pin all your hopes of happiness on others you could be riding for a fall. You may suffer disappointment more than most or experience loss and disillusionment more than you should. Find and nurture your happiness from within and counter external events with your internal resolve and inner contentment. Seek your own deepest passion or love. This can include a person but only if they can help you find or follow the purpose that is right for you, the something deep inside you which you know will bring you inner peace and contentment despite external events.

To place your entire sense of meaning and stability in life on a compulsive love of another is to rely upon a fragile foundation. You will be dependent on that other person and they will feel the pressure of that dependency. Because you are so irrationally attached, because your life-happiness eggs are all in one basket, you will live in fear of the loss of this love. Because this is all you have, you may become paranoid about it and seek to control it, enslave it and, along with your own meaning in life, ultimately destroy it.

This is not inner contentment but anguish. You are placing all your hopes and dreams on external factors not inner belief. This will not give you the internal strength to face suffering or disappointment.

In addition, this neediness, this supine expectation of another to shoulder the responsibility for your life happiness will not be attractive to an existing or potential life partner. People are drawn to people who are happy within themselves, who exhibit a healthy self-worth and independence, not to people who crave another person simply to fill a lack of meaning in their own lives or to give them a reason to exist.

The art of living is not about possessing another human being or wealth accumulation nor is it about consumption or a rich lifestyle. It is about finding self-worth and self-meaning despite other people, external events and circumstances, not because of them.

'The stubborn reoccurrence of misery means the development of a workable approach to it must outstrip the value of any utopian quest for happiness.' Proust.

Action: Accept there will be some unhappiness in your life but do not let it define you. Don't rely on others, know that only your own inner strength will allow you to face suffering, find logic in it, grow from it and move forward.

I'M NOT GOOD ENOUGH, I HAVE NOTHING TO OFFER

If you feel like this you are probably trying too hard at the wrong thing. Everyone has something to offer that is why we are here but we cannot all offer the same thing.

We are all naturally good at some things where the work we are engaged in seems easy, enjoyable and effortless. Conversely, we are all naturally less able at other tasks. Here we find the work tedious, we struggle to concentrate and to find meaning in it, we expend lots of energy but it remains stubbornly difficult. For us, it is not natural or flowing. Choosing this difficult way is arguably justifiable for progressing through an exam system to enable us to get to a stage where we can specialize or when attempting temporary, unimportant tasks such as hanging wallpaper or assembling flat-pack furniture but is totally unacceptable when seeking your true purpose in life. It leads to throwing your rattle out of the pram, to pitching your shovel over the hedge; it leads to frustration and disillusionment.

Do not base your life purpose on flawed assumptions or reasoning. Do not join the armed forces because the money and security are good and you will get to travel, if in your soul you abhor violence or find communal living distasteful. Don't try to master written Greek just to prove your intellectual prowess or impress others if the exercise holds no meaning or interest for you. Certainly don't chose a career or life purpose solely because you think it will make the most money and by accumulating this aspect of wealth you will miraculously accumulate happiness and contentment at the same time.

Equally, do not automatically default to what is expected (or not) of you by parents and teachers or be limited by culture and environment and all the other outside influences upon you. Don't let your ego or social, outer self make these crucial decisions for you. It should be your deep inner self, the essential self of your soul and subconscious that decides. You must look to what you love doing above all else as this is the clearest guide you have to your true purpose and life happiness.

When you seek the spiritual path of least resistance (doing something you love), when you attune your life with the laws of nature and the universe instead of going against them; you will detach yourself from specific outcomes, you won't feel the need to force solutions but instinctively know that resolutions will happen and you will strive less but accomplish more. If you are tune with yourself you will be calm and patient, you will intuitively appreciate that it is the evolutionary way of nature and the universe to bring order from chaos. Even in difficult situations, you will accept the moment is as it is meant to be and learn from it.

You will not feel superior or inferior. You will not envy you friend's luxury cars and large houses as you feel no need of these things and you will relish the journey you are on without worrying about the destination. Because you are contented and fulfilled, you will be happy to share this well-being by way of giving to others. You will understand you can offer and give plenty of things that do not involve money. Time, helpful words, kind thoughts and blessings cost nothing. This all achieved by walking in step with the reason you exist; doing something you love and moving the world forward.

Everyone has something to offer, you just have to follow your internal guidebook to find what it is. Do not battle to be a master of the universe but rather be at one with it. For you, this is the surest way to bring success (including money) and happiness.

'When we understand these (spiritual) laws and apply them in our lives, anything we want can be created; because the same laws that nature uses to create a planet, or a galaxy, or a star, or a human being can also bring the fulfillment of our greatest desires.' Deepak Chopra.

Action: Solitude, silence and deep thought will guide you to your true path in life. Although you will accumulate money by following your true purpose, you will appreciate on a profound level that money is only one of the many constituents of wealth.

FEEL THE FEAR AND DO IT ANYWAY

The title of a famous self-help text that is so powerful and precise it has been accepted into our common speech.

What is fear? At one level, it is the adrenaline rush that enables us to run away from a tsunami instead of being frozen to the spot, the decision of flight over fight. On another, it is an uncomfortable, almost painful emotion felt when facing danger or risk of pain. However, at the most commonly experienced level it is simply a powerful apprehension about the unknown. If we have no experience of something we fear it as we don't know how we will cope with it.

Being human, we err on the side of caution or negativity (fear, it will be painful) instead of the equally possible positive outcome (nothing to fear, it will be pleasurable). Fear, in this sense, pollutes our thinking and creates inertia in the same way as worrying too much and like our worries, most of our fears are unfounded.

Accept fear or apprehension as a necessary part of your personal growth. Overcoming the fear or ignorance of something will always increase your sense of well-being and self-esteem. Ask yourself why you always feel good when you have overcome a personal challenge such as an exam, a mountain climb, a first flight, or even a difficult conversation. It is because you know that you have learned something, you realize you have added to your internal bank of experience, you have developed as a person and become more self-confident. This self-knowledge will ensure you feel less helpless and more able to cope with life and the uncertainties it will throw at you. The more you challenge yourself; the more experiences you have. The more faithful leaps into the unknown you make; the more mentally vigorous and positive you will become.

It is ironic that those of us who never take risks, remain in their zone, and never feel the fear and do it anyway live in irrational dread of something going wrong. So, bottle that feeling you have when you have challenged yourself and succeeded and make it your default emotion.

'Pushing through fear is less frightening than living with the underlying fear that comes from a feeling of helplessness.' Susan Jeffers

Action: Try new pathways in life and seek self-knowledge. Get out of your comfort zone and become a more complete person. Greater experience will bring greater confidence. You will develop a positive 'can do' attitude rather than a negative 'better not' one.

LIFE IS A GAME

Like any game, the game of life has rules and if you want to succeed at it you had better know them.

The first rule is that no-one is going to win this game for you. Others may try to lead or teach you but the ultimate decision on whether to play will come from you.

The second rule is you must understand human nature and work with it not against it. Be in the game to do your best, no-one will respect you, or even be interested, if you are not trying. Don't submit to a victim mentality, understand that, whatever your circumstances, you have the responsibility for your life and you alone.

The third rule is to be realistic about yourself and how the world operates. Start by seeing your life and who you are as it really is. There is a Chinese proverb: 'The beginning of wisdom is to call things by their right names.' So, acknowledge where you are now and be realistic about what you want to achieve. Delve deeply into who you are and what will make you happy. Name and accept any obstacles or personal limitations you may foresee and have a plan to overcome or circumvent them.

The fourth rule is a consolidation of the first three. Understand that your motivation must come from within and it ourselves who teach people how to treat us. In addition, be aware the game of life requires a clear strategy from the players if they are to have any chance of success.

'The winners in this life know the rules of the game and have a plan, so their efficiency is exponential to those who don't. No big mystery, just fact.' Philip McGraw.

Action: You are the master of your life destiny so take responsibility for it today. Banish denial as you cannot change what you do not acknowledge. Think deeply about a realistic, achievable plan for your life.

I FEEL IT IN MY SOUL

If you feel something in your soul, you are feeling it at the deepest level you can. As your soul is your essence, the essential you, the epitome of what you are; you must listen to its urgings and act upon them. This idea that your soul is your essence has been around since the time of Aristotle who was born in 394 BC. He described it as: 'what you are by your very nature' or 'it is those of your properties which you cannot lose without ceasing to be yourself.'

The soul is unbounded. It accepts no borders or restrictions and it is within our souls and subconscious that we can connect with the deepest meaning of self and our link with all in the universe. It is the mark on the universe that we leave behind.

Good relationships, purposeful work, forgiveness, personal happiness and well-being and mindfulness are all gifts of the soul. It is also where our greatest asset of hope resides; and to travel through life without hope is to travel with nothing at all. So, it is important we should take care to cultivate and listen to our souls.

One way to exercise and cultivate our souls is to meditate on things that happen to us whether they are good or bad. Accept these things have happened and try to find meaning or learning in them. Banish negative, debilitating thoughts about things you dislike or people you disapprove of and, as an alternative, think deeply about why things have got to this stage or why you think the way you do. With deep thought you may be able to see some logic or meaning, you will question whether what you are feeling is worth it or has validity or benefit. By doing this, you will find a way toward eradicating any polluting, negative emotions that are clouding your soul and subconscious. Additionally, your soul will know your true purpose in life and who you really want to be. When, during deep thought, you drill down into it you will know what is right for you because you soul will reveal it to you. Working this way with your soul can make you feel better surprisingly quickly and easily.

Our souls or inner selves are different to our ego or outer selves. The imaginative and mysterious aspect of the soul where all possibilities lie will guide us to our true desires and purpose whereas our mechanical and more socially savvy ego will plan and organize the route to these desires. We need our outer selves to be able to function in the world but in equal measure we need the eternal and mysterious aspects of our unique souls to define who were are and where we want to go.

To really know your true self you should make your reference point your essential spirit or soul. This is the internal self-knowledge that gives you the power of self-referral. The opposite is object referral where your reference points are external and you are always influenced by outside forces.

'There is one spectacle grander than the sea; that is the sky. There is one spectacle grander than the sky; that is the interior of the soul.' Victor Hugo.

Action: The soul is the mysterious depth of your individual essence and meaning of your existence. Cultivate it as your personal guidebook to who you really are and what your purpose is in life.

WHO SAID LIFE WAS EASY?

Many large problems we face in life are the result of putting off or ignoring lesser ones. We are indecisive, we procrastinate or we hide our heads in the sand. Because we are not self-disciplined enough to face our problems we incubate and nourish them until eventually they have grown so strong they overwhelm us. Individuals, societies and great empires have done this for millennia.

People continue to baulk at this responsibility and delude themselves that problems will disappear of their own accord. This is misguided thinking, if history cannot always point out the way forward we should at least deduce from it what to avoid.

We must exert self-discipline and self-control to confront the obstacles or problems we are destined to meet in life. We must take responsibility for our actions, learn from our mistakes and have the strength of will to deal with our worries. If we crave personal freedom and value individuality, we must show heightened not lessened traits of self-discipline, self-control and responsibility to achieve it. After all, the man who lives alone in the wilderness needs more self-discipline to survive than the man living in a warm flat above a supermarket.

Do not be surprised that life feels difficult sometimes. It is not easy to forge the self-discipline required for true mental freedom and happiness; it is easier to let things slide, let others take responsibility so we can blame them when things go wrong. But although it takes effort, high standards and clear purpose, the goal of genuine inner happiness is so superior to the alternatives on offer it is vital we pursue it.

'Most do not fully see the truth that life is difficult. Instead they moan more or less incessantly, noisily or subtly, about the enormity of their problems, their burdens, their difficulties in life as if life was generally easy, as if life should be easy.' M. Scott Peck.

Action: If we really want to be mentally free and achieve our individual true purpose we must instill responsibility and discipline into our thoughts and actions.

I'VE GOT IT ALL BUT AM STILL UNHAPPY

We have already established that happiness is a state of mind. True happiness is a permanent and stable state of mind. On the other hand, pleasure is a temporary, superficial happiness with a sell-by date. Where true happiness is created from within, most pleasure is purchased or sourced externally. Usually it involves the consumption or purchase of something which provides a temporary stimulus to our mood. A new designer outfit, the latest car or an exotic holiday are all pleasurable but they have a time limit on them, the excitement of them soon dulls.

Pleasures are fine in themselves but if they are all we have as our source of meaning and true purpose - our source of true happiness – we soon default to our usual setting of discontent. Of course, when the excitement fades, we can go out and buy more pleasure, and we do, but that will take more money and more work we may dislike to earn it. It will also only paper over the underlying cracks and so the unsatisfactory cycle will continue.

Everything and everyone within the universe has a divine design or true pathway in life. To Greek philosopher Plato it was: 'their perfect pattern.' Most of us do not really know what it is and, in the absence of this self-knowledge, pursue pathways in life that are inherently wrong for us. They may turn out to be financially rewarding and enable us to consume in compensation but they fail to give us any essential meaning, any true sense of purpose.

We instinctively dislike these pathways but we feel locked into them to maintain our financial and family security. However, our soul and subconscious will whisper constantly that this life is not the real us and we will worry and nag at it. Our minds will be turbulent, our thoughts volatile, our wants addictive and we will not have the inner contentment to cope with our problems in life. This is why many people who are outwardly 'successful and rich' remain unhappy and unfulfilled or burn out or become addicted to alcohol or drugs (more purchased pleasures) and spiral out of control. Equally, many successful people have found their true path but then for various reasons have veered away from it. The rock star who began just enjoying creating his or her own music now finds their time dominated by agents, accountants, managers and the demands of record companies. A famous actor who was once happy just to hone his art in a provincial theatre is now a valuable world commodity to be controlled by film studios and their PR machines and is stalked constantly by a voracious media.

Even a simple promotion within a career you love could push you off track. If you loved selling, meeting people and being on the road responsible only for yourself it might not be a great move for you to become a desk-bound manager who hires and fires whatever the increase in pay and status offered, and the list could go on. Many people have started off creating their own vision but they find it has been corrupted and they have been pushed off course. It is as important to stick to your true path once found as it is to find it in the first place. You do this by having real self-knowledge.

Just for a moment imagine life without meaning or purpose. It would involve a life-long search for a substitute, a replica, an ersatz replacement. If you had money it could mean an endless round of buying temporary highs at increasingly greater levels as each additional one would offer less satisfaction than the last. This would lead, in varying degrees, to self-destruction. Another aspect of a life with no personal meaning is that you may lose sight of who you really are. You would be defined, by yourself and others, as a reflection of what you own or as a mirror of your status as that is what you have become - you have no other measure of meaning you can use.

At the other end of the scale, if you have no possessions or position you are summarily dismissed as a failure because in the absence of any other meaning you are defined by your circumstances. Furthermore, how many times have you heard people who are famous say they are misunderstood and we don't know the real them? Of course, there is an inherent phoneyness to celebrity anyway but irrespective of that, one could argue this is because they realize they no longer understand or know the real them either. This is as equally valid point if you are in a more normal career or lifestyle.

Next time you feel the compulsion to spend to compensate yourself for your life, instead of reinforcing your present incarceration by purchasing more temporary pleasure buy some space and time instead. After all, Plato himself considered leisure essential to wisdom. Give yourself six months off and really think about what is important in your life and how you wish to spend the rest of it. If, among other things, you can imagine how difficult it would be to win £100 million or how potentially life-ruining to be famous instead of automatically assuming that either would solve all your problems and assure your life happiness, then you will be beginning to understand true happiness.

'People are simultaneously drawn along one road by their intellect, reason and prudence and along another road by their passions.' Author.

Action: Take stock of what offers real meaning in your life. Understand that true happiness is derived from true purpose and comes from within; a deep inner contentment and not external stimuli. Find quiet and solitude and enter a state of deep meditation. Really drill down into your subconscious and soul to find your true self and what works for you. Then act upon your findings.

TALENT ISN'T RARE, PERSISTENCE IS

History is awash with people who have achieved great things despite poor and difficult beginnings; ordinary people who have succeeded in spite of obstacles and debilitating disadvantage. It is equally awash with people who were born into great advantage, faced no great obstacles in life but have achieved little more than mediocrity, mere existence or self-destruction.

This apparent contradiction in the natural order of things is explained by finding meaning and true purpose. If you have found your true purpose you will have the persistence and motivation to achieve it whatever your background. You will also have the mindfulness to know how important it is to your happiness.

Most of what we call 'genius' or an almost supernatural abundance of talent, is nothing of the sort. It is the result of hard work, commitment and steadfastness in the face of failures and obstacles. Similarly, 'overnight success', a term we use constantly, does not exist. Success happens after a period of trial and error, sustained effort and persistence not by a kind of magic as the minute hand passes midnight.

We are all talented. We all have hidden powers. There is something all of us are good at. Some talent may be more sought-after or lucrative than others but the fact remains we are all good at something however well disguised it may be. We all have something to offer mankind and the universe. So, talent is common. What is uncommon is to discover that intrinsic talent and armed with it undertake our true purpose. If we can do that we will find we have the persistence and will to succeed.

However, many of us don't do this instead choosing other life pathways that for various reasons or with no reasoning at all, we (or those who influence us) deem more important or worthwhile. Then we find we struggle at them, it proves hard to persist with them when faced with obstacles, hard to be motivated. Instead of being in bliss or in flow as you are when doing something you love, you are in a stop-start, doubting turmoil. With massive effort we plough on to maybe achieve some sort of success, usually a limited financial reward, or we give up defeated and disillusioned. We know our heart isn't in it but as our minds are turbulent we see no alternatives.

Another advantage of walking your true path is you will have an instinctive, inner trust that you will succeed. This persona of character and trust and your obvious independence and integrity in what you do will be very attractive to others with whom you must deal.

So, talent is common but steadfast persistence in the face of set-backs is rare. You already possess the former so ensure you inherit the latter by finding your true purpose. Finally, do not make your choice based upon what society or culture advises or others expect of you. You choice must be dictated by what will bring *you* inner meaning and happiness.

'No laws, however stringent, can make the idle industrious, the thriftless provident or the drunken sober. Such reform can only be affected by individual action……….' Samuel Smiles.

Action: Believe that you have something to offer and base your purpose in life on something you love doing. Then not only will you enjoy the journey but you will naturally possess the commitment and persistence to succeed.

STOP THE WORLD! I WANT TO GET OFF

Many of us will say this to ourselves at some time in our lives. Equally, many of us will mean it when we say it, will grasp the understanding that locked into our busy, 24/7 lives we have somewhere along the line lost the essence of ourselves and don't know how to get it back. We resolve to do something about it but then the demands of our lifestyle kick in again and we don't. The rollercoaster rolls on.

The realization can creep up on you that you have accumulated lots of titles by which you are described but none of them seem anything to do with the real you. You are father, mother, husband, wife, manager, carer, lover, breadwinner, dutiful consumer, family banker, good citizen, cook, gardener, cleaner or your children's driver.

Additionally, you are your job title, social status, address and what you own. Possibly all very laudable, but worryingly all these titles seem to indicate some kind of ownership of you as though owning yourself, having your own personal identity, is not an option. So, who is the real you? You were somebody that existed before you acquired all these titles. Where has that person gone? When did their individual hopes and dreams become subjugated? Where has the unbridled optimism and positive expectation of your youth gone? What happened to your personal desires and dreams? Are you living your own life or have you let convention, culture and other people mould one for you?

If you don't take time to step off the rollercoaster of life, to stop *doing* all the while and try *being* then you will never achieve the peace of mind to question where your own true happiness lies. Your true purpose has not gone away or been substituted by your current value or benefit to others. It is still there in your soul and subconscious and remains your best guide to finding contentment and happiness. Irrespective of what age you are you have an obligation to yourself and the rest of us to seek your true identity, your true title. If you do not, society, culture and other people will do it for you. The trouble with that is society doesn't value individualism and dreams, it values conformity. It values acceptance of your lot, even expecting a sense of gratitude from you for the limited (but just enough to keep us docile) rewards on offer. It cares little for the uniqueness, beauty and freedom of the individual; its purpose is to maintain a generic framework that holds together (or down) the mass.

By finding the real you, by being your own man or woman, you can free yourself from a nagging discontentment with life and the negative, see-sawing emotions that discontent brings. Do not accept a mindset of mediocrity or conformity, free and elevate your mind to think about your true self and seek awareness of your true purpose. True happiness comes from within and you have a responsibility to yourself and those around you to seek it.

'The only defence against numbing conformity is to find and walk the trail of uniqueness.' Ralph Waldo Emerson.

Action: Do not let society, convention, culture or other people mould you into something you are not. Detach yourself from these external pressures and seek what you love doing, what offers you real meaning. Do not accept being a title, rediscover the real you and, for a change, be a little selfish about it.

I WANT TO BE ALONE

I don't blame you. We all need to remove ourselves from the mindless rush of life from time to time and try that strange experiment of human being instead of human doing.

If you want to be alone your subconscious is telling you the pressure and noise around you is getting too much. It is urgently warning you that you need quiet and solitude so you can allow deep reflection and peace to enter your mind. This is not mystic, mythological or spiritual frippery but rather one of our body's key defences.

We all need to be alone and quiet sometimes. It is as natural a gift to our mental state as breathing is to our physical one. Mankind has done it for all of time. However, western society can view it as odd or reclusive, seeing it as out of step. Spouses or partners, family and friends misunderstand it, thinking it may be rejection of them. But this time to ourselves, away from everything life demands of us, is a vital bolt-hole.

The person obsessed with the accumulation of material reward and status has a price to pay. They must accept their time and mental energy will be wholly absorbed with that goal. It will be a single-minded pursuit that can imagine no alternatives. They ignore the beauty and peace of deep thought or the self-knowledge from the soul that solitude, meditation and silence brings. They ignore the possibility there is another way for them which is far happier and easier. If you try this meditation it may lead you to question whether working at something that drains your soul to perpetuate a meaningless cycle of ever greater consumption is a good or sustainable idea after all. It might pose the question why you feel the need to have all these compensations in life. If you answer that you deserve it because you spend most of your time working hard at an unfulfilling job then question why you are devoting so much of your life to what you don't like and so little to what you do.

I urge to you to take time out and rediscover the total freedom of mind you enjoyed as a child. Cast aside all the indoctrination you have accumulated and also discard the expectations of society and others. Shine a coruscating light into yourself to see what life you want as opposed to what life can make you the most money or what society or others think you should do. Step back and think would it really be that terrible to take a pay cut or drive an older car or live in a smaller house in order to enjoy life, attain inner happiness and contentment and break that vicious circle of compensatory need. If you require any further impetus consider most studies consistently show that after a certain level (when we have achieved the basic needs of security, shelter and food for ourselves and family) the happiness that spending power brings drops off dramatically.

You could argue from this there is a plateau of money that is required to contribute toward our life happiness and no more. Above this level, yet further accumulation of money and possessions becomes increasingly meaningless in terms of happiness.

If you take this decision to change your life you may initially be looked on as odd. To start with you will almost certainly face some opposition from those around you. But when people realize how much happier and contented you have become by following your inner guide to true purpose and meaning they will want to know your secret.

'The mass of men lead lives of quiet desperation.' Henry David Thoreau.

'If man does not keep pace with his companions, perhaps it is because he hears a different drummer. Let him step to the music he hears, however measured or far away.'
Henry David Thoreau.

Action: Get out of the mental crush and conditioning of modern life. Take time to reassess your life and who you are. Don't follow the crowd in the mistaken belief that because they are many it makes them wise. A truth remains a truth if only known to one man.

True Purpose

Don't flog a dead horse

Follow your dreams

There must be more to it than this

Men will be men

It's the same old story

Don't follow the crowd

Don't go with the flow, go with your flow

I am an individual, not a number

I don't know why I'm here

I never have time

Smell the roses

They are the same as us, only different

DON'T FLOG A DEAD HORSE

Have you ever asked yourself: 'Why am I doing this?' Have you ever thought sod it! and abandoned a task in frustration. Ever felt like just another cog in a meaningless wheel? Have you ever felt like this about your career or daily life?

I caught the bus and train to a job I disliked one day as I had done a few hundred times before. When I reached the entrance to my workplace I suddenly stopped dead in my tracks. Something had snapped inside of me, I couldn't go in. I turned around jumped on the same train then bus and went home. I changed out of my work suit into my normal clothes and spent the rest of the day walking and thinking in the countryside. Although I had bills to pay and responsibilities, I felt elated not worried and I never went back. If you feel like this about your chosen work, then you are almost certainly trying too hard at the wrong thing. You are on a journey that isn't yours. You may experience an epiphany like I did or the realization might creep up on you slowly. However the penny drops, you need to change direction.

Your right direction will involve something that gives you unconditional happiness, something you would do willingly not even thinking about the rewards it might bring. It is a task or project you will lose track of time doing and you will find easy and natural to accomplish. Eastern philosophy would explain this as *non-action* or *the path of least resistance*; more modern psychologists would describe it as *flow*.

Whatever description you prefer it is when you are not battling or struggling to do something you know in your heart isn't for you, but rather when engaged in work your mind and body instinctively knows is right. It is so right in fact, you are not even concerned about outcomes; you have faith they will sort themselves out. Don't be worried if you can't change directly to your true purpose just accept you will have to travel indirectly for a while. Nor should you concern yourself about finding exactly the right road first time, there might be few wrong turnings; just make a start and get as near as you can.

Be aware of the competing forces within your head. These are your ego or social self which is pitched against your subconscious, soul or essential self. Both are vital to us but they have different agendas. Our social self allows us to mechanically function and interact with the world but it is susceptible to the indoctrination of conformity, societal and parental pressure, culture and environment. It works in what it thinks is our best interest but it is cautious and protective, it is safe and steady, it is risk adverse. In that job or career we dislike it will whisper things like: 'Hang in there, it will get better' or 'If you get a pay rise you will enjoy it more' or 'It's better to be safe in a job with your mortgage to pay.'

Our essential self, the dreams and meanings that lie deep in our soul and subconscious, is more interested in us than society or conformity. It knows what will make us happy and contented and it wants to lead us there. It will whisper: 'It won't get better, nothing will change,' or 'the extra money won't buy you any more happiness,' or 'sod the mortgage, follow your dream.' To achieve real happiness and contentment in life you must listen to your essential, inner voice and choose the pathway or vision it suggests to you. Then you can let your mechanical, social ego organize the details.

Not only will your essential self nag at you if it thinks you are working at the wrong thing and should change direction, but your body will rebel as well. Although, with the heavy armament at its disposal, the ego seems all-powerful it will be rocked back when your body and essential self have had enough. The body's rebellion will manifest itself in physical malaise, lack of energy and even illness. It could mean increased drinking or overeating or drug dependency whether prescriptive or otherwise. The subconscious will cut off the flow of motivation, enthusiasm and positive thought. You could become tetchy, argumentative and unreasonable. If that is not enough, it could make you self-implode in varying degrees. This may range from losing your temper with your boss and telling him to stick his job to deliberately messing up a promotion exam or interview. In my case, it physically stopped me entering my workplace ever again. You must really listen to and watch out for these signals from your soul, your essential self.

I have left lots of jobs in my working life and never once felt sad about leaving. I have sometimes felt chastened about the circumstances of leaving but on every occasion felt a sense of freedom, release and elation when I drove out of the gates or walked through the door. This was because I knew in my heart I had left something that wasn't right for me and by doing so I now had the freedom to seek something that was.

Write a list of anything and everything you do where you find peace, contentment, or fulfillment; where you instinctively feel right with yourself and the world. Just for a time completely dismiss any everyday worries or self-doubt you may have and ignore external pressures. This is an exercise between you and your essential self, your ego or safe head isn't invited.

'The soul is like an eye resting upon that which truth and being shine. The soul perceives and understands, and is radiant with intelligence.' Plato.

Action: Practice a period of silence and meditation daily. Find some solitude in nature to de-clutter your mind from outside pressure and expectation. Only when your mind is still and receptive can you introduce ideas into it.

FOLLOW YOUR DREAMS

It is right to follow your dreams. In fact, it is incumbent upon you to do so for the betterment of yourself and mankind. However, be compassionate and thoughtful about it. In following your dreams, be minded not to tread on or extinguish the dreams of others.

Equally, do not think you can just withdraw from life and avoid making any life choices at all because you must not. An aimless, feckless, desultory life holds no meaning at all and if nothing in the universe holds any meaning for you there is no reason for your existence. You add nothing of value so you will receive nothing of value.

On your dream journey be aware that as we are living beings we cannot avoid our thoughts and actions and the effect they have on our lives and the lives of others. This is our *karma*, the natural law of cause and effect. What we are today is the product of our previous thoughts and actions; where we are in the future will be the product of how we think and act now.

When seeking your dreams do not make the mistake of simply wanting things you perceive successful people have. Question whether the acquisition of material wealth on its own, without attendant meaning or fulfillment, is worth the journey. Do not use your intelligence only but your reason as well. Animals and machines exhibit intelligence but only humans have the advanced reasoning power to fathom who they really are and what will bring them happiness and contentment.

When following your dream always take the long view. Don't shackle yourself with time limits or specific outcomes. Don't worry about day-to-day problems and keep your focus on your vision. Remember intermittent failure when following a clear course of action is not failure at all but simply a progression through stages of learning where we stop, reflect and adjust.

Don't be surprised if in following your dreams you face opposition. This maybe well-intentioned or could be for less charitable reasons such as envy. We have a tendency in our society to feel happier with the gallant loser than the winner. It is probably because the majority of us can identify more readily with the former. Neither be surprised when following your dream how much mediocrity and conformity you will have to confront. Sadly, in the workplace it is more normal than not. Not because people are naturally unintelligent or mediocre but because they are in the wrong jobs for the wrong reasons and, therefore, have no spirit or motivation to excel. They conform because they have not considered an alternative route. They follow because they have not opened their minds sufficiently to lead.

By finding and taking your true path and following your dreams you may only become a leader of one but that is better than only being one of the led.

Lastly, do not allow yourself to be deflected by other people ridiculing your dreams. Ideas, dreams or desires are like new truths. Firstly they are ridiculed then they are opposed until finally, they are accepted as being self-evident all along.

'With perfect meditation comes perfect act' The Bhagavad-Gita.

Action: The way to find your dream is mediate deeply on what is really important to you, what really resonates with your soul or essence. Find silence and solitude daily to do this. The way to follow your dream is to take the long-view, treat others fairly en-route and detach yourself from specific outcomes or fear of failure.

THERE MUST BE MORE TO IT THAN THIS

If you are voicing this concern you are acknowledging that all is not well with your life. Your essential self is nagging at you that something is missing and you are not leading the life you could. In accepting this, in ignoring your ego voice and listening to your inner one, you have already taken an important step toward achieving more out of your life.

However, acceptance is not enough. You must believe you can achieve want you want, believe both in yourself and in the greater intelligence and power of the universe.

It does not matter if you accept the Big Bang theory or you hold the view that a God created all things, what is indisputable is the evolution and expansion since the beginning. If you note what has been created from 'nothing' since that explosion of energy or divine creation and if you ponder what yet might be created as the universe continues to expand along its infinite timeline it is not hard to believe there is a grand plan, a unifying greater intelligence at work. The only alternative to this explanation is that everything we know of, everything we can conceive of has happened by pure chance. Everything that was uncreated which is now created, everything that now is but wasn't before is purely the result of a haphazard, unconnected, unplanned, disordered, accidental series of events. To me, this is even more difficult to believe.

We must have faith that we are an integral part of this process and intelligence. A belief we are a part of the evolutionary product of all that has gone before and what we will achieve in our present incarnation will form part of the total creative product that lies ahead. We are at one with the universe, we share the same constituents and energy; physiologically and psychologically we are part of that before, that now, and that after.

Both eastern and western spiritual or religious texts offer us a vision and pathway to a more enlightened life. This offer promises that, with faith in our unity and essential oneness with a higher intelligence or God, our lives can be changed; that there can be a better tomorrow.

This was quite a radical proposal in its day. Prior to this people accepted their lot in life and got on with it on a daily basis accepting the fates dealt them by various fickle gods. They made sacrifice and offerings to try to influence individual events but the possibility of personal advancement or enlightenment remained an alien concept.

Some might argue these religious and spiritual texts were the first life transformation manuals. By saying life does not have to be like this and going on to say that faith in a higher intelligence to guide us will move us forward to a happier alternative, they underpin all the philosophical and self-help writing that followed.

This age-old call to faith is no different to having faith in the spoken, written or visual affirmations advocated in modern self-help literature. But it's all a con I hear you say. They can offer you anything and blame it on your insufficient faith when it doesn't work out. This, of course, 'they' can; nevertheless please name me a working alternative to belief if you have one. If you have no instinctive faith or belief in yourself or what you are doing or, worse still, hold no beliefs at all, you will never do or begin anything.

'The lord is my shepherd, I shall not want; he makes me lie down in green pastures, he leads me besides still waters, he restores my soul.' Psalm 23.

Action: We find our link to the higher intelligence in our soul and subconscious. We access it by silence, solitude and meditation. This is also where we discover there is more to life than this and we can achieve it.

MEN WILL BE MEN

Many men have become confused with their role in life. In the movement to their new man persona of harmony, heightened compassion, peacefulness and empathy there remains an uncertainty in their lives about their essential masculinity. Having moved toward a more feminine side, they have realized women do not want men to become an emotional mirror or an acquiescent reflection of the female consciousness. While women appreciate the line of travel to a more gentle thoughtfulness, they don't want their man to abjectly surrender his masculinity; the essential aspects that mark him as a male of the species and what attracts them in the first place. Men must understand that women are generally contemptuous of the emasculated male. In a relationship, women will probe and test and jostle in order to influence and so they should but, ultimately, they need to know where a man's boundaries lie.

So, man finds himself in a confused, middle ground, aptly a no-man's land. However, the way forward is not a return to callousness or unthinking brutalism but rather by finding an even balance between the greater thoughtfulness of the new receptive man and the age-old power and vitality of the warrior. If masculine warrior energy festers and is not directed toward a true purpose it can turn inward and become corrupted expressing itself as sullen mood or short temper at one end of the scale to external or domestic cruelty or other anti-social behaviour at the other. However much of a new man you may be, you have to be aware of this aspect of your psyche.

Male initiation ceremonies across all cultures remove young men from the feminine cocoon of their mothers and force them to live with older men. This teaches them survival, self-worth and is considered important to enhance their masculine traits. Through varying trials it also introduces them to the darker side of life which is vital for their development. Arguably, in the 20th century of the western world this was accomplished by taking men to war and in peace time, to a lesser degree, by conscripting them into the armed forces at age eighteen. In the 21st century, this avenue for men to recognize their masculinity and channel it in the right way is largely absent. It remains, however, important that men do not subjugate their masculinity or become convinced it is redundant in our age. Recognize the inner strength it provides then utilize it in a non-destructive way.

'The male in the past twenty years has become more thoughtful, more gentle. But by this process he has not become more free. He is a nice boy who pleases not only his mother but also the young women he is living with.' Robert Bly.

Action: All men have to leave the protection of childhood at some stage and stand up to be counted, to face the world as it is. Welcome the new sensitivity within you but also accept the presence of the age-old warrior. Understand that women do want empathy but their deepest needs remain love, security and protection.

IT'S THE SAME OLD STORY

Men have searched for their bliss or right journey or true direction throughout the ages. The bliss they searched for is no different to that which we seek today. It is that vision, activity, career or purpose which we are passionate about, endlessly intrigued by and which feels instinctively right for us. It may be something you have thought about for years but have resisted or you may have been lucky enough to find it earlier in life. Or you may still be looking.

Ancient or classical mythology, the stories told and retold countless times around the firesides burning throughout millennia, can give us a modern day insight into our lives and how we can handle them. There is a reason why these stories have endured and been passed down to us over the years and it is because they continue to fire our imaginations.

By increasing our knowledge of past cultures and mythology we can see and sense ourselves in the larger history of human thought, hope and expectation. We can find some sense of being part of a continuance, a pattern to life even and appreciate the problems and obstacles, not dissimilar to our own, that have been faced and solved by our ancestors. We will understand the questions we now ask of ourselves have always been posed by man.

Consider the phrase, 'wheel of fortune.' This has been around for centuries and is still freely used today. Not only do we use the expression but we immediately grasp its significance. It is a normal wheel with a hub and a rim. As it turns through time and space we grimly hang on to the rim enduring an unending revolution of ups and downs. In our modern age, chasing our tails for money, status, possessions or instant gratifications is rim hanging.

It would be far better to change our position to the hub of the wheel where the movement is less turbulent and where our minds and emotions are not spinning out of control. Here we are at the centre and focus of the wheel of life where everything is less frantic instead of revolving wildly along its outside edge. The analogy with true purpose is evident.

Appreciate the myths and stories of old as they reassure us our problems are not new or singular to us and they infuse our imaginations with the value of following our bliss.

'To teach how to live without certainty, and yet without being paralysed by hesitation, is perhaps, the chief thing that philosophy, in our age, can still do for those who study it.' Bertrand Russell.

Action: We can all have the hero's journey so beloved of our mythology. Do not accept the disenchantment of an inauthentic life. Just like the mythical hero, use your imagination, determination and courage to follow your bliss.

DON'T FOLLOW THE CROWD

With any faithful expectation they have any better idea where they are going.

Even if some in the crowd do have a sense of direction it will not necessarily be yours. Everyone has a destiny to pursue that is independent of other people.

This destiny is more profound than romantic love or simply perpetuating the human race. If you think you have discovered the real meaning of your life by falling in love and raising children then you may be disappointed. You might have found one meaning but it is not, necessarily, *the* meaning.

Romantic love is worth seeking for the happiness it will hopefully provide, at least in the short-term, but romantic love is not all-important. Without the meaningful purpose in your life which is your destiny it will not be enough. Hence, the initial radiance of it dulls, discord and disenchantment set it and the divorce lawyers move to bigger houses. However close you feel to someone, your personal destiny is just that - it is detached from other people and unique to you. Unless your life partner can help you search for and then achieve your life's special journey then you may be better off on your own.

Of course, you may say I don't want to be on my own or that being a husband and father or wife and mother is enough for me. That this personal destiny stuff sounds selfish and too big a sacrifice for my taste. That, of course, is your right and masses of people in the world exercise it. Whether these masses are truly fulfilled and happy is the question you need to ask yourself. You would also be right in thinking it takes sacrifice and a little selfishness. But the fact remains that true personal happiness comes from within not without and your own true purpose is an essential part of who you are, your personal identity; the reason for and meaning of your being.

It is a given of your life that you will sometimes face difficulty whatever decisions you do or do not make. This being self-evident why not face life's difficulties with the strength and resolve of knowing you are on your true path with the mental freedom, conviction and clear sightedness that brings. Your dreams may have a price but isn't there a larger toll to pay in not living them?

I grant you it is easier to follow the crowd. It is safer to fit in, there is less thinking to be done, less personal responsibility to shoulder and more people to share the blame when things go wrong. I can understand why most of us are seduced. To follow your individual path takes courage and you must be prepared (but not destined) to sacrifice conventional ideas of comfort and security. However, the rewards can be worldly as well as spiritual. Uniqueness and specialism is a valuable commodity in the 21st century. Today, the greater financial rewards are not to be found as a ubiquitous cog in the industrial/commercial wheel but by offering something different, something rare. Dare I suggest - something individual and unique.

'Whatever you can do, or dream you can, begin it – boldness has genius, power and magic in it.' Goethe.

Action: Know that in fulfilling you personal destiny you are being true to yourself which is the only honest way to be true to others. Be courageous and live the life that is yours, the life that has been preordained for you.

DON'T JUST GO WITH THE FLOW, GO WITH YOUR FLOW

Going with the flow is similar to following the crowd, it means you are happy not to make a decision but will accept the consensus – the collective decision of the many. At an unimportant level this may be just your easy-going nature saying I don't mind if we go to the beach or the park or the cinema or the pub and that is harmless. It could also be about allowing your current thinking and situation, however unconventional, to take you where it will and this can be a useful exploration. However, to obediently follow the flow and not consider where your individual true meaning and purpose may lie is anything but harmless or useful. It is a surrender of personal responsibility and identity which can have significant life-long consequences. At this deeper level you need to disregard the general flow and concentrate on your own flow.

Have you ever asked yourself when it is you're at your happiest and most contented? Ever questioned what it is you do which brings about the most satisfaction, enjoyment and inner harmony? If you have really thought about this you will conclude it is not when engaged in temporary highs such as sex or alcohol or other forms of consumption. Admittedly, they may bring ephemeral pleasure but they will not provide lasting, inner happiness. That will be found in an activity, vision, purpose or even just an idea that completely works for you, feels absolutely right and gives you inherent happiness and fulfillment without the need for external stimuli. That is when you are in flow - your flow.

You will have known and felt this yourself but psychiatric experiments back it up. They have shown we are at our happiest when involved in activities that hold the highest value for us. When completing these activities, we stop clock watching, we are genuinely absorbed and we are in a place where external worries are blocked out. We do not question or doubt whether what we are doing is right or workable and we seem to achieve or succeed without really thinking about it.

Psychologists call this optimal experience or flow. Do not ignore this feeling as it is your key indicator in seeking your true purpose and subsequent happiness in life.

Your flow will be personal to you. What intrigues you will bore another. What you find easy and are flowing in others will struggle and sweat over. Flow is also the natural order of things. Undertaking the task allotted to you which is the task that *you* do best is what happens in nature. You will recognize whether you are in flow by various emotions such as an inner contentment, an ordered and focused mind and clear objectives. There will be no internal dialogue of procrastination or justification, no doubts about whether you are doing the right thing. The activity becomes automatic, you stop thinking and just do, and you do without conscious effort.

Being in flow will give you a sense of purpose, meaning and knowledge of yourself all of which are vital components of happiness. Believe that the meaning of life, on the personal and most important level, is doing what is meaningful for you. Loving what you are doing most of the time will enable you to love most of your time.

'As far as we can discern, the sole purpose of human existence is to kindle a light in the darkness of mere being.' Carl Jung.

Action: Accept it can be difficult to be happy as external events have a tendency to conspire against it. But this is an even greater reason to seek your flow activities. Distinguish between true happiness and mere pleasure and think deeply about what your flow activities are.

I AM AN INDIVIDUAL, NOT A NUMBER

If you have uttered these words to yourself or others and railed against the blueprint for man and woman that our industrial or commercial or political society seeks to impose then you are thinking in the right way.

You are aware, or becoming so, of the fact you are unique; you exist for a special reason independent of other people or what society has in mind for you. You appreciate your small role in the universe has a special purpose and you must achieve that purpose whatever the dictates of your culture or environment. If you think like this, or are beginning to, then you have taken a huge step toward self-knowledge and achieving true happiness.

We learn about ourselves in various ways. One is by suffering and experience which is fine if we are positive about it. The danger lies however, if we fall into the 'why me' syndrome where only negative things are learned. A second way we approach self-knowledge is to attempt to put some order and direction into our lives. In other words, we set ourselves goals. Again, these are fine if they are the right ones but we could condemn ourselves to a life-long struggle if they are not. By far the best way to knowing ourselves is to seek enlightenment (self-knowledge) and happiness by walking in step with our true purpose. We will then understand that everything in nature and the universe has a specific purpose or reason for being and we find ours. In this way we walk in step with nature, order and reason not against it.

Use that independence of mind which is your personal gift. Do not allow yourself to be a helpless reflection of your society or environment. Allow only a positive mindset and seek that meaning for your life which is unique to you. Words like prosperity and scarcity are not definitions set in stone but merely personal states of mind. People can be 'rich' in many ways, it depends on how they view things, how they calibrate the meaning of 'richness' in their belief systems. Concentrate on the greater reward the work or direction which is uniquely yours will bring not on the expectation of best possible financial outcome.

Don't worry about what has gone before nor be concerned about the position and status you are starting from. Your true purpose remains out there for you whatever position you are in now. As any car salesman will instantly understand; 'It's not where we start that matters, it's where we finish.'

'The great and glorious masterpiece of man is to live with purpose.' Montaigne.

Action: Write down and meditate over everything you love doing in life. Listen to your persistent inner voice and intuition. Seek the true pathway that is yours and commence your individual walk of life.

I DON'T KNOW WHY I'M HERE

When everything you try goes wrong, when every road you expectantly travel leads to a dead-end or where the relationship that *this* time you felt sure was right comes to an acrimonious full-stop you may question why you bother, why you are here at all.

It is at these moments when you seem to be going nowhere fast that you must slow down, reflect and be at your most positive. In each of these periods in your life you confront a potential tipping point where you decide either to fall deeper into a self-pitying mental abyss or you decide to use your unique independence of mind, your individual will and character and, most of all, your belief in yourself to step back from the brink and move on. Our lives are not supposed to be an untroubled, uninterrupted stroll toward broad, sunlit uplands. No-one has had a life trajectory that hasn't at one point been cruelly deflected. Without set-backs we would never self-examine or reflect or take stock. Without this self-examination we would never grow, become more confident, or learn as a person. So, appreciate that set-backs do not happen only to you, they do not question your existence and yours alone.

If everything you try goes pear-shaped it is not because you are useless but rather that you are working at the wrong things. If you keep coming up against dead-ends that exhaust your motivation you are simply on the wrong road or have taken a wrong turning on the right one – find your reverse gear and turn around. If relationships are not working out it may be because, in the absence of any other, you are trying to put all your life's meaning into them thereby forcing issues instead of letting them develop naturally. Or, thankfully you may simply have saved yourself a basket-full of future grief by off-loading someone who, for your life journey, is totally unsuited to you.

So, never be despondent or feel worthless if you find yourself at yet another crossroads, you now have one of the most exciting emotions known to us all, something we all envy - freedom and opportunity. Freedom and blessed release from what wasn't working for you and exciting opportunities to seek all kinds of possibilities that will. If you don't believe me ask anybody stuck in rut what they would desire most. You have moved from the realm of limited possibility and low expectation to suddenly having a myriad of exciting choices.

You are here because you are needed. As in nature, you exist because you have role to play and a skill to contribute. Within us all, whether in our souls, subconscious or heart, we retain an image of what we can be, an illustration of the life we can lead. History is littered with examples of ordinary people whose inner vision has driven them forward unrestricted or undeterred by set-back or circumstance.

'Callings' are not restricted to missionaries, explorers or doctors, we all have a call from our soul to live out our true purpose. This call of the soul is the invisible guiding force within us and we should never ignore it. The Ancient Greeks called it *daimon* and the Romans had an even better name for it; *genius*. This genius is within us all.

You have a duty to yourself to retain your self-esteem not least because you are a unique creation. We are not simply the result and mirror of the vagaries of our genes and environment. We have a wholly individual identity apart from those reference points; we are what our imaginations and souls tell us we are. We are not products of places and events nor are we a product of our parents in the sense that it is inevitable we will be just like them. All of the above, of course, are factors that can shape us (if we allow them to) but they pale into insignificance when compared with the power our individual minds and souls have to define ourselves. Consider the thought for a moment that we don't exist because our parents engaged in sex, but rather they engaged in sex because of the necessity of bringing us into existence. You are *that* important.

'At the outset we need to make clear that today's framework for understanding a human life, the interplay of genetics and environment, omits something essential – the particularity (that) you feel to be you.' James Hillman.'

Action: You are needed, you can offer something, you are part of the story, there is a reason you are here. Never let external events or other people steal your sense of self and genius. Listen to the calling of your soul and enact its message.

I NEVER HAVE TIME

This phrase along with the infinite varieties of, 'If only' must rank at the very top of the list of excuses we make for not doing more of what we love.

We struggle with the concept of time; it is both abstract and definite to us. We also have a strange relationship with it, almost as if it presented a physical challenge or was a constant opponent with which to do battle. I'm not even sure we grasp what real time is and we certainly don't know how to use it effectively.

Time in the modern age is artificial, it is man-made. With a few adjustments, we still use a calendar of time adopted by a 16th century pope. Additionally, our industrial/commercial society plays around with it; twice a year in the UK it either goes backwards or forwards in order we have enough daylight to get to work. So, time has been made to be what we want it to be. Once we worked with time but now time works on us. We used to get up when it was light, we worked and sustained ourselves with food and drink as required and went to sleep when it was dark. Night and day and our physiological clock were all we needed. Now we have a gratefully received lunch time where we are supposed to eat whether our bodies require it or not or we use it to rush around doing the things our working hours prevent. We have work time, leisure time and home time. Things to be done are now allotted a certain time, whether we actually want to use that time to do them is considered unimportant.

We also struggle with our perception of time. When we are waiting for something exciting to happen we feel time purposely slows down, it drags. Conversely, on our week's annual holiday away from a depressing job, purely out of spite it speeds up - the seven days pass in a veritable blur!

Another mixed message we carry around is that although we readily accept the infinite nature of time the universe represents, we cling to a more-or-less consistent mindset that time is short. But time isn't short or long or fat or thin, like space, it just is. Yet even as we complain that time is short, we conspire to shorten it further. In the chronology of the universe, our existence on earth measured as a proportion of what has gone before and what stretches ahead lasts for a miniscule amount of real time. Instead of appreciating this and trying to stretch it out, to try and use this 'shortness' of time as effectively as we can; we shorten it further by gleefully slicing it into smaller and smaller segments of different activity which we can then rush between.

Worst of all we become busy. Dear Lord, please preserve me from the person who finds the time to accost my ears with the phrase, 'I am sooo busy,' as if it is something I will be unhesitatingly impressed by. I feel like screaming, 'Busy doing what?' but I don't. I nod and smile and mutter something inane like, 'That's good' while actually thinking the opposite. I wonder if they could be busy doing anything worthwhile, rewarding or for the common good; anything that is personally fulfilling or advances their self-knowledge. God forbid, could they even be doing something they love which makes them happy and fulfilled?

'Busy' people use the word busy as if it is a justification in itself, as if it creates something and has meaning in isolation. What we are busy at we seem to spend less of our precious time thinking about. It is said that if you want something done you should ask a busy person. Well I wouldn't, they are too busy being 'busy' for me.

I get asked if I'm busy all of the time. People even use it as a greeting, 'How are you, keeping busy?' Sometimes I answer, 'Yes, I am busy doing nothing but thinking,' then note the expressions of disappointment, confusion and finally sympathy that drift across their faces.

The point of this preamble is to suggest that we spend far too much time doing what we don't like and far too little time doing what we do. Doing what we love and, therefore, creating our happiness takes up precious few hours of our day. Think about what really makes you happy and fulfilled in life, when you naturally feel all is right with the world, that this is how it should be. Now consider how much time you allocate to the activities that inspire these warm feelings within you. A rule of thumb for most of us is that we allocate only 20% of our time to doing the things we love. Put another way, for 80% of our time we willingly forego the activities that inspire happiness in order to be 'busy' with things which do not. This mirrors Italian economist Pareto's economic rule that 80% of results derive from 20% of effort. This economic rule is an observation of reality and is equally real when applied to life.

Time seems short to us because we allocate our time too widely and to the wrong things. If we spent more time doing the things we really love, a purpose, work or activity where we are in flow, then time will cease to matter – there will be an abundance of it. The reality is that we are awash with time but just waste most of it doing the wrong things.

This economic principle applied to life works whether you believe in it or not. Agnostics may apply, there is no faith required. We find it hard to believe because we are conditioned to doubt it. To most of us, the 50/50 principle of you-get-out-what-you-put-in has been a powerful indoctrination. That hard work (even if you loathe it) will provide a level of reward commensurate with the effort applied. As we know how effortlessly effective we can be when engaged in our true purpose, this is patent nonsense. It is all to do with political and societal cohesion and nothing to do with the desires of the individual. It is more about creating a passive, stable and unthinking society, where mediocrity is accepted and conformity rewarded, than allowing an individual to follow their true purpose in life.

'Most people try too hard at the wrong things………only by fulfilling oneself is anything of extraordinary value created.' Richard Koch.

Action: Allocate more of your time to what you love doing. Do not confuse being busy with having true purpose and meaning in your life. Do something that comes easily and naturally to you where you can be in flow without conscious effort. This will be your unique offering to our world and the contribution which will hold inherent value for you and rarity value for others.

SMELL THE ROSES

You don't have to love gardening or even have a garden to smell the roses. No horticultural interest is necessary. You simply need to stop, take time out and just *be* sometimes instead of constantly rushing around *doing*. All of us require some solitude and silence on a regular basis in order to quiet our minds so we may actually hold on to an important thought and let it soar. We need to banish the frantic, tick-box mentality of our usual mental state and calm our body and mind. Don't only smell the roses, look at them anew and at the same time take a new look at yourself.

When we are quiet, when we find some solitude and peace; we immediately feel better. If we ever treat ourselves to a leisurely walk on the beach, a ramble through the countryside or just a stroll through an urban park, we experience a smoothing-out of our mental patterns such as a wave-tossed sea returning to calm after a storm. We actually feel our stress levels lowering. Not only do we instinctively know this but science and clinical study backs it up. What is happening is we are regaining our natural pace; we are stepping in time with nature and the universe. Instead of battling against time and the way of nature -the natural regulator of the world – we become more attuned with it, more at one, closer to where we should be.

A carpenter would not work against the grain of the wood and nor should you work against the grain of nature and the universe. If your life seems a constant struggle, a manic striving, a frantic treading of water simply to avoid going under; then you need to stop and reassess.

You need to quickly ring the bell for the end of the round and slump down on to your stool at the corner of the ring and take a breather. Reflect deeply on the possibility of there being another way for you, another life which is much more focused on what will make you happy, another life that is simpler, easier and less effort. This will not be easy, but with regular silence, solitude and meditation it is achievable.

'Be still, and allow the mud to settle. Remain still, until it is time to act.' Tao Te Ching.

When you find the life you were meant to lead, the contribution you were meant to make you will be in tune with the natural, unifying flow of the universe and higher intelligence. This only works if you work only at what works for you. If you do this you will flow around obstacles rather than splinter against them, you will succeed effortlessly without struggle or anguish. You actually know this to be true. It has happened to you when experiencing yourself in flow engaged in an activity you love. Believe there is an essential oneness of the universe of which you are part and understand you have a unique role within it. If what you are doing now requires an effort of will to accomplish anything or it involves the exploitation of another it will not be the right way for you, you will be out of step with the higher intelligence of the universe.

So take a step back instead of forward. To take this time out instead of increasing your efforts and to stop pushing the pace or forcing issues and, instead, slowing everything down, may to some, seem strange advice for achieving success.

Not only does this eastern philosophy of waiting and letting the oneness of the universe guide you, conflict with our ingrained work ethic and the effort/reward equation we all assume but it also seems at odds with some modern self-help literature. These are the modern writers that extol positive, committed and physical steps to take control of our lives - action and movement not patience and calm. So, who do we believe? Which way is best?

To intensely strive to achieve or to go with the flow of the universe and see what transpires? As usual it comes down to the beliefs of the individual and where your faith lies. Do you acknowledge the oneness of the universe and that a higher intelligence will help you? Do you believe that you have a true purpose in life, a code from the soul which is worth seeking? Or, do you believe you stand alone with no commonality with anything else, that you exist in isolation of nature's purpose and reason and you are engaged in a battle with everything and everyone to achieve your aims?

In the introduction to this book I asked you to believe. Now you must decide.

'The wise stand out because they see themselves as part of the whole. They shine, because they don't want to impress. They achieve great things, because they don't look for recognition. Their wisdom is contained in what they are, not their opinions. They refuse to argue, so no-one argues with them.' Tao Te Ching.

Action: Think deeply about the idea of oneness, a unifying and reciprocal exchange of energy within the universe. Roll the thought over in your mind that the universe is naturally abundant and can provide for everyone and everything.

Consider the bizarre logic of having a natural order which is designed purposely so life will be a colossal effort or constantly attritional. If you had millions of years to design something the very least you would expect is that it not only worked, but it worked effortlessly.

THEY ARE THE SAME AS US, ONLY DIFFERENT

If you have ever travelled, you will know that far from people from other parts of the world being foreign to us in the sense of being alien, they are pretty much the same. There are many more similarities than there are differences. Their aspirations and hopes, although they may differ in levels of expectation, are the same as ours. They want a purpose in life, they want to better themselves, they want to provide for their families and they seek some meaning for their lives just as we do. We are much more alike than we think; there is a human commonality of values, thought, intention and desire.

If you recognize the fact that at the same time as being unique within this world you are also at one with the rest of mankind you also realize your true path or expression in life is part of everyone's evolution or progress. You will understand and accept that we do fit into a higher and larger scheme of things and our job is to find out where.

We are now evolved to a level of civilization in the developed world where most of us have achieved our basic human needs of security, shelter and food. At this stage of our evolution we must strive to push our imaginations beyond simply survival or superficial gratification and concentrate them on the deeper meanings of our existence. It is no longer enough to accept Darwinian evolution theory and move no further, we now need to know *why* we evolved from apes.

As a proportion of the time continuum from the Big Bang or divine creation, the concept of 'humankind' in the sense of a collection of people essentially the same, is a pretty new idea. Although the violent religious, cultural and political divisions of the last 3000 years of history points to anything but this collective mutuality, the concept has become entrenched. That we now do not question this concept, despite continuing violent conflicts, is a measure of our higher understanding, our evolution. We have moved beyond purely personal, local or regional concerns to concern for the whole of humankind. We now understand what affects the rest affects us also. This concept is so established within our minds that we accept there is no progress to be achieved for humankind by individuals or groups trying to transcend it, destabilise it or subjugate it to another concept. We understand, when we really think about it, that we will never evolve by being out of step with its unifying oneness or by denying all of our fellow club members the opportunity to express their own potential in full. Everyone is needed and we move forward together or, as an evolutionary concept, we don't move forward at all.

Much as we have our physical stratosphere, as long ago as 1925 the term Noosphere was coined by a Jesuit priest named Pierre Teilhard de Chardin. This described an invisible layer of imaginative thought around our earth representing the sum total of accumulated human knowledge and spirituality. The same writer predicted that localism would become less important and people in the future would need the resources of the whole planet and the people within it to sustain them intellectually and materially. This prophecy would also work in reverse in that individuals would add to this stratus of intelligence to willingly share their personal knowledge and insight in order to influence and benefit the progress of mankind. Crucially, the knowledge and prowess they had achieved would now be available to people way beyond their immediate circle, locality or nation.
60 years later came globalization and the internet.

'Modern man no longer knows what to do with the potentialities he has unleashed….sometimes we are tempted to trample this super abundance back into the matter from which it sprang without stopping to think how monstrous such an act against nature (that) would be.' Pierre Teilhard de Chardin.

Action: Understand that we all have a role in our evolution. We may be individual and have a unique true purpose but we share a common cause and obligation and all of humankind is important for that.

Printed in Great Britain
by Amazon

MORE PARANORMAL ROMANCE FROM
ZOE CHANT

Outback Shifters Series

Hector

Callan

Euan

Trent

Rhys

The Lost Dragons Series

A Mate for the Dragon

Fated for the Dragon

Destined for the Dragon

A Bride for the Dragon

Bound to the Dragon

See Zoe Chant's complete list of books here!

A NOTE FROM ZOE CHANT

Thank you for buying my book! I hope you enjoyed it. If you'd like to be emailed when I release my next book, please click here to be added to my mailing list.

Please consider reviewing *Chimeras and Christmas Cakes* even if you only write a line or two. I appreciate all reviews, whether positive or negative.

You are also invited to join my VIP Readers Group on Facebook!

The cover of *Chimeras and Christmas Cakes* was designed by Isabelle Arden.

ZOE CHANT

"… Maybe I can wait a few minutes to open my present," she murmured, pulling him into the room.

"Just a few?" he replied, mock-insulted. "I'd hope it'd take a bit longer than that."

"I suppose it depends on how long it takes me to unwrap you," she said thoughtfully.

"Well, I guess we'd better get to it," Levi said, as the clock outside struck twelve. "So that you can get to unwrapping everything you want. That *is* what Christmas morning is about, after all."

"You'll just have to teach me," she said with a smile. The playful edge melted away, replaced by pure sincerity.

"Merry Christmas, Levi," she said. "I love you. Thank you for everything you've done for me."

"Merry Christmas to you, Margot," he murmured back. "And thank *you*." He looked into her eyes, his gaze intense. "I love you, too."

"Merry Christmas," she said again, inanely, before pulling him in for another kiss, stumbling back into the room.

Yes, she thought dreamily, as Levi lifted her up into his arms, *Christmas surely is the grandest of all the holidays.*

Thank you so much for reading! If you enjoyed this book, you may also enjoy the other books in the series! They can be found here:

Unicorns and Honey Cakes (Sylvie and Gale's story)
Dragons and Cupcakes (Kira and Caleb's story)
Griffins and Apple Pies (Natasha and Kieran's story)
Hellhounds and Angel Cakes (Henry and Luna's story)

CHIMERAS AND CHRISTMAS CAKES

Margot pouted. "Technically, it *will* be morning."

"That's true," Levi laughed. "Lead the way."

She stood up and moved toward the bedroom, where they had each placed their carefully wrapped presents. As she passed through the doorway, she stopped, noticing something new.

A sprig of mistletoe hung over the door.

She blinked at it. No, that definitely hadn't been there earlier!

She turned to Levi, confused. "Is your house sprouting again? This seems to be becoming an ongoing issue."

"What? No!" Levi shook his head. "Are you telling me that in all your research about Christmas, you never read about mistletoe?"

"I did, but..." She racked her brains, trying to remember. She hadn't seen much – just a quick mention – but now that she thought about it...

"Oh." She could feel her cheeks turning warm, and it wasn't just from the nog. "Did you put that there?"

"Well, I certainly hope no one else entered my home and tried to steal a kiss from you," Levi said with an arched eyebrow. "Is this a Christmas tradition that you think you would enjoy?"

"Only with you," she breathed, wrapping one arm around his waist and using the other hand to pull his head down for a searing kiss. It took her breath away every time, each kiss even better than the last, his warmth seeming to fill her entire being.

I have a whole lifetime of kisses to look forward to, she thought dazedly, even as she kissed him again.

Eventually she had to pull back for air, and she opened her eyes, looking up at him, his cheeks flushed slightly pink, his stormy blue eyes hooded with lust.

ZOE CHANT

texture and moistness balanced so that it practically melted in her mouth, the flavors of the fruits and spices combining to create a heavenly feast for her tastebuds, offset by the subtlest hint of candied orange and lemon peel.

She followed it up with a mouthful of eggnog, before nodding decisively.

"The other Christmas cakes were wonderful, but *this* one is my favorite."

Levi laughed. "I should've known you'd be a traditionalist."

Margot held out the plate to him. "Would you like some?"

He shook his head. "Thanks, but I think I'll leave it to you. While I'm sure Sylvie's baking is amazing, I'm sure you're still going to enjoy it much more than I would. You keep that one for yourself – there's plenty of other cakes here I can enjoy."

The two of them sat like that for some time, just enjoying each other's quiet company and the cake and the nog, the wind whistling gently outside and the enormous clock that stood in the corner ticking stoically away.

Margot found the ticking almost hypnotic, watching the hand as it moved around and around – she wasn't used to clocks like this, but it was a wonderful way to record the passing of seconds, minutes, and hours.

Honestly, she would have fallen asleep right there and then, lulled by the clock and the warm drink, if not for the fact that she knew it was so very nearly Christmas. She couldn't just sleep through her first one!

Eventually, the clock ticked over until it was very nearly twelve, and she couldn't contain the excitement anymore.

"Can we go and exchange the presents now?"

Levi smiled. "It's traditional in these parts to wait until morning, but since this is your first Christmas, I think we can do it now."

CHIMERAS AND CHRISTMAS CAKES

SHIFTERS AND SWEETS BOOK FIVE

ZOE CHANT

AUTHOR'S NOTE

This book stands alone. However, it's the fifth in the sweet, exciting and heartwarming Shifters and Sweets series. Each book features a new couple, with a completely standalone adventure featuring sweet romance and a big helping of delicious baked goods. If you'd like to read the series in order, they are:

Unicorns and Honey Cakes (Sylvie and Gale's book) - also available on audiobook
Dragons and Cupcakes (Kira and Caleb's book)
Griffins and Apple Pies (Natasha and Kieran's book)
Hellhounds and Angel Cakes (Henry and Luna's book)

You can also buy the first three books of the series here in one boxset:

Shifters and Sweets Collection Volume One

CHAPTER 1

This is your last chance. If you don't do this, everything is going to be over. Forever.

Margot's fingers tightened into fists, even as a more rational voice inside her head gently suggested that maybe she was being just a *little* bit over-dramatic.

And who knew – maybe the voice was right. Maybe her own perception of her problems was a little overblown, and actually all of this was perfectly surmountable.

… Or maybe things were even worse than she'd originally thought, and not only was she condemned to a life of misery and failure, but she was also going to inadvertently cause the heat death of the universe, or something similarly horrendous.

She stifled a sigh, and made a conscious effort to unclench her hands.

What's with all the doom and gloom? I'm not normally like this. Sure, I can get a bit anxious occasionally, but I've usually got my head on at least reasonably straight.

That was all true… but then again, she usually wasn't operating under a do-or-die ultimatum. Or, at least, a do-or-

fail ultimatum, which wasn't exactly much better. Which one was worse – death, or humiliation?

Because that was what was on the line, here. Complete and utter embarrassment. Shame and disgrace to her family, all her ancestors, and probably any descendants that may one day come after her.

Because really, when your dad was a bigwig in magical research – specifically *the* go-to guy for all things levitation and telekinesis – and your mom was running the single biggest magical university in the world, well, expectations were that you would have managed to graduate from your course of study in practical magic before the age of twenty-six.

At the very least, it was expected that you wouldn't somehow manage to set your professor's beard on fire. Especially when you weren't even in pyromancy class.

It was a little impressive, she supposed, that she'd managed to summon a kind of magic that she'd never even once been trained in. The purple flames in Professor Imari's beard, unfortunately, had been even more impressive still, and she was lucky that he'd been able to douse them immediately – not with a spell, but by dunking his beard into the large-mouthed bottle of water that had been sitting on his lectern.

Not many things from the non-magical world filtered through to the magical world, but in this case, it had been fortunate that Professor Imari had been caught up in the non-magical world's craze for oversized bottles of water. *Hydration is important*, he'd always said. Little had he known how true that would turn out to be.

Luckier still was that Margot hadn't been suspended or expelled on the spot. She suspected that the only thing that had saved her was that because everyone knew she was so

CHIMERAS AND CHRISTMAS CAKES

bad at magic, they all knew that there was no way she could have done such a thing on purpose.

Still, the punishment she'd received had almost been worse.

Being expelled, horribly soul-crushing though it would have been, would have at least brought a definite end to things. She would've slid to the bottom rung of magical society, barely able to find a way to survive beyond the bare essentials, but at least she wouldn't have to go back to class anymore. She just wasn't cut out for magic, and she knew it.

But no, instead of being expelled, she was being given a second chance. A second chance that involved a major magical research project, which, should she pass it, would be enough to scrape her through to an overall passing grade.

If it had just been research, she could've maybe done it. While she didn't consider herself *skilled* at research per se, she was at least passable at it. But magical research always involved a practical element – you had to prove what you were researching, after all – and it was this element that filled her with dread.

She'd wanted to tell them no. To beg them to please just let her bow out with as much dignity as she could muster, meager though it would be.

But it would've killed her parents. They'd been so supportive of her studies over the years, making sure she had access to whatever materials she needed, tutoring her at home in their scarce spare time, and generally just being so wonderfully encouraging that she knew it would break their hearts if she dropped out.

And how would it look, if the daughter of two of the most powerful witches and wizards in the world couldn't even pass the most basic of magical studies? She didn't know anyone who had failed.

Ever.

ZOE CHANT

There were occasional whispers of people who never mastered basic magic and just locked themselves away, living as recluses, or who went out to the non-magical world in order to try their luck. But it was all very hush-hush, and most definitely not something to aspire to. The complete opposite, in fact.

No. She had to go through with it. She had to pass. Not just for her, but for her parents.

Which was how she'd ended up here, on this bus, looking out the window as the snow grew thicker and thicker on the ground as the bus chugged up the winding mountain road, making grumbling noises on the steeper bits.

If nothing else, she supposed that she was having an adventure.

She'd never been on a bus before, and had barely seen snow, having grown up in warmer climes. The magical world wasn't really quite part of the non-magical world, existing alongside it but not quite in it. It wasn't in a physically different place – it was more just slightly out of phase with it.

A different state of mind, was how she thought it was most easily described. There were things going on in each world that the others just weren't aware of, slipping past on the edge of a person's consciousness.

The only difference was that magical people could move into the non-magical world when they chose to, while non-magical people didn't have the choice. Sometimes they might catch something magical out the corner of their eye and be confused for a moment, but then they'd shake it off as a moving shadow, or their mind playing tricks on them, or anything other than what it actually was: the presence of magic, just beyond their perception.

Given that she was incapable of safely traveling long distances via magical means, she had no choice but to go out into the non-magical world and interact with non-magical

4

CHIMERAS AND CHRISTMAS CAKES

people – and so here she was, on a bus, heading to a town she'd never heard of. It was interesting, watching the world go by for hours on end, although she could've done without the part where her knees were brushing the seat in front of her and her butt was slowly going numb.

An irritatingly familiar voice intruded on her thoughts.

Are you going to spend this entire trip finding things to complain about? Because if you are, let me know now, so I can tune you out.

Margot's nose scrunched up in mild annoyance. *You already 'tune me out,' as you so euphemistically put it. 'Ignore me constantly' would be more accurate.*

Her familiar, Monty, turned his cat nose up at her in disdain as he strutted along the headrest of the seat in front of her, his whiskers twitching, large fluffy tail wiggling.

Maybe I would pay more attention to you if you had something worthwhile to say.

Margot bit her lip to keep from answering out loud. In the magical world, it would have been perfectly normal for her to reply to him – even though the witches and wizards around her wouldn't have been able to hear what he said, they would have been able to see him, and would have known that they could communicate.

But her parents had warned her that in the non-magical world, people did not have familiars. They couldn't even *see* Monty – he was more of a *spiritual* cat than an *actual* cat. Regular people could only see him if he chose to be perceived.

She supposed that there might be circumstances under which his invisibility would be handy... and being on this non-magic bus was probably one of them, given the way he was currently sitting on the back of the seat in front of her, presumably flicking his tail around in the face of the person sitting in it.

Ahead of her, she heard the man sneeze.

Maybe Monty's invisible tail got up his nose.

Margot might have wondered if that was even possible, but right now, she was just trying to remember not to talk aloud to Monty. A long-time habit of chatting away to her familiar, snooty and superior though he could act, was hard to break!

His presence, annoying as it was, reminded her of her mission, and she sobered once more. It wasn't just her and her family's pride that was at stake – it was Monty's entire presence in her life.

Familiars were only granted provisionally to those who studied magic, with the lifetime's relationship only guaranteed upon the witch or wizard's graduation as a full-fledged magic user. If she flunked out, Monty would be reallocated to some other up-and-coming magical practitioner.

And that was something that she simply could not even contemplate. Not for a moment.

It didn't matter how much he got on her nerves, or delivered snide running commentaries, or put holes in her favorite clothes. He was her closest companion in the world, and the thought of having to give him up to someone else was more than she could bear.

No, she thought, her resolve strengthening. *I have to graduate. For him, if no one else.*

Well, she was almost at her destination – this town known as Girdwood Springs. She'd never heard of it before beginning her research – at least, not by that name – but then again, there were a lot of places she hadn't heard of.

She was here to look for a rare flower – the rarest flower in the world, in fact: the *flos nivis*. The snow flower.

So named because it bloomed only once a year, on the coldest nights of the year, when the snow was at its heaviest.

And it was so rare that no one was *really* sure where it

CHIMERAS AND CHRISTMAS CAKES

grew, and there were only a few – nebulous and doubtful – reports to go on, written long ago in ancient tomes locked away in dusty libraries.

Ordinarily, Margot might not even bother with what was so obviously a forlorn hope, but she'd known she'd needed to pull something truly spectacular out of the bag in order to have any hope of passing her studies.

So she'd spent her whole semester break poring over those ancient tomes locked away in dusty libraries, until she *thought* she had a… very vague, rough, probably totally wrong idea about where the *flos nivis* might be found.

And if I can find it...

Well, if she could find it, she'd never have to worry about her studies again. She would gain her degree, and then try to put all the years of frustration and disappointment behind her.

Legends bestowed upon the *flos nivis* a wide array of magical properties, some more outlandish than others – everything from granting a witch or wizard the ability to create mighty magical earth tremors, to enhancing their powers to untold new heights, to curing the common cold within an instant.

Margot didn't know what to believe about any of it, but she supposed that that was the entire point of the research project – to find the flower, and determine what it could actually *do*. If it was capable of even a tenth of what had been attributed to it over the years, then that would be more than enough for her to spend the rest of her life studying it.

Well. Probably someone else *could spend the rest of their life studying it. Several someone elses, even. I don't think I'd be the best candidate for carrying out magical research on a rare and precious flower. But just bringing it back would be such a gift to magical society I could coast on it for a good long while,* Margot thought.

Professor Imari had jumped at the chance to approve her

research project – but Margot had a feeling that was just to get her as far away as possible from him, and his still slightly singed beard.

And to be honest, Margot didn't have much faith in her own ability to carry out her own research task.

But I have to try, she thought, biting her lip. *Monty is counting on me.*

I most certainly am not, Monty informed her haughtily, as he finally stopped wiggling his tail around in the man in front of her's face and leapt gracefully down, his spiritual form coasting down through the air to land weightlessly on her lap. *Do you think I, me, moi, need to rely on anyone?*

"Oh, of course not, Monty," Margot said, momentarily forgetting in her haste to soothe his ruffled feathers that she wasn't supposed to talk to him out loud. "I know you're more than capable of taking care of yourself."

She giggled a little as she ruffled her fingers through the soft black fur of his belly, just the way she knew he loved, as he tried – and absolutely failed – to keep his dignity as he writhed around on her lap, purring like an idiot.

Margot forgot all about the spectacle she must be making of herself until she happened to catch the odd look the old lady sitting across the aisle was giving her, and gulped.

She couldn't imagine what a picture she must make to a non-magical person. To another witch, she was *obviously* tickling her fingers over her familiar's belly while he yowled and wriggled as if he hated it, even though he literally loved it.

But to a non-magical person...

Jerking her hands back from Monty's fluffy tummy, Margot attempted a smile, hoping she wasn't coming off as *too* crazy. It was just way too hard to remember not to do certain things when she'd been doing them her whole life. The man at the bus station had asked her where her luggage

was, and she'd blinked at him, dumbfounded, about to say *Well, obviously everything I need for travel is right here in my tote* – which, technically it wasn't, of course, it was just short-hand for the fact that her tote had a pocket dimension inside it, with everything she'd need for her journey in it.

Luckily, she'd caught herself at the last minute and just said, *Oh no, I'm traveling light!* and sauntered her way onto the bus as if she didn't have a care in the world.

But being unable to resist giving Monty's belly a good scritch had now been her undoing.

Her heartbeat sped up. Had she blown it already? Was this lady going to report her as a witch to the police? Margot had heard that was a thing that could happen here in the non-magical world.

But thankfully, after a rather strained pause, the old lady returned her smile, even if it was a little bit warily.

"Where are you heading then, dearie?" the old lady asked after a moment – maybe she was assuming Margot *was* soft in the head, and was starting to feel sorry for staring.

"Oh, um, Girdwood Springs," Margot managed to stutter out, as Monty, clearly in a huff at being deprived of his belly rubs, stood up, shoving his ineffable cat butthole in her face, before leaping off to prowl about the seats, invisibly annoying the other passengers.

"Ah, lovely little town," the lady said a little more warmly now. "I have family there. It'll be lovely this time of year – you must be going for your Christmas vacation."

Margot blinked, opening her mouth and then closing it again.

Christmas?

She was about to say *I'm sorry but – what's Christmas?* when finally her brain caught up with her mouth.

You've read about Christmas! You know *what that is!*

And she did – sort of?

ZOE CHANT

She *had* read about it – she'd read as much as she could about non-magical culture before she'd departed for this journey, but that had had the effect of making her head feel so overloaded with information that she had to spend some time rummaging around for what she wanted.

Maybe there is such a thing as being overprepared, she thought, even as she fixed a bright smile on her face.

"Oh yes!" she said, hoping she sounded suitably excited. She'd read, after all, that Christmas was a time to celebrate, filled with joy and excitement. "I *definitely* am! I'm so looking forward to – um –"

Ah, fiddlesticks.

Margot realized, to her horror, that she couldn't actually remember, specifically, what non-magical people did on Christmas.

What was it again?

"To… to hunt for my… my Christmas eggs, after the Christmas stork delivers them for me, and um, to carve a pumpkin in the shape of… of… a reindeer," she managed to stutter out finally.

There. That's right, isn't it?

Or, she reconsidered, after seeing the expression on the lady's face, maybe not.

"Well, folks must do Christmas a little differently where you're from," the old lady said, after yet another *very* uncomfortable pause. "But as long as you're having fun and enjoying the holiday season."

Margot deflated a little as the old lady turned away, whispering a little to the equally old man next to her – probably about the poor, confused woman she'd just been talking to.

Clearly, Margot decided, she was going to have to study up a bit more on non-magic traditions before she tried to interact with anyone else, or she wasn't going to fit in here at all.

CHIMERAS AND CHRISTMAS CAKES

Not that she really needed to, since she was determined to find the *flos nivis* as quickly as possible and go home, and hopefully never leave the magical world, shame her parents, or set anyone's beard on fire ever again.

"Girdwood Springs Main Street is our next stop – if you're getting off at Girdwood Springs Main Street, make sure you have all your belongings with you and prepare to exit the bus at the next stop."

Thankfully, the driver's announcement – and *that* had been a bit of a shock to her system too, a mode of transport that needed a driver! Crazy! – cut any further conversation she might have had with the old lady short.

She shot up in her seat as Monty made his graceful way back to her, leaping weightlessly from seat back to seat back, before winding his way around her shoulders like a living, very fluffy scarf.

Time to get off, is it? he asked as he nestled comfortingly against her cheek, blinking his big yellow eyes.

Yes, Margot told him in her mind – *not* out loud – as, determinedly, she marched toward the front of the bus. *Now, all I have to do is try not to mess everything up.*

I'm sure you won't, Monty reassured her, as the bus came to a stop.

Margot raised an eyebrow. *Are you actually sure about that?*

Nope, Monty said cheerfully, as he wafted his tail in her face. *Not even slightly.*

Well, that was fairly typical of Monty, Margot thought as she went down the steps, resisting the urge to roll her eyes. He'd *seem* to say something encouraging, only for – for –

"What – what – *what?!*"

This time, Margot *did* speak out loud – but it was mainly because she surely couldn't keep her thoughts in her head this time. She was *way* too overwhelmed by the sight in front of her for that!

11

ZOE CHANT

What is *all this?!*

She stared around her, blinking in disbelief, as if she expected everything to disappear in the split second her eyes were closed.

For spread out before her, in a glittering, wondrous display, was the most amazing thing she had ever seen.

The town – Girdwood Springs, presumably – was draped in snow and bedecked in a wild array of color and light, glittering like some precious and multifaceted jewel. Margot barely knew where to look first.

She gazed at the scene before her, trying to take it all in. The snow was deep and fluffy where it lay along the ground, and was of the purest white, with tiny sparkles where the light caught it. Icicles glimmered along the eaves of the buildings.

But beyond the natural beauty, there was the *light* and the *color* – strings of vibrant, twinkling lights seemed to adorn every possible surface, even the bare branches of the trees, casting gentle pale patches of red and green and gold onto the snow.

It took her breath away. There was nothing like this back home! Sure, magical light displays were a dime a dozen – which was a saying she'd read they used in the non-magical world – but Margot had to admit that she was a bit bored of them at this point. Each was bigger and more spectacular than the last, and while she admired the mastery of those who performed the feats, it had all gotten a bit… dull.

You could do anything with magic after all, but…

The people in this town did all this… without *magic?!*

There was something about these lights and the sheer *physicality* of them that just tugged at her heart in the most wonderful way, even as she marveled at how they could even work. They seemed to be joined together by little black

strings. She couldn't help but wonder at where those strings went and what they did.

Not that she was *completely* detached from how the non-magical world did things – she had caught glimpses in the past, and there were witches and wizards who used 'technology' to enhance their magic. There had just never been much reason, or opportunity, for her to learn about these things.

She stood there and watched, entranced, knowing full well her mouth was hanging open, as the lights blinked on and off. She was only dimly aware of the bus pulling away behind her and Monty insistently headbutting the side of her head from his perch upon her shoulder.

It really was lovely.

The lights, not the headbutting.

Eventually, she dragged her eyes away from the light display so that she could take in the rest of the decorations. Everywhere she looked, there was something new and strange and wonderful to see: giant red-and-white-striped hooks, a fat old man in red pajamas, holly wreaths, colorful round balls, strings of a glittering metallic substance, a herd of reindeer.

Ha! she thought triumphantly. *I knew I was right about the reindeer!*

There's a first time for everything, Monty sniffed.

You say that like a cat who doesn't want to get his treat, she shot back.

Monty shut up real fast. For a cat that spent most of his time as an invisible specter and technically didn't actually need food, he sure did like to scarf down a piece of fish – or ten – when he was in his physical form.

Margot continued to look for a while longer, just happy to bask in the strangeness and wonder of it all, and to breathe in the crisp, clean mountain air.

"Excuse me, miss –"

ZOE CHANT

Margot jumped at the sound of a voice behind her, and realized, to her slight mortification, that she'd simply been standing in the middle of the public thoroughfare, blocking the passers-by who were clearly just trying to go about their day.

"Sorry! I'm sorry!" she babbled, as she jumped out of the way of a young couple and their two apple-cheeked children, bundled up in woolen hats and scarves, their jackets making them round as pumpkins.

Margot couldn't help but stare as they passed. If the weather got a bit nippy in the magical world, she and everyone else she knew just cast a spell to keep a bubble of warm air around them as they moved about. The spell was so simple that even *she* could do it easily. There wasn't any need to bundle up so much!

But *everyone* seemed to be dressed like that – everyone had on earmuffs and woolen scarves and gloves and long coats and jackets.

Okay, note to self: in the interest of blending, make sure I wear some of those things, Margot thought, as she turned in a circle on the spot, simply trying to take it all in.

It was clear, however, that all the cultural preparation she *thought* she'd done back home was manifestly inadequate.

I need to know more! And – she thought, shivering, and realizing just how cold her cheeks were getting – *I need to get inside and figure out where to go from here.*

She did have a magical map she could follow – one not created by her, obviously, since her sense of direction wasn't the best – but she decided to put it aside for a bit and just wander. She could always get it out if she needed to, but for the moment she was content to see where her feet would take her.

Also, she realized suddenly, she could smell the most

incredible smell. Quite possibly the best smell she'd ever encountered in her life.

She drifted dreamily down the snow-lined street, letting her nose guide her, only half-noticing as Monty trailed little snowy pawprints in his wake. The smell, somehow, got even better.

Is there anything about Girdwood Springs that isn't *amazing?!*

In the end, she didn't have to go far at all – just to the next shop, in fact.

That's it, she thought happily as she read the sign above the door.

That's the smell.

Looming before her, dark and wooden and old – and, oddly, completely devoid of Christmas cheer – was the source of the wonderful smell:

Thorne's Antique Booksellers.

If there could have been any doubt about the store's contents, the area just outside the front door was stacked high with boxes of old books, barely protected from the snow by a striped awning.

A small wave of indignation rose within her at the sight. Who would dare to treat books so shabbily, leaving them out in the snow to freeze?!

Well, maybe she would just have to rescue them.

Despite the cold, the front door was propped open, and she peered inside. Piles of ancient tomes teetered precariously in the dreary gloom, and she couldn't suppress a blissful sigh.

Stomping the snow off her shoes, she took in another deep breath of that heavenly old book smell, and entered.

CHAPTER 2

*G*reat. *Wonderful. Fantastic.* More *books.*

Well, to be honest, Levi wasn't sure exactly what else he should have expected to find in a box shoved up the back of his great aunt's old bookshop but even more books... but, still.

He hadn't asked for this – any of this.

He'd always known about his Great Aunt Aida, who'd left their chimera village to strike it out on her own in the human world. It hadn't exactly been a *secret*, but then, no one in the village had actually approved of her choice either – even if she was one of those shifters who, due to the ornery and secretive nature of their shifter type, had never actually managed to shift, and take on the form of her chimera.

It wasn't exactly an uncommon problem amongst chimeras – unlike other shifter types, chimeras preferred to keep themselves to themselves, and that included not revealing themselves to the world until they really, *really* felt like it. And sometimes, that *until they felt like it* never actually came.

Great Aunt Aida had been one of those unfortunate

16

CHIMERAS AND CHRISTMAS CAKES

shifters whose chimera had chosen to remain hidden – and once she'd hit a certain age and still hadn't shifted, she'd announced to the whole village that she was taking off and finding her own way in the world. It was just never going to be all that comfortable living in a chimera village, as a shifter who couldn't shift.

Just like me.

Levi shook his head.

No, not just like me.

But as much as he tried to deny it, he had to admit, with every year that passed, he was losing more and more hope.

At twenty-seven, he was well past the age that most chimera shifters finally figured out how to coax their inner chimera to the surface. And yet, his remained stubbornly curled up inside him, refusing to come out, refusing to even *speak* to him a lot of the time, except to offer him some cantankerous, unhelpful advice or snarky comment, before going straight back to sleep, its scaled tail curled around its lion's head, its giant eagle's wings folded around its body.

Just like his great aunt, he too was a shifter who couldn't shift. Even his parents had stopped bringing it up, and resigned themselves to the fact that he'd be just like Aida.

Except, Levi thought, as he started lifting dusty old books out the box he'd found shoved under the shelves, *I'd never run away from the chimera village to open a bookshop in a human village, and then send a note out of the blue one day to my family saying I'd met an unbelievably handsome silver-haired dragon shifter on my annual vacation to Florida and was off on a whirlwind round-the-world honeymoon with him, so can you please go and sort out my stock and shut up shop because I won't be back!*

So now, this shop and everything in it was simply someone else's problem.

Namely, his.

In some ways, Levi had to grudgingly admit, he did kind

ZOE CHANT

of admire Aida. She did what she wanted, when she wanted. Even if it meant he was now in possession of a bookshop he'd never asked for, since his family had decided for whatever reason that the mess Aida had left behind was *his* job to sort out.

True, he was the only one of his siblings who didn't have children yet, and so wasn't in the midst of trying to prepare what seemed like endless Christmas celebrations and getting their present shopping done, so he *supposed* he could see where they were coming from.

And at the time, Levi had thought it might be a good chance to get away from all that. It wasn't that he didn't love his brothers and sisters and what seemed like their immense horde of children – it just felt like a constant reminder, at this time of year especially, of everything he'd never have.

No one would choose a chimera who couldn't shift as their partner.

He knew it – it was unspoken, but it was generally just *known* that chimeras who never managed to figure out how to bring out their shifted forms just weren't really considered marriage material.

Levi wondered if that was part of the reason Aida had decided to run off. She'd known it'd never happen for her, so she'd gone to find her own happiness – a different kind of happiness.

Until the ripe old age of sixty-three, when she suddenly met her dragon shifter fancy man, apparently, Levi thought, shaking his head.

He sighed as he sifted through yet *more* books with disgustingly cheerful caroling children on the cover, holding candles and delighting homeowners – who had probably just been trying to enjoy their dinner before these kids showed up – with their merry songs. He *did* have to wonder about her taste in books.

18

He'd never liked Christmas, and being here now in Great Aunt Aida's bookshop, trying to sort through the stock she'd unceremoniously dumped on him, he was finding nothing in particular to endear it to him.

He'd never thought about it particularly hard in the past, but now that he'd been thrust into this situation, it struck him that it was kind of... *weird*... how much chimeras liked Christmas. Not only did they tend to be a bit grumpy and antisocial by nature, but they weren't overly integrated into human society, either – while they didn't keep themselves fully apart from it, they did more or less keep mainly to themselves, and follow their own traditions.

Except for Christmas, it seemed. And a couple of other random things that had carried over somehow, like water polo, Arbor Day, and root beer floats. Levi could only assume that some overly enthusiastic chimeras in the past had brought these things in from the outside world, and made them into a *thing*. He guessed that when your community was small, it didn't take much for certain crazes to take over.

But Christmas was the biggest one of them all. Chimeras *loved* Christmas. It was like it gave them all an excuse to shed their cranky, antisocial exteriors and become their cheeriest, most festive selves.

Levi hated it.

Well, 'hate' was probably a strong word. But it wasn't that far off the mark. He'd just never been able to get into the Christmas spirit. Why should he start acting chirpy just because the time of year dictated it? There was no need for it. If he was going to be happy, it was going to be on his terms.

Even as a kid, he'd never gotten it. His parents had rolled their eyes in fond exasperation as he'd crossed his arms and huffed, exclaiming that he'd *never* like Christmas, *never EVER*. They'd told him that he'd understand one day, but that day had never come. If anything, he liked it even less now. Now,

ZOE CHANT

as an adult, Christmas came with expectations that he would actively contribute to the charade, and he wanted no part of it.

No, it being Christmas was just the cherry on top of this whole situation. He sighed as he looked at the insufferably festive book.

Don't suppose you'd feel like helping? he asked his chimera where it was curled into a tight ball inside him.

It twitched its scaled tail, ruffled its feathered wings, and Levi thought he caught a glimpse of a golden lion's eye.

Nope, it said.

Then it went back to sleep.

No. Of course not.

Levi wasn't even sure why he'd bothered to ask. His chimera had made itself clear: the outside world held no interest to it whatsoever.

Irritated, he scrawled the word 'FREE' onto a box and then tossed the book into it with a satisfying *thump.* The sooner he could get rid of this stuff, the sooner he could get out of here and stop looking at pictures of jaunty-looking elves and prancing reindeer.

Of course, this store had been here for decades, and he doubted that the good people of this town – *what was it called again? Kirkwood Springs?* – would happily whisk away several thousand books out of the goodness of their hearts. So he was going to have to sort out how the hell he was going to get rid of all the leftovers as well, not to mention trying to sell a dark, dusty, musty old shop in the middle of nowhere.

Thanks, Great Aunt Aida, he thought sourly. *Thanks so much for jetting off with your age-appropriate boy toy and leaving me to deal with your mess.*

His nose twitched in annoyance... or possibly an impending sneeze from all the dust he was stirring up.

Nope, definitely a sneeze. He pressed his tongue to the

CHIMERAS AND CHRISTMAS CAKES

roof of his mouth, stifling the sneeze in its tracks, his eyes watering just a bit.

Levi paused a moment, waiting to see if the sneeze would come back, and that was when he heard it – the tread of feet on creaky floorboards.

A customer? But the shop's closed up!

Had he forgotten to close the door when he took the last box of books outside? He didn't want customers – he just wanted people to take the boxed-up books away somewhere, anywhere, as long as it wasn't here.

But no, somebody had obviously wandered in – and, if the increasing volume of the footsteps was any indication, they were wandering farther and farther into the labyrinthine corridors of the store. The place was so stuffed with books and shelves and who knew what else that a person could easily get lost.

Levi pinched the bridge of his nose.

Great. Fantastic. Just what I need – some nosy person who'll come in and ask me why the books are being packed up, and where Aida is, and who I am, and a bunch of other stuff I neither know how nor care to answer. Just take your free books and go. Go. Shoo.

He remained stock-still as the footsteps stopped and started, and stifled a groan. Any remaining hopes he had of the person wandering off were being well and truly dashed.

"Hello? Is anyone here?" a voice called out, and Levi barely restrained an annoyed groan. It was a woman's voice, and she sounded friendly.

Levi didn't like *friendly*. *Friendly* invariably led to *chatty*.

He slid back farther into the dark corner, blocking his nose against the gentle rain of dust that fell upon him, and listened with growing irritation to the approaching voice as it muttered to itself.

"Where's the reference section?" the woman said thoughtfully. "Or… oh, this is a cookbook! I could use one of those…

21

ZOE CHANT

oh, a book on… knitting? And this book is about Hanukkah! That's a holiday, right?"

Levi blinked at the sudden jumping from topic to topic. What exactly was this woman looking for? He was almost tempted to go out and try to help her find whatever it was – the sooner she left, the sooner he could go back to clearing this place out, instead of hiding in the corner.

No. Not hiding. Strategically waiting.

He continued to strategically wait, but to no avail, as the woman was clearly now a few short feet away, just on the other side of the shelves. She came to a halt directly across from him, and he scowled.

"So if Santa has reindeer that help him deliver hot cross buns, and they've been doing so for many years," she mused, "then they must be pretty old. Where does he get the new ones to replace them from? Does he breed them? Or maybe they're magical reindeer. They must be magical, if they can fly."

Levi blocked his nose against another incoming sneeze, even as he wondered what the hell this woman was trying to accomplish. His Great Aunt Aida had a lot of books about Christmas, but he was pretty sure that none of them covered Santa's reindeer breeding regime.

Could he sneak out past her, and come back later once she'd gone? Or maybe she'd take the shop off his hands – she seemed like she would be happy to wander the stacks forever.

Once I'm done here, I'm definitely rewarding myself with something. Like a hot dog.

Hot dogs were one thing chimeras didn't seem to have bought into, but Levi had to admit that he liked them.

Yes, he'd reward himself with a hot dog after all this was done. He thought he deserved it.

As he contemplated his soon-to-be reward of mouthwa-

22

CHIMERAS AND CHRISTMAS CAKES

teringly delicious processed meat in an absolutely un-nutritious white bun, hoping his unwanted customer would finish up whatever she was doing and leave, he suddenly became aware of the shelf in front of him wobbling precariously – followed by the woman's surprised cry of *whoops!*

Whoops?! Levi had time to think – a moment before a pile of very large, very heavy, very dusty books came toppling down from above him, landing squarely on his head.

Make that two hot dogs, he thought grimly. *With extra onions. And a very large beer.*

"Ow," he muttered without thinking, rubbing his head, and the woman on the other side of the shelves suddenly fell silent.

The silence grew longer, and then longer still. Levi thought that if he just stayed silent, maybe she would think she'd hallucinated his voice and wander off elsewhere.

"Hello?" she called hesitantly. "Did I hurt you? I'm sorry!"

No such luck, then. He stayed silent, trying to blend with the shadows, though he knew it was probably a lost cause. He didn't exactly *blend* easily at the best of times, being a six-foot-five chimera shifter, but there was no way he could blend with a bookshelf, no matter how much dust he was now coated in.

And speaking of dust…

Oh no. Not now. Not now –

The sneeze, of course, paid no heed to his request, and chose that moment to make itself known. It trumpeted through the silence of the store, followed quickly by another, and then another.

The sounds reverberated off the walls for a moment, before silence descended once more.

Well. She probably won't think she hallucinated that.

Levi was weighing up whether he could just leave the

23

ZOE CHANT

store out the back way before she saw him, when suddenly one of the books in the shelf slid backward, creating a gap.

"Oh!" said the voice. "So there *is* someone here. I am so, so sorry. I can't say how sorry I am. I'm such a klutz, oh my goodness." Her voice lowered to a barely audible mutter. "This is so typical. Drop books on the handsome man, why don't you, Margot?"

Levi shook his head, confused, and then bent down to look through the gap in the books. An eye peered back at him. As far as eyes went, he had to admit that it was interesting – a pale green, flecked with gold, with darker green at the edges. He found himself staring into it.

"Hi!" the voice said, sounding a little surprised, and the eye blinked rapidly. "I'm Margot! I'm, uh, really sorry about before. Are you okay?"

It would be churlish of him not to respond, he supposed. Even though he really, really hated small talk.

"I'm okay," he said, trying not to sound *too* much like he would rather be literally anywhere else in the world right now. "It wasn't your fault. This place is an OSHA nightmare."

"Oh… uh… sure, I guess. OSHA," she said, repeating it as if she'd never heard the word before, and now it was Levi's turn to blink. This Margot was a bit of a strange one. Probably exactly the type of person to frequent a moldy old bookstore. And yet, as much as he hated to admit it, he found her oddly fascinating.

While he was trying to work out how to respond, she spoke up again. "You know, this is a bit silly, the two of us talking through a gap like this. Is it okay if I come around there?"

Before he could reply – and really, it would be a bit much to say no, even for him – the eye disappeared, and then a few moments later a woman rounded the corner.

"Oh! There you are!" she said brightly, her face breaking

24

CHIMERAS AND CHRISTMAS CAKES

into a smile. Her gaze drifted up to his face. "Wow, you're tall!"

"I guess I am," he said helplessly, unable to think of a better response. She looked a little embarrassed, probably realizing that she had just stated the obvious, her cheeks turning a light shade of pink.

It was... *cute*. Which wasn't a word he would normally use, but he couldn't think of a better way to describe it.

She was pretty cute all around, in fact, with her big green eyes and long blonde hair, some of which fell almost to her waist, while the rest was arranged in elaborate plaits. A long, multi-colored skirt swished around her sensibly-booted ankles, and a shawl was wrapped around her shoulders.

So, besides *cute*, he could probably add *eccentric* to the list. And also *gorgeous* –

That stopped him cold. Since when did he go around thinking that kind of thing about random women he'd just met? And random women who'd just dumped dusty old tomes on his head, at that?

But there was no denying it – there was something about her that just grabbed his attention in a way that no one else ever had. He couldn't quite put his finger on it, but it was indisputable.

He realized that he was staring at her in a way that was also definitely not like him. The only redeeming factor was that she was staring as well – their eyes locked for a moment, and he found it almost impossible to look away.

What on earth is going on here?

A movement in the corner of his vision grabbed his attention, and he gratefully took the opportunity to look away from her – admittedly beautiful – eyes.

A black cat meandered down the aisle, weaving around the piles of books and brushing against Margot's leg. He didn't *think* it had been here earlier, and he knew that Great

25

ZOE CHANT

Aunt Aida definitely would've mentioned it if there was a cat living at the store. It also seemed pretty comfy around Margot, so surely it had to be her cat.

He would've been surprised, but he was rapidly getting the impression that Margot was the kind of person who *would* take a cat shopping without a second thought.

In any case, it was a good distraction. He cleared his throat, partially because it was still full of dust, and partially because this Margot made him feel oddly self-conscious.

"Is that your cat?" he asked. The cat stopped its wanderings and stared at him.

Margot's eyes widened in delight. "You can see Monty?" she exclaimed. "Oh! *Oh!* Then you must be – oh thank goodness. That makes things so much easier, oh my goodness."

Levi frowned. She was… surprised he could see her cat? Her very large, very fluffy cat?

He moved *eccentric* up to the top of the list of words that best described her, and mentally underlined it a few times for good measure.

"This is great," Margot went on. "If you've been living here, you can help me learn about these people and their customs. I've been doing my research, but I'm so confused! Someone like you would be such a help, you have no idea."

"I'd like to help you how I can… *if* I can," Levi said quickly, before she could get the wrong idea and carry the conversation off in a direction that it would be hard to backtrack from.

And he didn't even want to think about what she meant by *these people and their customs…* though he was starting to get the impression that maybe she was from a completely different place.

And he didn't even know why he'd offered to help her. He didn't even know her! And he had enough on his hands already, without doing good deeds for beautiful strangers.

26

CHIMERAS AND CHRISTMAS CAKES

Strangers, he mentally amended. *It doesn't matter that she's beautiful, it's still trouble I don't need.*

Margot opened her mouth, looking for all the world like she was about to launch into ten questions at once, and Levi quickly spoke up before she could start talking again.

"Your cat is, uh…" he said lamely, mentally flailing around for the appropriate word. Finally, he settled on, "Cute."

It had been the right thing to say, apparently – a brilliant smile spread across her face, lighting up her eyes. At her feet, Monty seemed to preen, and Levi reminded himself not to get caught up anthropomorphizing the creature – it wasn't like it could understand what was being said about it.

"Monty *is* cute, aren't you, Monty?" Margot crooned, scooping up the cat and scratching him under his chin. She turned to face Levi. "Do you want to pet him?"

"Well, I –" Levi said, before he cut himself off. He'd been about to say no, but Margot looked so hopeful. He hated the idea that he could let her down.

Where is any of this even coming from? he thought desperately. *I just met her! And she almost knocked me out!*

"Please?" said Margot, looking at him beseechingly. "I feel so bad about dropping those books on you, so if you'd like a little bit of cat time, it's the least I can do."

Really, how could he say no to that?

Her smile was already starting to fade ever so slightly as he failed to respond, and he found that he hated that. He didn't know why, but the sight of her looking anything other than blissfully happy made *him* feel unhappy.

He made his way over, hesitating for a second before he reached out and touched Monty's belly, which was just as soft as it looked.

He'd never had a cat of his own, and he knew they could be vicious if they felt threatened, but Monty seemed

ZOE CHANT

perfectly happy having his belly rubbed, if his deep, rumbling purr was any confirmation.

"He likes you," Margot said, and Levi looked up to see her brilliant smile once again.

Wow. I could get used to that.

He gazed at her for a long moment, before he suddenly became aware of the fact that Monty was now grabbing his hand with his front legs and bunny-kicking at it with his hind legs.

"He's jealous because you stopped paying attention to him," Margot said with a laugh, "Monty, that's enough. Don't kick at the nice man."

Monty responded by gnawing at his fingers, which Levi thought was much more in character with his general expectations of cat behavior. He carefully extricated himself from Monty's deadly grasp, and Margot lowered the cat to the floor.

"Sorry, he can be a bit of an attention hog," Margot said apologetically. "Between that and the books, I fear that I've caused you quite a lot of injuries in the past five minutes."

Levi shook his head. "It's nothing. Don't worry about it."

He was finding that it was a little easier to talk to Margot than it normally was to talk to people he'd only just met, though he had no idea why. Maybe this had all just been so unusual that it had shocked him out of his normal responses, or lack thereof.

Amazingly, instead of trying to find some excuse to hurry her out of the store, he found himself actually asking her a question.

"You said I could help you. What was it exactly you needed help with?" He grimaced a little. "Not that I think I'd actually be much help, since I don't know where anything is and don't actually work here."

Her brow creased in confusion. "You don't work here?"

28

CHIMERAS AND CHRISTMAS CAKES

"Well, it's a long story," he said. "The short version is that my great aunt owned this place, but now she doesn't want it, and I certainly don't have any experience with bookshops. Don't live in the area, either. So I'm sorting through everything and throwing it out so this place can be sold."

He gestured at the general mess of books with his arm, vaguely aware that he'd said more words in the past few minutes than he often would in a day. "If you see anything you want, just take it. Please. You'd be doing me a favor."

Margot stared at him, dismay clear on her face. "You're throwing out all these books and selling the shop? But this is… this is *heaven!*"

He shrugged. "If you want to buy it, feel free. And like I said, take what you want of the books. But I can't just turn my life on its head to become a bookseller because my great aunt decided she'd rather spend her time working on her tan with her new boyfriend."

Margot looked confused for a moment as she tried to follow along, before understanding dawned and she nodded. "I get it. I do. I can't just pack up and buy this place either, as much as I'd like to, so I can't really expect you to pack up your life for it, I guess. It's such a shame, though. I wish we could swap lives. You'd be so much better at my life than I am."

Levi wasn't sure why on earth she'd think that, but at least she'd given him an opening. "What are you looking for here, anyway? Like I said, I don't think I can help much, but I guess you never know."

Margot looked cagey for a moment, which wasn't an expression he would have expected from her. When she spoke, he felt like he wasn't getting the full story.

"Well," she said, "I'm in town for a bit of a research assignment. But then I saw the town all lit up for Christmas, and then I saw the books here about Christmas, and I

29

ZOE CHANT

figured this would be the place to learn more about it. I think I may have already embarrassed myself when I was talking to someone else about Christmas. My study did not prepare me."

Levi managed to hide his wince. *Oh God. I knew she had to have some kind of flaw. I just can't escape from the Christmas people. Why are they so obsessed with this holiday?!*

"The town was just so beautiful," Margot went on. "There's nothing like it where I'm from. I would really love to know more about it." She gazed up at him, her eyes imploring. "Will you teach me about Christmas?"

She looked so hopeful. How could he say no?

"Okay," he managed to get out through his gritted teeth eventually, hoping that he didn't sound actively unhappy about it. "Yeah, I can do that."

Her face lit up even brighter, and okay, yeah, he could do this. But he was definitely going to get some fries and pickles to go with those hot dogs. He one hundred percent deserved it.

"Thank you so much!" Margot said, bouncing a little on her toes. "Did you hear that, Monty? We're going to learn about Christmas from – from –" She faltered. "Uh, sorry, but I don't think I caught your name earlier. What was it again?"

It was kind of her to pretend that he hadn't been so rude as to just not introduce himself.

"Levi," he replied. "Levi Thorne."

"We're going to learn about Christmas from our friend Levi here," Margot continued. "And then maybe if we get time, he can tell us a bit about Easter as well!"

Levi thought he did a pretty good job of stifling his groan... though at least chimeras weren't completely obsessed with Easter, so it wasn't such a problem. He didn't actually know a lot about it himself.

"Well, should we go out and have a look at the town, and

you can tell me about Christmas?" Margot asked. "I'll buy you something to eat as recompense."

The thought of wandering through the snow with Margot had already sounded nice, but he had to admit that the added incentive of food was definitely a bonus. He'd been boxing up books for hours, and, he suddenly realized, he was ravenous.

Still, he didn't want her to feel like she had to pay. "Are you sure? I can get myself something to eat."

She shook her head. "Please. I insist. I practically concussed you, and then my cat attacked you, and now you're teaching me important cultural learnings. It's the least I can do."

She was obviously determined, and he didn't think she'd take no for an answer. What choice did he have, but to say, "Sure. It would be my pleasure."

"Great!" she said happily. "That's sorted out, then. Let's go. You'll have to lead the way, though, since I have no idea how to get out of here."

"That makes two of us," he said, and Margot laughed.

"Oh, wait," she said, as he went to move past her. "You've got some dust in your hair. A *lot* of dust in your hair."

Before he could react, she brushed at his hair absently, sending dust flying up into the air. That was startling enough, but then the slightest contact of her fingertip against his temple sent a bolt of electricity shooting straight through his body, radiating all the way to his fingers and toes, and he stopped short, stunned.

He knew what this was.

My mate. She's my mate.

Levi stood there, stock-still.

Within him, his chimera had actually lifted its head, blinking as if someone had just roused it from a deep slumber.

ZOE CHANT

Our mate? Our mate is here?

It was the most interest Levi had ever felt from it about what was going on outside of whatever dreams it had while it was curled away inside him.

It can't be true.

But even as he thought it, he knew it was.

And – and could this mean –

Will meeting my mate finally *mean my chimera reveals itself?*

Right now, his chimera didn't seem inclined to actually emerge – but it *was* interested.

And Levi knew, the only thing he could do now was to follow Margot.

No matter how... how odd *she seems.*

"Come on, slowpoke!" she laughed as she grabbed his hand, practically dragging him down the aisle. "You can explain to me the meaning of the jingling bells, and then we can partake of the nog!"

He followed as if in a daze, barely conscious of the movement of his legs.

This strange, beautiful, bewildering woman is my mate.

CHAPTER 3

My first bit of good luck since... well, ever! Meeting a wizard-errant who can show me around this strange – but amazing – place.

Margot knew there were some witches and wizards who chose to keep themselves separate and live full-time in the non-magical world, for various reasons of their own. It was a little contentious, actually, since most witches and wizards had long ago decided to simply keep themselves to themselves. But Margot had always thought it sounded quite romantic and exciting to strike out by yourself.

Too bad I would never be able to, she thought, biting her lip and stealing a glance at the man walking next to her – Levi Thorne, he'd said his name was.

She could right away see why *he* had decided to live independently. He was calm, cool, confident – and *strong*-looking too. He could clearly handle whatever situation he might be thrown into.

And... um, he's kind of handsome as well...

Kind of was putting it a little mildly, Margot thought, as

ZOE CHANT

she looked away, feeling a flush creeping up her cheeks. Levi was unlike any of her classmates at the university, that was for sure – he was tall and rugged, with larger muscles than she had ever seen. A lot of wizards didn't tend to be all that physically strong, given that they could use magic to easily accomplish whatever it was they wanted, but clearly Levi hadn't chosen that path.

He looked like even if he lost his magical abilities somehow, he'd be able to survive perfectly fine in the wilderness on his own – catching his own food, building his own shelter, doing bare-handed battle with a pack of wolves to keep Margot safe from harm…

She shivered, even as she berated herself. She'd only just met this man! She had a job to do! She didn't need to be wasting her time fantasizing about him!

But she found that this was easier said than done.

It didn't help that Levi was just also incredibly good-looking – with hair as black as night, piercing blue eyes, and a strong jaw with just a hint of stubble. She'd never thought of herself as being interested in the strong, silent, protective type, but now that she'd met Levi, she couldn't imagine being interested in anything else. Any*one* else.

I bet he'd somehow look even more handsome if he smiled.

Margot blinked in surprise at her own train of thought. It really was none of her business as to whether he smiled or not… but, she had to admit, the fact that he hadn't smiled once since she'd met him was a little disappointing. Hopefully she wasn't *that* terrible of a companion!

Well, maybe she would just have to make sure to do her part to be a good companion as well. Admittedly, she was spending a lot of her time *ooh*ing and *aah*ing over all the decorations and festivities, and asking questions about Christmas. She hadn't really asked him much about himself.

34

CHIMERAS AND CHRISTMAS CAKES

She resolved to change the topic… right after he finished telling her about advent calendars.

"So, each day you open the corresponding window in the calendar," he said, with what appeared to be a mild grimace. She wasn't sure quite why he wouldn't like advent calendars – they sounded quite delightful to her! – but then again, she didn't know his background. Maybe his magic was based around numerology or telling the future, and he didn't like associating a particular number with a particular unknown object. Magic users could be quite strange sometimes in what they did and didn't like, depending on their magic. She wouldn't have picked Levi as an eccentric type, but appearances could be deceiving.

In any case, he was providing her with vital information, and she really should have been paying close attention, instead of contemplating the way his light eyes contrasted with his dark lashes, or admiring the juxtaposition of the pure white snow against his black hair.

She made sure to nod extra enthusiastically. "And then what happens when you get to 25? Do you summon Santa Claus, or does he just appear on his own?"

He looked at her a bit strangely, then shook his head. "No, you just get another piece of cheap candy that's gone past its best-before date. Or whatever it is that you get in your calendar – they have all kinds of stuff these days."

"Oh." It seemed like a bit of an anti-climax – but then again, she supposed that it was just an accessory item that allowed children to build up some excitement in the lead-up to the big day. She brightened. "I would very much like to have an advent calendar."

Levi shrugged. "Well, it's almost Christmas, so it wouldn't be much good now… but you could get one going cheap, at least."

"Maybe I shall." With determination, she changed the

35

ZOE CHANT

subject so that Levi would have a chance to talk about himself – and, admittedly, so that she could satiate her curiosity about him. "So, what made you decide to come out here on your own, and leave behind your own people?"

He stopped in his tracks and looked at her with an expression that was somewhere between curiosity, caution, and confusion. After a moment, he said, "What do you mean, 'my own people'?"

Margot was aware that the magic world was largely a secret in the non-magic world, and so she dropped her voice to a whisper, painfully aware of how close she had to lean to him – and how much taller than her he was! "You know. Outside of the realm of regular human existence."

Now he definitely looked taken aback. "You can tell? How do you know about that?"

"Of course I can tell!" she said, feeling a surge of triumph at having worked it out.

I knew it! I knew he was a wizard!

She had already been almost certain – after all, he could see Monty, and he'd offered to help her despite the fact that he was busy with his great aunt's bookshop. The wizards-errant of the stories she'd grown up with were always going out of their way to help people, even when it wasn't in their own best interests.

But now… now she knew for sure. He was a wizard, *and* he knew about human culture – if anyone could help her find the *flos nivis*, it was him.

She practically floated as they walked along the path that weaved through the town, sometimes passing charming little cottages, sometimes winding through the trees. It really was like a little slice of heaven, the snow crunching under their boots, the sky turning clear and blue as the clouds lifted, the stark branches of the trees dotted with color as little pink-and-gray birds scurried about. The air

36

was so crisp and clear that it invigorated her with each breath.

Levi must have noticed her staring up at the birds in the trees, because he turned his head to look as well. "They're rosy finches, I think," he said absently. "My great aunt mentioned them once in a letter she sent."

"Rosy finches," Margot repeated, staring in rapt wonder. They really were lovely, with their little round pink bellies, all fluffed up and warm for the winter. "Are they a Christmas thing?"

"Just more of a winter thing, I think," Levi said, squinting up at them against the glare of the sun.

"Well, I think they're wonderful," Margot said. And she did. She'd always been warned against the grime and crime and general untrustworthiness of the non-magical world, but she thought that it was positively enchanting. Even the bus had been a new experience!

They watched for a couple of minutes more before the birds flitted off, and then continued down the path. Margot could hear a distant clamor up ahead, of people chattering happily and other noises she couldn't quite pick out, and she picked up her pace. Maybe there was some more Christmas culture to be discovered!

Levi caught up to her in a couple of long strides. "Where are you off to now?"

"To whatever that sound is!" Margot said giddily, high-stepping through the snow. "Perhaps there will be some eggnog!"

Margot thought she could hear the slightest exasperated sigh behind her, but surely she was mistaken. Who wouldn't be excited to go on a mission to search out some Christmas cheer?

"Oh, hey," Levi said suddenly. "Is, uh, your cat okay? I haven't seen him for a while."

ZOE CHANT

"Oh, Monty?" Margot replied, feeling touched that he would think to check on Monty's wellbeing, even as she was confused as to why he would do so – all wizards knew that familiars could look after themselves, after all. "Yes, he's fine. He'll catch up at some point."

"Are you sure?" Levi asked as he looked around, his expression dubious. "It's freezing, and he doesn't know the area."

"Positive," said Margot, even as she called out mentally to Monty to come back from wherever he'd gotten to. She knew he was fine, but apparently it was bothering Levi enough that it was weighing on his mind. It was kind of sweet, really.

Yes, yes, I'm coming, Monty said with a world-weary sigh, and Margot turned to see him trotting up the path behind her. He'd clearly been rolling around in the snow for some reason, if the state of his fur was anything to go by.

"Here he is!" she exclaimed, scooping him up so he could perch on her shoulder like some giant hairy gargoyle.

I have no need of such modes of transportation, he huffed.

Well, go on then, she said placidly. *Hop down, if my shoulder isn't good enough for you.*

Monty sniffed. *It will suffice, I suppose. But I'm only here because it pleases you, and I am nothing if not magnanimous.*

Mm-hmm, Margot said, nodding a little. *It has nothing to do with you warming your paws on my shawl.*

Naturally.

In any case, she saw a brief flash of relief on Levi's face, before it resettled into its habitual… well, not *scowl*, exactly, but certainly he wasn't the exuberant type.

It made her stomach glow a little with a happy warmth. She wasn't sure *why* she cared so much that he was concerned for Monty's wellbeing, but she did.

"Let's go!" she said, racing forward once more. Now that

38

she was closer, she could smell all kinds of wonderful things – food this time, not books – and she suddenly realized that she was *ravenous*.

The trees became less dense around her, and she found herself out in the open once more – to see a dazzling array of stalls spread out before her, each more enticing than the last, decorated in lanterns and lights and baubles and – and all *sorts* of things! Everything was decked out in green and red, which, thanks to Levi, she knew meant only one thing: *Christmas*.

Meats were sizzling and sending steam up into the frigid air; people were serving up cups of something that smelled warm and spiced; children were running around excitedly clutching on to what she now recognized as *candy canes*. An enormous tree towered above it all, shimmering with tiny twinkling lights and with a golden star perched on the very top. Heavy clouds were rolling in over the mountain once more, tiny flakes of snow just beginning to tumble down.

All of the research she had done hadn't begun to prepare her for just how marvelous it all was! She felt like she was in a waking dream, dazed and amazed.

Where should I even start?!

Luckily, Levi seemed to realize that she was feeling a bit overwhelmed.

"You said you wanted to try eggnog?" he said gruffly.

"Oh – yes! I've read about it – the book said it was like the nectar of heaven," Margot said, excited at the idea of finally getting to try the foods she'd only ever read about. "And then, perhaps… some roasted Christmas turkey? With stuffing? And all the trimmings?" She didn't know what trimmings actually *were*, but she knew she wanted to try them.

Levi's frown deepened a little. "Well. I'm not sure we'll be able to get a whole turkey with stuffing and trimmings, but

ZOE CHANT

we should be able to get *something* to eat. And there must be an eggnog stall here somewhere."

"I'm very happy to give anything a try," Margot told him, meaning it. She *knew* she should be off looking for the *flos nivis*, but she'd only just arrived. Surely no one could begrudge her spending just one afternoon indulging her curiosity – and stomach?

Levi glanced around, before pointing at a stall with a red and white awning, festooned with trailing holly leaves and dripping with sparkling lights. "Well… there's a goulash stand over there that smells pretty good. How about that?"

"Goulash?" Margot asked, never having heard of it. "That sounds wonderful. Lead the way!"

Was it her imagination, or did Levi's face twitch *just* a little as she impulsively grabbed his hand, towing him over to the stall he'd pointed out, and from which a truly amazing scent was emanating?

Um.

She really hadn't meant to do that, she thought, wondering if she could discreetly drop his hand… though would that just be even more awkward somehow than just keeping hold of it? His hand was so warm, and it felt nice in hers… like they'd been made to fit together.

And now I'm just having silly fantasies again, Margot scolded herself as they reached the stall. *Please just stay focused, Margot!*

Monty's claws in her shawl seemed to be the timely reminder she needed, and she quickly slipped her hand out of Levi's when they reached the stall. If Levi minded, he hadn't said anything – but Margot *did* notice him staring down at his hand after she'd let it go.

"Welcome to Kovacs's Goulash Stand!" The man behind the stall's counter beamed at them. "What can I get for you today?"

CHIMERAS AND CHRISTMAS CAKES

"Oh… well, it'll have to be goulash, surely," Margot said, watching as the man lifted a lid from a massive cast-iron pot, letting a rush of steam carry the truly amazing scents of beef, cinnamon, cloves, paprika, garlic, and many other things Margot wasn't sure she could identify up with it.

"Good choice, considering that's all we have," the man behind the counter chuckled. "Here you go – two serves."

He ladled the thick, creamy-looking stew into two bowls, and then placed two steaming-hot bread rolls on a couple of plates. Margot could feel her stomach growling louder and louder with every passing moment.

"That'll be ten dollars," the man said, once he'd passed the tray with the goulash and rolls to Margot.

"Oh… um, of course!" Margot said. She'd read about this too, of course – things didn't work here like they did in the magical world, where people mainly just bartered or traded items for what they needed. No – here, they used *money*.

"Don't worry, I'll get this."

Before she could find a place to put the tray and begin rummaging in her tote for this *money*, Levi had gotten out his own wallet and paid the man. Margot gave the wallet a glance – it looked like just a regular wallet, no pocket dimension included. But she supposed it wasn't always needed, and if he was used to living here, then Levi probably just didn't bother with such things for his everyday life.

"Oh, that's very… very gentlemanly of you," Margot said, smiling up at him. It must have been true, what they said about wizards-errant: they really were helpful and kind.

"It's nothing," Levi muttered, though Margot thought she could see just the tiniest hint of a blush beneath the very manly stubble on his cheeks. "Should we find a place to eat?"

You know how I feel about human food, and yet, I admit that this goulash does smell quite delicious, Monty told Margot as she followed Levi through the tables of red and gold decorated

ZOE CHANT

wooden tables, most of them filled with laughing families all enjoying the food the Christmas market had to offer.

How delightful, Margot thought as she gazed around. So far, Christmas had been even more amazing than she'd imagined.

Levi led her over to a table that was slightly apart from the others, in a less full section of the eating area, and at the foot of the decorated pine tree with a blazing star adorning its point.

"We can sit here," he said, as he took his bowl and plate from her tray. "I have a few things I'd like to ask you."

"Oh, anything," Margot said as she sat across from him. "I guess I should also explain myself too – like why I'm here, and how you can help me. I promise, I'll be sure to tell everyone when I return how gallant you were. It will look very good on your record of achievements and good deeds."

Levi opened his mouth, then closed it again. Then he picked up his bread roll and dipped it into his goulash.

Margot followed suit. She wanted to make sure she did things right.

But the moment she put the roll in her mouth, all thoughts of propriety flew straight out of her head.

The flavors!

She'd never tasted anything quite like this before. It was spicy and savory at once, thick and creamy, hearty and nourishing. The bread roll was toasty crisp on the outside and warm and soft in the middle, the perfect accompaniment to the incredible stew.

"Wow, this is amazing! An incredibly good choice!" Margot said, belatedly realizing she was talking with her mouth full.

Levi nodded, chewing on his own mouthful of goulash. He at least remembered to swallow first before he said,

42

CHIMERAS AND CHRISTMAS CAKES

"Okay, I have to admit, that *is* good. I guess I can say there's a few good things about Christmas after all."

"Isn't everything about Christmas good?" Margot asked, tilting her head a little. Levi had said it as if he didn't think so.

"Well… let's not get into that right now," Levi said, before scooping up another mouthful of goulash with his spoon. Margot shivered a little as he licked his lips in evident pleasure. "Right now, what I really wanted to ask you was… how do you know what I am?"

Margot blinked in surprise, even as she savored another taste of her goulash.

What did he mean by that? He could see Monty – who was currently sitting on the edge of the table, batting lazily at a little horse ornament that dangled from one of the boughs of the tree – after all. Maybe he just hadn't been expecting a witch to show up and request a boon from him?

"Oh… well, I guess I just figured it out," she said. "After you said you could see Monty, well, it was just kind of obvious."

"You keep saying that I can see Monty," Levi said, frowning. "But… he's right there? He's a little hard to miss."

Margot smiled fondly at her familiar. She supposed it was true – he *was* a pretty big cat, and very fluffy to boot. It was definitely good that only witches and wizards could see him right now, as he climbed his way slowly up the Christmas tree, poking at shining ornaments as he went.

"I suppose he is," she said, as Monty moved on to sniffing at a silver bauble, poking at it curiously with his nose. "But you know what I mean. He's not revealing himself to people right now. I read that animals aren't always welcome everywhere. But since Monty's not *really* an animal I thought it would be okay to bring him."

Again, Levi opened his mouth and then closed it again,

43

ZOE CHANT

before giving Monty a very hard look, as if he was trying to figure something out.

"He's not a shifter though," he said at last. "And neither are you. So how –"

"Warm spiced wine! Get it here! Warm yourself up on this snowy day! Ho ho ho!"

Whatever Levi had been about to say, he was cut off by the sudden arrival of a man by their table, a tray of steaming hot drinks attached to a strap around his neck. From each of the cups, there flowed the scent of anise, cinnamon and orange.

"I'll take two!" Margot said, unable to let this incredible scent go by. And this time, she managed to get her money out of her tote before Levi could move, handing the piece of paper to the man with the tray. Margot was still a little unclear about how a piece of paper with some little drawings on it could be traded for such delicious food, but if that was the way things were done here, then she wanted to stick to it.

"Uh... you wouldn't happen to have anything smaller, would you?" the man asked, looking down at the paper in his hand. "It's only two bucks a cup, and this is a hundred."

"Oh…" Margot said, feeling a little crestfallen. "I'm afraid they're all like that."

"No problem, I'll handle it," Levi said, once again taking out his wallet.

Margot felt a little embarrassed. She didn't want Levi to use up *all* his little papers with pictures on them on her.

But then... he said something about shifters, didn't he? What do shifters have to do with anything? she thought, as Levi paid the man for the drinks.

Of course, Margot knew about shifters – there were plenty of shifters who were also witches and wizards, mainly ones who had strong magical abilities, like unicorns, pegasi, and wyverns.

44

CHIMERAS AND CHRISTMAS CAKES

But she couldn't for the life of her work out why he had brought up the idea of her or Monty being shifters. She hadn't said or done anything to give that impression, surely?

Confused, she took the cup of wine with a murmur of thanks, and brought it to her lips to buy a few seconds while she thought.

Part of her wanted to savor the heavenly, heady aroma forever, while the other part of her just wanted to tip the whole lot into her mouth right now, scalded tongue be damned.

In the end, she compromised, and took a tentative sip, letting the sweet, spicy wine warm her from the inside out. Her eyes slid closed in pure contentment.

"Mmm," she said happily. "This is the most unmagical thing I've ever tasted. Thank you so much for procuring and paying for it – I will return the favor tenfold, I swear!"

She opened her eyes just in time to see Levi blinking in confusion as he took a sip of his own wine. He seemed to do a lot of that – she wasn't quite sure why. Maybe he had been out in the non-magical world for too long, and had forgotten how wizards and witches tended to talk to each other?

"No problem," he muttered.

She watched, entranced, as he appeared to undertake some kind of arduous battle within his own mind. What was it that he was thinking about? Margot honestly had no idea.

Eventually, he seemed to come to some kind of conclusion, because he squared his shoulders, set his jaw, and raised his head to look her in the eye. His gaze was intense, and she couldn't help but shiver just a little.

"Margot, look," he said, his voice low, just for her. "I feel like there have been some misunderstandings here on both our sides, and I think we should clear them up before we go on any further."

ZOE CHANT

Taking a deep breath, he plowed on. "Hi Margot, I'm Levi Thorne. I'm a chimera shifter. Nice to meet you."

He held out one arm across the table, his hand pointing toward her, and Margot took a moment to take everything in. A wizard *and* a chimera shifter? He had to be very powerful indeed!

Still, maybe that explained why he was so taciturn. Chimeras were notoriously private, isolation-loving beings – the fact that he had offered to help her at all was quite an honor.

She didn't know what to do about the hand he was holding out to her, though – and the longer he held it out, the more his face fell. Not that there was much change in his expression, but there was enough that she could tell he was disappointed.

But what did he want her to do?

In the end, she reached out and took his hand in both of hers, and his eyes widened slightly in surprise. A nice little warm thrill went through her fingers at the contact.

"Hi, Levi," she replied. "I'm Margot Delgard, and I'm a witch, of course. It's nice to meet you, too."

His eyes widened still further. "A witch?" he said, pausing for a long moment. "... Well. That makes a lot more sense."

"And you're a wizard," she continued, still enjoying the feeling of his hand in hers. "A chimera wizard is highly unusual – I've never met one before."

"Wait – what?" Levi jumped a little. "A wizard? No. I'm just a chimera shifter. And not even much of a chimera shifter at that."

Margot's stomach dropped.

What? He's not a wizard? How did I get it so wrong?!

"You're – you're not?" she exclaimed, acutely aware of how hard she was gripping his hand. "But of course you are. How could you not be? You can see Monty!"

46

CHIMERAS AND CHRISTMAS CAKES

"Why wouldn't I be able to see him?" he asked, eyebrows pulling up in confusion... before, suddenly, understanding spread across his face. "I think I get it. Monty is your familiar, isn't he?"

Monty stuck his nose in the air. *I prefer to think of* you *as* my *familiar, but whatever helps you to sleep at night, I suppose.*

Zip it, Monty! she yelled. *This is not the time!*

"Yes," she said, barely aware of the words that were tumbling out of her mouth. "Yes, he's my familiar. And you're... you're really not a wizard?"

She forced herself to look up at Levi's face again. He shook his head, solemn. At least he didn't seem angry, but, still – Margot had never been so embarrassed in all her life, and that included the time she accidentally committed magical arson.

Chimeras were reclusive and mercurial creatures. They generally didn't want anything to do with anybody. The fact that she'd been nattering away all day to a chimera she'd only just met – and asking him about *Christmas*, of all things – well, she was positively mortified. The only reason she had bothered him so much was because she had thought he was a wizard-errant!

"I'm so sorry," she said, loosening her grip on his hand with a force of will. "Please forgive me my intrusions – I will leave you to go about your day." She dug about hurriedly in her tote, pulling out a fistful of paper money and shoving it toward him. "Here. Please take this – I hope it covers the food you so kindly purchased for me, as well as the time I've caused you to waste."

"What?" Levi said, and the stupefied look on his face would have been funny if she hadn't felt so awful. He gently pushed her hand away. "I don't want your –" He looked again, his eyes widening. "Your *eight hundred dollars?*"

"Please," she begged. "It's the least I can do."

47

ZOE CHANT

"Look," Levi said with a sigh, still refusing to take the money. "I wouldn't have come along with you if I hadn't wanted to, okay? I admit that Christmas isn't my favorite thing in the world, but... I *did* want to know more about you. To spend time with you."

He was almost mumbling by the end of his little speech, but Margot barely noticed, she was so over the moon.

He – he wants to spend time with me? Because he wants to, not because he feels obligated?

"Really?" she whispered, barely daring to believe it.

He nodded. "Really." A ghost of a smile crept over his face, and she couldn't help but smile back. Even Monty sticking his tail in her face couldn't dampen her joy.

They say that Christmas is a time when wonderful things happen... and they're right!

She was so happy that she could feel it in her stomach, a warm, joyous tingling. Her life had been so overwhelming lately, the threat of failure hanging heavily over her head... and now, this handsome, kind, wonderful man wanted to spend time with her. Such things would have felt impossible just a few short hours ago.

"So," she said, barely daring to believe that today was really real. "What do we do now?"

Levi took another sip of his wine. "Well, you said you wanted to try some eggnog, so how about we go see if we can find some? And then you can tell me more about this research assignment of yours. Now that we both know what each other's deal is, maybe I can help you out. I don't know much about magic, but I do at least have a bit of experience dealing with regular humans. Maybe between the two of us, we'll have a chance."

"You mean that?" Margot said, unable to keep the silly grin off her face. "You don't have to get back to the bookshop?"

48

CHIMERAS AND CHRISTMAS CAKES

"It can wait a day," Levi said quickly. If Margot didn't know better, she would've thought that he didn't want to go back there. But who *wouldn't* want to go to such a wondrous place?

"Okay," she said, downing the rest of her rapidly cooling wine. "Let's go find some nog."

CHAPTER 4

*S*he's a witch. Of course *she's a witch. How did I not get that right away?*

Levi glanced across at Margot as she walked beside him – or perhaps *floated* beside him might have been a better word. She didn't really seem bound by things like *reality* or *the laws of physics*.

Her long blonde hair seemed to drift behind her in shining waves, and Levi would not have been the slightest bit surprised if, when he looked down, he found her feet weren't actually touching the ground at all, but she'd somehow found a way to walk on sunbeams.

That's pretty much what she is. A walking sunbeam.

Levi scowled at the thought.

He was not the type to try to put these kinds of thoughts into words, and now, every attempt he made to try to describe the way Margot made him feel just made him aware of how inadequate he was at expressing himself.

The bond you feel with your mate can't be vocalized, his chimera woke itself from its slumber to inform him. *It simply is.*

CHIMERAS AND CHRISTMAS CAKES

Well, Levi thought, he'd have to find a way to vocalize it pretty soon, if he was ever going to try to get Margot to understand what they were to each other – what she was to *him*.

But then... would that be welcome news to her?

Levi had to admit, he didn't know much about witches. But he knew that most of them didn't really live here in the world of humans, or amongst shifters.

They had their own domain, and given Margot's fascination with all things Christmas, her request for his help in understanding the non-magical world, and the fact she didn't seem to think there was anything wrong with shoving eight hundred dollars at him in payment – which he didn't actually want or need – for about twenty minutes of his time told him she was probably not a witch who'd spent a lot of time among non-magical folks.

But if that's the case, surely she'll just want to go home once she's finished whatever this magical research assignment is?

Could he tell her they were mates then, knowing what kind of dilemma it might place her in?

Maybe if he was a regular shifter, he would have considered it more seriously. If he'd been a unicorn or a pegasus or a wyvern, something with magical powers – and that he could also, you know, *actually shift into* – he thought the decision would have been a little easier.

If he'd been a shifter who could shift, then he thought he might have something more to offer Margot.

But that just wasn't the case. And how could he ask her to give up her life in the magical world for a chimera that he couldn't even turn into? And if he went with her to her world, wouldn't he just be a burden to her? He didn't have any powers that might have made him useful in the magical world.

He couldn't even coax dead plants back to life again like a

ZOE CHANT

unicorn could, or use his uncanny good luck to locate lost tomes and parchments even in the darkest depths of a library, like a dragon could. Hell, he couldn't even summon a storm or cause springs of life-giving water to gush from the earth with a tap of his hooves, like a pegasus could!

I'd just be a burden to her, no matter where we went, Levi thought, despair rising up inside him. *Just like I am to my own family back home.*

A shifter who couldn't shift, his own chimera village had made it clear to him, wasn't really of any use to anyone.

So how can I ask her to tie her life to mine? Especially when she's so... so...

"Oh my goodness!" Margot cried, her brilliant green eyes lighting up as she spied something that apparently interested her in the stalls. "Does that say *Christmas Cake*? Is there a cake that's just especially for Christmas?"

"Uh, yeah," Levi said, after he remembered how to speak – it was kind of hard when he was staring at the delicate pink flush of her cheeks, her excited eyes, the way she just seemed to be utterly *enchanted* by everything she saw. It almost – *almost* – made him feel just the tiniest bit excited for Christmas too, as if her excitement was infectious. "But I have to say, I really don't like it."

Margot's face fell a little, and Levi could have kicked himself.

"That's not to say you still can't try some," Levi went on quickly. "But I don't really know how to describe it – it's kind of alcoholic, with dried fruit and nuts in it. And some-times they serve it with custard to sweeten it up. It wasn't my favorite when I was a kid, I have to say."

"Oh, I see," Margot said, nodding, but she still looked a little wistfully at the cake stand. It had a big sign above it reading *Sylvie's Sweets and Bakery* – Levi had seen the shopfront for this place the first day he'd arrived in town. It

52

was on the main street, a little way down the road from Great Aunt Aida's bookshop, though that was right at the end of the street, whereas Sylvie's was the central location.

And it had seemed absolutely buzzing when Levi had walked past it too – enough so that despite the fact the bakery itself had smelled incredible, he had resolved never to go in. There were just far too many people inside.

But perhaps this was a chance to sample some of the cakes now – he was already here, after all, crowds or not, and Margot *had* asked him to teach her about Christmas.

And, as her mate, how could he refuse even the smallest of her requests?

"We can go check it out," Levi said. "You did say you wanted to learn about Christmas, and that includes the kind of gross cakes, I guess."

"I'd very much like that." Margot beamed up at him. "Perhaps they'll sell other things too – it does smell amazing. Like sugar and spice and all things nice!"

Just like Margot, Levi couldn't help but think as he followed her to the stall. Her familiar, Monty, seemed to have wandered off again somewhere, but now that Levi understood his true nature he wasn't so worried. A witch's familiar could most certainly take care of itself.

On reaching the stall, Levi could see that Margot had been right about there being a bigger selection of cakes to choose from.

The array of them was almost overwhelming, in fact: there didn't seem to be any end to the kinds of cakes that were laid out on red and green checked tablecloths, golden tinsel dangling from the awning above, fixed in place with green sprigs of holly.

Levi wasn't any kind of expert in human cuisine, but even he could name some of the cakes that were in front of him now. Aside from the vast array of donuts – cinnamon sprin-

ZOE CHANT

kled, chocolate frosted, strawberry frosted, lemon frosted, each with a little icing holly leaf and berries – he could see angel cakes with the fluffiest-looking whipped cream he'd ever seen, chocolate cake with thick frosting and decorated with strawberries and tiny wildflowers, layered honey cakes that smelled of butterscotch and caramel.

And then there were the pies – despite the fact he didn't have full access to all of a shifter's heightened senses, his nose was still far more sensitive than a regular human's, and he could smell the bay leaf and thyme that rose up from the piping hot apple pies, the sweet sugary crust on the pastry lattices on the cherry pies, and the lavender syrup that infused the lemon pies.

It was, to put it mildly, *heavenly*.

Levi had never smelled cakes and pies like these before. Whoever this Sylvie who owned the bakery was, Levi was beginning to wonder if she might not be a witch herself – cakes and sweets this good *had* to be made by magic, right?

"Hi, and welcome to Sylvie's Sweets and Bakery – or at least, our Christmas market stall," a voice interrupted his thoughts, and his incredulous staring. "Is there anything I can get for you today?"

Levi blinked, looking up to see a short, dark-haired woman in a cape and apron, who, going by the tag on the front of her shirt, must be Sylvie.

"Uh," he began, but Margot, her wide eyes twinkling, jumped in before him.

"Oh wow, I don't know how I could even begin to choose," she said, looking back and forth across the wide counter. "I guess I came here to sample Christmas cake, but now that I'm here…"

"Well, if it's Christmas cake you're after, then I might have a little treat for you," Sylvie said, with a wide smile. "I've been taste testing my new recipe for Christmas cake – a new kind

of Christmas cake. My secret recipe, of course – or *recipes.* But I've been asking people to sample each kind and vote on their favorite. The winning recipe will be the one I make available for Christmas orders. Care to take part in the selection process?"

"Oh yes, I definitely would!" Margot said, her own smile spreading across her face in an instant. "Would you also like to take part, Levi? But oh –" Margot's smile dropped a little. "I forgot – you said you don't really like Christmas cake."

No, forget I ever said that, Levi wanted to tell her. For her, to affix her smile in place again, he'd eat about an acre of Christmas cake.

"No pressure or anything, but this isn't your grandma's Christmas cake," Sylvie said. "Not that I'm insulting your grandmother's cooking," she added quickly. "It's just that I'm not using the traditional recipes. This is all new, *à la* Sylvie. You should try it – you might be surprised."

"Well, I guess it can't hurt," Levi said, nodding. "I'll give it a shot."

Well, don't sound so enthusiastic, his chimera said, its eyes glinting in the darkness.

Like you've been any help, Levi snarled at it. *You won't even come out and let me shift, so I'd be a worthy mate for Margot. And now you're telling me off about not sounding enthused enough about eating some cake?*

The chimera had no reply for that, apparently, only retreating further within him, as it did when he'd especially offended it. Not that it mattered, since, it seemed, it was never going to allow him to take on its form anyway.

Turning his attention back to Sylvie, he found her laying out several plates in front of her, each with a different kind of cake.

He had to admit, however, they did certainly look like the traditional kind of Christmas cake he knew – round and

covered in icing, with little holly leaves on top. But they certainly didn't *smell* like the Christmas cake he knew at all.

"Okay, cake number one," Sylvie said, slicing off two tiny slivers of cake and handing them over to Margot and Levi. "Butterscotch and cinnamon, with pecan and walnuts."

Margot's eyes were the size of saucers as she lifted the cake to her lips, taking a tiny, delicate bite.

"*Mm.* Oh my goodness," she murmured, her eyes fluttering shut in delight. "That is *delicious.* Goodness!"

Levi managed to tear his eyes away from the sight of Margot's enraptured expression for long enough to take a bite of his own slice of cake – and then, he had to admit, Margot had a point.

This is... possibly the most delicious thing I have ever tasted in my whole entire life, he thought, as the tangy butterscotch and the spicy cinnamon rolled over his tongue. The nuts gave it just enough crunch to keep it interesting, and rounded out the flavor with their mild, creamy taste.

Sylvie was right – this was definitely *not* the Christmas cake he knew.

But then, a moment later, realization hit him, and his chimera blinked to life within him again.

This is... wait a moment. A unicorn had a hand in making this!

Levi had, as far as he knew, never met a unicorn before, but he *did* know that fruits, vegetables and spices tended by unicorns were far more lush and flavorful than anything that could be raised by human hands.

And yet, he could tell just by looking at Sylvie that she was a regular human – he couldn't sense anything about her that told him she was a shifter.

So perhaps she knows a unicorn, Levi thought, glancing over his shoulder as if he expected to see it prancing through the bustling crowds of the Christmas market, its golden horn twinkling in the fairy lights.

Well, maybe her supplier is a unicorn, and it doesn't live here at all, Levi thought, frowning a little. It wouldn't be the first time a unicorn had set up a fruit and vegetable business, after all. Sylvie might not even realize it – in fact, she probably didn't.

"What did you think?" Sylvie asked, breaking off his chain of thought.

"Delicious," Levi said, without thinking – but it was true. Sylvie had been speaking the absolute truth when she'd said that this wasn't the Christmas cake he was used to.

"*Absolutely* delicious," Margot said, nodding. "But I want to try the others before I declare it the winner, even though I have no idea how anything could beat that."

"Well, have some chamomile tea as a palate cleanser, and then we'll see about that," Sylvie said with a laugh, before handing them a small cup of steaming tea. "Okay, ready for more?"

The next cake was chocolate, sour cherry and almond – and Levi had to admit, even he, with this complete lack of a sweet tooth, found it delicious.

The sour cherries were still, somehow, juicy and soft after being baked in the chocolate cake, and they tempered the sweetness of the cake itself, making it taste almost smokey. And the cake itself was smooth as silk – he'd never tasted chocolate cake that was quite so rich and yet, somehow, not *too* rich before in his life.

I could probably eat about a hundred of these, he thought, eyeing the cake Sylvie had cut the sample slivers from hungrily.

One look at Margot's face told him she was feeling pretty much the same way he was – her eyes were closed, her cheeks infused with pink, a blissful expression on her face as she clearly savored her cake with gusto.

"Oh my… oh my… now *that* really is something," Margot

ZOE CHANT

gasped, when she finally opened her eyes again. "How can I be expected to choose between the two of those? Can I just vote for both?"

"Well, you haven't tried the last one yet," Sylvie told her, her eyes twinkling. "Perhaps that'll be the winner."

"What's this one?" Margot asked, her eyes wide as Sylvie cut small slices of the final Christmas cake.

"This one is vanilla cake, with apricot and nutmeg," Sylvie said as she handed them their napkins. "Once you've tried it, you can vote on your favorite by circling its name on that paper over there, and then dropping the paper in the box at the end of the counter."

Margot's eyes somehow widened even further at the knowledge that she was going to not only be offered a third type of cake to try, but that she was then going to be able to vote on which one was her favorite. Her joy at what seemed to him to be a fairly run-of-the-mill – if delicious – situation was, he had to admit, incredibly endearing.

And the cake itself was, of course, delicious – like with all the others, it was velvety and not too sweet, somehow managing to taste like all the best parts of a traditional Christmas cake while still offering something completely different. Whoever this Sylvie was, she was clearly a genius baker, even above and beyond the boost her food was – perhaps unknowingly – getting from the unicorn-enhanced ingredients. All three would have been the best Christmas cake he'd ever experienced even without that, and he certainly didn't mean that as damning with faint praise.

Margot too was licking her fingers as if she was trying to get every last possible scrap of flavor off of them, so he had to assume that this one was also a winner with her.

"I do hope you'll consider voting for your favorite," Sylvie said with a smile, even as Margot practically bounced from foot to foot with anticipation.

58

CHIMERAS AND CHRISTMAS CAKES

"But of course!" she exclaimed. "Just as soon as I work out which one I'm going to vote for. I don't possibly know how I can decide!"

"Well, as delicious as they all were, I know which one I'm voting for," Levi said, picking up a ballot paper and circling his choice, before stuffing the ballot into the box.

"A man of conviction," Sylvie said approvingly.

"Okay," Margot said, nodding with determination. Her hand hovered over the paper for several seconds, before finally she made her choice, placing her paper in the box. "All right! All done."

"Well, let's hope your favorite wins," Sylvie said with a laugh. "But I'll let you in on a little secret – I'll still be making the other ones, no matter the winner. So make sure you drop by the bakery on time to pick one up for Christmas!"

"Oh." Margot's face fell a little. "I'm not sure I'll still be here by then."

Levi blinked, glancing at her in surprise.

She may not be here at Christmas? But that's only a little over a week away.

His heart clenched at the thought. Of course, he'd already known that Margot, being a witch, most likely wouldn't be staying here long. She'd have to get home – and, despite her evident enthusiasm for Christmas, she probably wouldn't even *want* to stay here much longer than that.

But still...

Still, he'd somehow thought he'd have a little more time with her than that.

But perhaps things are for the best this way.

Even if she was his mate, he'd already known he couldn't offer her anything a normal shifter could. If she hung around for any longer, he knew it'd only be all the more difficult to let her go; it'd only be all the more difficult to keep the secret of their mate bond to himself.

59

ZOE CHANT

Desperately, he looked inward to his chimera – surely, if anything was going to awaken it, then the prospect of his mate's departure would surely be it.

But no, it remained sleeping, not even bothering to uncurl its scaled tail from in front of its lion's face, yawn, and offer some biting comment.

"Well, that's a shame," Sylvie said, breaking into Levi's bleak thoughts. "But that's no reason why you can't still enjoy some good cakes."

Margot nodded. "I hope so – I honestly don't know very much about Christmas. I've been trying to read up about it, and Levi here has been so wonderful, telling me all about how Christmas works despite the fact that we just met, but there's still so much more to learn!"

If Sylvie thought it was odd that Margot didn't know much about Christmas, it didn't show on her face. "Well, one of the most important things about Christmas is that it's a time of year in which you give gifts to other people." She picked up a large box from behind the counter, and started to place an array of cakes into it. "And so, in that spirit, I'd like to give you some more free samples."

Margot stared in astonishment. "Free cake? For me? This is a Christmas tradition?"

Levi opened his mouth, wanting to protest the truly insane amount of free cake that Sylvie was putting into the box – but he also didn't want to see Margot disappointed, and so he closed his mouth again. If Sylvie really wanted to let Margot have all of this amazing-looking cake for free, he didn't think he had it in his heart to stop her.

Just as long as Margot didn't try to pay Sylvie eight hundred bucks for it, he supposed it was all good. Though with the number of cakes that were going into the box, it probably wasn't that far off the mark.

"For you and your friend here," Sylvie said, with an

expression that Levi could only describe as *knowing*.

Margot looked up at Levi hopefully, as if wanting his confirmation that this really was normal and okay amongst humans.

I don't think this is very normal, Levi thought, even as he gave Margot a reassuring nod, *but if Sylvie is happy, then it's more than okay.*

"Thank you so much," Margot said fervently. "I don't know how I can thank you enough."

"No need for thanks," Sylvie said. "It's all just part of the Christmas experience." She picked up one last cake – a small Christmas cake – and placed it in the box. "Although I'm branching out with new Christmas cakes, I *did* make a few traditional ones, because I have some regulars who like them. Since it's your first Christmas, I think you should be able to try the original version as well, if you want to." She laughed, handing over the box. "No obligation, of course!"

Margot stared down at the box, cradling it as if it contained a precious treasure, before looking up at Sylvie with sparkling eyes.

"I am certain that it will be wonderful," she said with great seriousness. "And I will pass on this – this Christmas tradition of gift-giving, if I can."

"It's a really nice tradition," said Sylvie. "Doing something to make someone else smile is my favorite part of Christmas."

"She certainly did give you a lot of cake," Levi said as they walked away, eyeing the large box in Margot's hands – it seemed Sylvie was willing to put her money where her mouth was when it came to saying gift-giving and making people smile were things she enjoyed. "Would it be better to drop that box back where you're staying, rather than carrying it around for the rest of the day?"

Levi could have kicked himself the moment the words

ZOE CHANT

were out of his mouth – he hadn't intended it that way, but, he realized, this was a perfect chance for him to find out where Margot was staying.

Or it *would* have been perfect if he had any intention of trying to court her, like he would if things had been different. But now, it only served to remind him just how far out of reach Margot was.

"Staying? Oh," Margot said, waving a hand vaguely. "I just thought I'd find a waystation."

Levi blinked. *A waystation?*

"We… don't really have those here," he said. Or at least, he didn't think so, since he wasn't really all that clear on what Margot actually meant. "Just… regular hotels. B&Bs. That kind of thing."

"Oh, then I guess I'll find one of those," Margot said. "Do you think I brought enough money?"

"Yeah, I think so," Levi replied – he definitely thought eight hundred dollars would cover a few days' accommodation in a small mountain town like Girdwood Springs. "But I don't know if that will be the issue. It's more that it might be difficult to find a place that has a room free."

It hadn't been an issue for him coming up here at a moment's notice, since he was staying in Great Aunt Aida's apartment above the bookshop, which she'd left in just as much disarray as the shop itself.

But given the crowds all around them for the Christmas markets and food, plus it being such good skiing conditions this year, or so he'd heard, Levi wondered if there'd be any place left for Margot to stay.

Sighing, he glanced over his shoulder. Sylvie had seemed helpful, and she was clearly a local business owner. He hated to ask her for yet another favor when she'd already been so helpful, but right now, he really wasn't sure who else to ask.

Sylvie was helping another customer when Levi and

CHIMERAS AND CHRISTMAS CAKES

Margot turned back, but she fixed them with a bright smile as soon as she was done. "Back again already?"

"Uh, yeah," Levi said, feeling uncomfortable, but aware he had to make sure Margot had someplace safe to stay. "Sorry to ask, especially after you've already given us a bunch of free cake. But my… my friend here had a… a mix-up with her accommodation. You wouldn't happen to know anywhere that might have a room free, would you?"

"Huh, I'm sorry to hear about the mix-up, but that might be a bit of a tough ask," Sylvie said, frowning. "As far as I know, everywhere is booked solid. It's a busy time of year, as I'm sure you can see. Oh – wait – let me just ask –" She raised a hand, waving to someone behind them. "Natasha! Do you have a moment?"

Levi turned to see a tall, well-dressed woman moving toward them through the crowd. She smiled as she approached.

Must be Natasha.

"What can I do for you, Sylvie?" she asked, as she came to a stop by Sylvie's stall.

"Well, not so much for me, but for a guest here who's found herself with nowhere to stay," Sylvie said, gesturing to Margot. "You wouldn't happen to have had any last-minute cancelations, or know of anyone else who has?"

"Oh gee, no, I'm seriously booked out right now," Natasha said. "And rushed off my feet with it, but you know I like to be busy. But I'm really sorry I can't help – and to be honest, I don't know anyone else who might be able to either. Me and the other guest house and B&B owners were just talking about it in our get-together this morning – we haven't had a season like this in *years*. The place is jumping!"

With every word she spoke, Levi's heart sunk deeper and deeper. It didn't look like there really was anywhere free for Margot to stay.

63

Except one place.

The times when Levi's chimera actually spoke up were so rare that it startled Levi to hear its voice now, entering his head as if it were his own thoughts.

Don't, he internally snarled at it, as soon as he figured out what it meant. *You're making things worse.*

And it was. There was no way he could invite Margot to stay in Aida's small, poky apartment above her shop. There was no spare room – and no spare bed. The place was only four rooms big – bedroom, living room, kitchen and bathroom – and every spare inch of it was covered in books.

Books – and dust, Levi thought, despairingly.

Even if there *had* been a spare room, Levi wasn't sure he'd want Margot staying in it; Great Aunt Aida probably just would have used it as a repository for more books anyway, as well as a menagerie of dust bunnies.

But nor, he realized, could he just leave Margot – literally – out in the cold.

Sylvie and Natasha clearly had their heads together, trying to figure out some solution to this problem, going over the list of people they knew who might have a spare room free – but, they were both agreeing, most people had family staying with them for Christmas, and probably didn't have room for one more.

But even if they did, how can I ask that of them? Levi thought. *Margot is my mate. And even if I'll never tell her that, how can I let someone else take care of her when she needs something?*

He knew he couldn't. And looking at Margot's hopeful face as she listened to Sylvie and Natasha's conversation only convinced him even further of that.

"Don't worry about it," he heard himself say, cutting into the conversation, and watching as Margot, Sylvie and Natasha's heads all turned toward him. "I think I know somewhere Margot can stay."

CHAPTER 5

"*A*nd... are you *completely* sure this is okay?"

Margot knew it was, perhaps, a little late to be asking this – again – now, as she was following Levi up the curving stairs that led from the shop she'd first met him in to the small – he'd told her about ten times how small it was – apartment above it.

She'd definitely have to let her mother know she'd been quite mistaken about the people in the non-magical world.

Her mother had warned her repeatedly before she'd set out on this journey about how dangerous the people were here, how Margot should watch her back at every turn and make sure to treat everyone she met with a healthy dose of skepticism, along with a lot of other dire imprecations besides. But everyone Margot had met so far had been so... well, nice!

Perhaps it's just Girdwood Springs? Margot thought, as Levi paused on the steps before a wooden door. Certainly, Margot thought if she lived in such a place, she'd find it quite easy to be in a good mood all the time too.

"It's really fine," Levi said, as he remained paused in front

65

ZOE CHANT

of the door. "I just don't want you to get the wrong idea. This place is… well, I guess you'll see. And believe me, I won't be offended if you want to find somewhere else after you see it."

Margot sincerely doubted *that*. Aside from anything else, it meant spending more time with Levi. She really never had met anyone like him before.

She'd known wizards so powerful their magical auras could be felt from miles away, and of course she'd met dozens of handsome men in the past too. But even if she'd noticed their looks, they hadn't, well… done much for her. Even if they'd noticed her to begin with, which most of them hadn't.

She simply wasn't a good enough witch to attract anyone's attention, Margot thought gloomily. Looks weren't everything, or really that important at all. While other witches her own age were getting offers of magical alliances or research partnerships, no one had ever asked *her* for anything like that. She'd kind of given up on the idea that anyone ever would.

No one would ever want her that way, and she knew it was a concern for her parents. That was why she had no choice but to succeed in her current mission, too. She didn't want to worry her parents – she knew their own magical alliance was one of the most celebrated in the whole of the magical world, and it had yielded so many magical discoveries it made her head spin to think about it.

She knew they'd had high hopes for her, too. But it seemed like she'd only ever been destined to disappoint them.

She was already twenty-six, and she still hadn't even managed to graduate from her course of study, at an age when most other witches and wizards had already made at least one or two discoveries that benefitted the study of magic, or at the very least graduated from their study.

So I have to find the flos nivis, Margot thought. *I simply don't have any other choice.*

Well, as soon as you stop eating cakes and cavorting around Christmas festivals.

Margot jumped at the sound of Monty's voice in her ear.

Montague Hieronymus Bosch! And where *exactly have you been?!*

Margot knew Monty was more than capable of looking after himself, but it was easier to scold him now than to admit that he kind of had a point.

She hadn't really needed to spend all that time eating cake and looking at the Christmas festivities. As much as she'd insisted it was research, Christmas really didn't have anything to do with finding the snow flower. She'd simply wanted to satisfy her own curiosity – and to spend more time with Levi, with his sleek dark hair, his chiseled cheek-bones, his absolutely *criminally* blue eyes and broad shoulders –

Margot cut her own thoughts off. She really didn't need to be thinking them right now, especially when Levi was now unlocking the door to the apartment he'd invited her to stay in, a slight grimace still on his face.

"Oh," he said, glancing back at her as he opened the wooden door. "Your cat's back."

"Yes! Finally," Margot grumbled, shooting Monty a glare. "Sometimes I feel like he's not so much a familiar as a… a cat who just wanders in and out as he pleases."

"Sounds just like a cat," Levi said, a small smile ghosting across his face. "Anyway, prepare yourself for what you're about to see, I guess."

Levi made it sound like she was about to see something dreadful – but what Margot saw when he opened the door was one of the most truly *amazing* things she'd ever seen in her life.

ZOE CHANT

The apartment was small, true, just like he'd said it would be. There were chintz curtains drawn across the windows, framed by heavier, dark red drapes that clashed a little with the mustard yellow wallpaper, patterned with small blue wildflowers. A worn green rug stretched across the scuffed wooden floorboards. Little glass-doored cabinets lined the walls, filled with small porcelain objects and other tiny curios. A sagging dark green velvet couch sat in the middle of the room, covered in knitted blankets and raggedy cushions.

But aside from that, almost every surface of it was covered in *books* – books big and small, long and short, tomes to novellas.

Margot blinked, staring around her.

"Sorry about all this," Levi said after a moment of silence, the grimace back on his face. "Like I said, I'll do anything I can to help you find somewhere better –"

"Are you kidding?" Margot burst out, before she could stop herself. "Where could be better than this?!"

Without thinking, she walked past him and into the room, picking up the first book she saw, something entitled *The Duke of Passion* and which had a kind of, uh, racy cover, featuring a shirtless man – who, Margot fancied, with his tumble of dark hair and chiseled features, rather resembled Levi himself – embracing a woman whose heaving breasts were barely contained by her ragged bodice – before she put it down and picked up the next one on the pile, which seemed to be a different kind of book altogether, the cover featuring a gloved hand holding a bloody knife poking through a doorway, the title *Death's Doorstep* splashed across the cover in bright red letters, followed by the words *Knock, knock... you're dead!*

Fascinated, Margot picked up book after book, each one more intriguing than the last.

68

"Wow. I guess you really are a book lover," Levi said, and Margot jumped a little at the sound of his voice.

"Oh – I'm sorry, I didn't mean to be rude," she said contritely, as Monty leapt from book pile to book pile, without, of course, disturbing a single one. "Do these all belong to you?"

"Well… technically yes, I guess they do, now," Levi said, coming to stand next to her, frowning a little as he examined the cover of *The Duke of Passion.* "But as I mentioned, this place was my great aunt's. It seems like she kept the books she couldn't bear to sell up here – or she just liked reading them before she sold them. But it seems like her 'To Read' pile had gotten a little out of hand."

"I can see why, with so many interesting things to read," Margot murmured, looking around, as Monty settled himself on what looked like the mantlepiece of a large fireplace – which was unusable, Margot thought, because the grate was, like everywhere else, completely filled with books.

"And I guess I can't say Great Aunt Aida was the most organized of people either," Levi said. "It'll take me a long time to sort through all of this stuff and get it packed up so I can sell the place."

Oh yes... of course. He mentioned that, Margot thought, as she put the books she'd impulsively grabbed back down. She supposed he must have had a whole life of his own, somewhere else. The thought made a coil of tightness wrap itself up inside her throat, though she couldn't say exactly why. *He probably has a... a wife, and children.*

The thought should have made her happy, the idea that Levi had a happy life elsewhere. And of course he must have – she couldn't imagine a man like Levi, so handsome and kind, wouldn't have been snapped up already by some lucky lady chimera shifter.

But instead, it only made her feel more depressed. She

ZOE CHANT

wished she could understand why, but Margot couldn't explain it to herself at all.

I suppose it's just because everyone else seems to have their life figured out, except me, she thought glumly. Even the woman on the cover of *The Duke of Passion* seemed to know exactly what she wanted, and was almost certainly getting it.

"I'm sorry. I did mention the place was small. I really can try to find somewhere else –"

Margot looked up, blinking in surprise, as Levi ran his fingers through his coal-black hair, a strangely desperate expression on his face.

She realized her glum thoughts must have been clearer than she realized on her own face, and that Levi must have interpreted them to mean she wasn't happy about staying here, now that she'd actually seen the place.

"Oh – no! This place is *wonderful*," she said, meaning it. "It's really very cozy and sweet. Of course, I'll have to clear a few of the books off the sofa so I can sleep on it, and –"

"Sleep on the sofa? No, that won't be happening. You'll be in my bed," Levi said, shaking his head.

Margot stared at him, feeling a flush creeping up her cheeks.

Did he just say... in his bed? With him? Surely he can't mean that – but then again –

"I mean… you'll be in *the* bed," Levi blurted out in the next moment, cutting off her thoughts before they could get too far away from her. "I won't sleep in it. I'll be the one on the sofa. Or downstairs, in the shop."

"Oh, I see," Margot said, her heart sinking a little. But then, of course, hadn't she just been thinking Levi must already have a partner? "No, no, that's perfectly proper. I didn't think otherwise! Your wife must be very lovely after all –"

70

CHIMERAS AND CHRISTMAS CAKES

She cut herself off as she noticed the odd look Levi was giving her.

"My..." He shook his head. "Margot, I'm not married. I don't have a wife."

Surprise rippled through Margot as she looked at him.

"How can that be possible?" she asked, before she could think better of it – but then, she often let her mouth run away with her, saying things before she had a chance to consider whether it was really a good idea or not. "You're so... so..."

She gestured helplessly at how *so* he was – just for once, she couldn't find the words to describe just how incredibly good-looking he was, or how kind he'd been to her. It made her heart speed up in her chest, just as he had from the very first moment she'd laid eyes on him through the book-sized gap in the shelf after she'd almost concussed him.

Levi coughed, turning away, but before he did, Margot thought she glimpsed a flash of pain in his eyes.

"Well, that's very nice of you," he said gruffly after a moment. "But it's just not the case. Where I come from, I'm not considered a catch, to say the least."

"But I can't imagine that's true," Margot blurted out – but really, she couldn't. Wouldn't *anyone* feel themselves lucky to have a man like Levi by their side?

"Well, it is." Levi's voice was hard, and Margot snapped her mouth shut so quickly her teeth clicked together.

He sighed, shaking his head a little. "I'm sorry. I didn't mean to snap at you."

"Oh... no, you didn't," Margot said – and really, he hadn't. "It's just that... well, I suppose I was a little surprised to hear you say that. You're just so... *kind*. I don't know how I would have gotten along without your help. To begin with, I'd be off trying to look for a waystation that, thanks to you, I now know I wouldn't have been able to find. And you took me to

ZOE CHANT

the Christmas markets where I got to experience something really magical and eat the best cake I've ever experienced in my life. And –"

"Margot, I can't shift," Levi said, cutting her off, and Margot could hear the deep throb of pain in his voice as he said it. "And where I come from, a chimera who can't shift isn't of any use, to any*one*. Not to other chimeras, and definitely not to –"

He cut himself off, shaking his head.

"Oh," Margot said, understanding finally rippling through her. She felt embarrassed now that she'd practically forced him to tell her something that obviously pained him so much. "Levi, I'm sorry. I truly am."

"Don't be," Levi said, shaking his head. "You didn't know. It's not something I really enjoy telling people – and I usually don't have to, since other chimeras can see it with a glance. You were only being... sweet. But it's just the way things are. It doesn't matter what else I am – or what you might think I am. Without being able to shift, I'm just a failure."

That's not true at all! Margot wanted to protest, but really, she felt she'd put her foot in her mouth enough for one evening when it came to Levi. It was saying things like that that had forced him to admit something he'd clearly been reluctant to tell her to begin with. She had no desire to cause him any more pain.

"You want to talk about failure, I'm sure you have nothing on me," she sighed instead, sinking down onto the one tiny bit of sofa that was relatively free of books. "It seems like I can't help but disappoint everyone around me at every turn."

Now it was Levi's turn to look baffled. "I don't see how that can be true," he said, his handsome brow creasing as his eyebrows drew together. "I don't see how anyone could ever feel anything other than happy when they're around you."

CHIMERAS AND CHRISTMAS CAKES

Margot *almost* smiled at his words, and certainly, her heart sped up a little.

"I guess now it's my turn to tell you something I'd rather not," she said, with a tiny, slightly bitter laugh. "I'm just not very good at magic. And my parents are… well, let's just say they're kind of a big deal in the magical world. They expect so many great things from me. But I just can't do it. Everything I do ends in disaster."

Levi was still frowning. "How bad could it possibly be?"

"I set my professor's beard on fire," Margot told him.

That at least gave Levi pause.

"Well… I'm sure you didn't mean to," he said after a moment.

"Maybe it would have been better if I *had* meant to," Margot muttered darkly. "At least that way I could have counted it a success."

Levi stared at her for a moment, then he burst into laughter. "Well, I have to admit, you make a good point."

Despite herself, Margot felt her own lips twitching into a smile. She couldn't help it – now that she thought about it, she realized that this was the first time since they'd met that she'd heard Levi's laugh – or, really, seen him smile, more than a small half-smile at best.

And, she realized, she'd really like to hear him laugh and see him smile more. As much as she possibly could, in fact.

"One day I should try to tell you about all my other attempts to do things that just ended up causing problems," she said, shaking her head. She'd gladly tell him all the stories she had, if it meant she got to see him smile that gorgeous smile, that made her heartbeat pound in her ears and her stomach grow tight with warmth. "Maybe the ones that caused less bodily harm to the people around me, though. Like the time I tried to develop a spell to make magical plants

grow more quickly, and just ended up blowing the roof off the herbology department's greenhouse."

"Sounds like quite the story," Levi said, still smiling. "I'm not sure I have anything that can compare to that."

"I got suspended, and kicked out of herbology class," Margot moaned, cradling her head in her hands. "It was so embarrassing!"

"You want to talk about embarrassing," Levi said, "Try hearing about the time I tried to – for the first and only time in my life – participate in the Christmas cooking with my family, and almost burned down the kitchen because I didn't realize flambe-ing Christmas pudding is not a skill most eleven-year-olds possess."

Despite herself, Margot cracked just the tiniest bit of a smile. "Well, at least you had the excuse of being eleven," she said, with a small giggle. "And I guess we have, well, setting things on fire that probably ought not be in common."

"That's true," Levi said, sighing a little. "Believe me, they never let me live that one down." He glanced at the box of cakes that Margot had set down on a pile of books when she'd impulsively snatched up *The Duke of Passion.* "Speaking of cake, though, perhaps we should get those into a more air-tight container."

"Oh... is that to keep them fresh? I was thinking I'd just, you know, cast an ageless spell on them," Margot said, cocking her head. "It won't last forever, of course, but it'll certainly stop them from getting stale for a couple of weeks."

Levi's eyebrows shot up, but then, he shook his head. "Oh – of course. That's what I always do with my leftovers. I'm always casting ageless spells on them."

He's teasing you, just so you know, Monty loftily informed her from his place on the mantelpiece, where he was haughtily cleaning his already always pristine paws.

I know that! Margot snapped at him. *But it wasn't in a mean*

way – he's being funny. Not that I expect you'd know anything about that.

Monty, for once, had nothing to say to that, so he turned away, his tail held high, as he usually did when he knew he was at a verbal disadvantage and didn't want to admit it.

"You can cast *that* spell without knocking the roof off, right?" Levi asked, and this time he *did* sound a little concerned, and Margot didn't really blame him.

"Oh yes, of course!" she hurried to reassure him. "It's a very simple spell. I've known it since I was a child – I've never blown anything up with it. Well… not yet, anyway."

She shut her mouth quickly, but she could see the crease between Levi's dark, handsome brows deepening.

Quick, cast the spell and show him you can at least do something *right!*

Raising her hand, Margot curved her fingers round in a waving motion into her palm, feeling her magic gathering within them, the spell a warm, glowing ball. Then, she released it, casting it toward the box of cake Sylvie had so generously gifted her, enveloping it for a moment in a blue, shimmering light that glowed brightly for a moment before fading away.

"There! All done. No explosions, roof still intact!" Margot said, turning to him with a smile. "It's really a very useful spell! Sometimes when I was studying especially hard, I'd make meals and forget about them – but thanks to that, they'd still be just as fresh as when I made them."

"Well, I can't deny the roof *is* still on the house," Levi said, with a smile. "And Sylvie really did give you too much cake for just one person to eat in any kind of timely fashion, so the spell really is a useful one. I have to admit, I was expecting you to say 'Alakazam' or 'Hocus-pocus' or something, though."

ZOE CHANT

Even though Levi's words were light and teasing, Margot couldn't help but feel her heart sink a little as he spoke.

Just one person? Does that mean he thinks I won't be sticking around to share it with him? But that was the whole point of Christmas! Sharing it with – with –

Margot's thoughts trailed off as she realized she wasn't quite sure *how* she should think of Levi. He was unbelievably kind, *astonishingly* handsome, and he'd let her into his home – even if, as he'd said, it was really his Great Aunt Aida's home – even though he didn't really know her at all.

And Margot had to admit, she'd been hoping she'd get to spend more time with him. Not just eating cake, either, if the heat that flared in her belly every time she looked at him was anything to go by.

And at some point, maybe you could remember why exactly you're here, Monty reminded her with a twitch of his fluffy tail, as he ambled his way across the rug, twining himself between the piles of books that littered the floor.

Margot blinked.

Of course. The flos nivis. *The snow flower.*

She couldn't forget about that. She *had* to find it, and then return to the magical world to show off her triumph.

But going back will mean –

Almost as if he'd read her mind, Levi said, "Well, you said you'd have to leave here before Christmas, so I guess you'll want to get an early night so you can be up bright and early to explore the Christmas market some more. Though if you're here to research Christmas, is there a reason you won't be sticking around to observe the day itself?"

"Oh… goodness," Margot stuttered, even as her dismay grew as she thought about the fact that finding the *flos nivis* and going back to the magical world would mean never seeing Levi again. "That's not really why I'm here. I have to admit, the Christmas thing is just… personal interest. No,

76

I'm supposed to be here for a research project that has nothing to do with that. I just let myself get distracted for a bit, I suppose."

Levi cocked his head. "So what's your project actually for, then?"

"I need to complete it in order to pass my studies and finally graduate as a full-fledged witch," Margot said, feeling hopelessness welling up inside her. She stared down at her hands, knotted in her lap. "But it won't be easy. I need to find a certain kind of flower, called the *flos nivis*, or snow flower – it's very rare. It only grows under certain conditions, and it flowers but once a year, when the season is at its coldest. It doesn't grow in many places, but when I was searching through the ancient tomes, they named this place as one of them."

"This place? You mean Girdwood Springs?" Levi asked, still frowning.

"Yes, though that isn't what it's called in the herbology tomes," Margot said. "There, it's called the Mountain of Sources – and I'm not even sure that this is the right place. I did as much cross-checking as I could, and had to match up a lot of different maps and instructions for how to get here. It's my best guess, though – but I guess I'll only be proved right if I can find the *flos nivis*. But even then, given it's so rare, even if I'm *right* I may not find it."

"I can imagine," Levi said, nodding. "So… this flower, I'm guessing, has magical properties of some kind?"

"Oh, yes," Margot said, nodding fervently. "Well, that's what the tomes say, anyway. But it's so rare and hard to find that it seems like no one's exactly sure what its magical properties are anymore, only that it's very powerful – that's why I want to find it. If I can bring one back, even a single bloom, it'll be something the whole of the magical world can study, to find out what it actually *does*."

ZOE CHANT

"I see," Levi said, his lips curving down into a frown as he gazed toward the window, with its half-drawn chintz curtains. Beyond the panes of glass, Margot could see flurries of snow falling from the sky – something she'd never seen before until today. It was enchanting.

"Well, the issue I can see here is that going up the mountain in this weather could get a little dangerous," Levi said after a moment of watching the snow. "All the hiking trails are very much closed at this time of year, and I'm guessing if this flower is so hard to find, you won't be finding it along any of those anyway. Or on any of the ski fields that are open at this time of year."

"Oh… I suppose you must be right," Margot said, deflating a little. This was yet another thing she'd read about, but, she guessed, she'd failed to appreciate the reality. She'd simply been so determined to find the snow flower she hadn't thought about, well… the snow.

"But I can't go back without it," she muttered after a moment, as her determination sprung to life within her once more. "I just can't. This is my last chance. If I don't pass my research project, then I won't graduate – I'll never be a proper witch. My parents will be so disappointed, and Monty will be reassigned as someone else's familiar. I really can't let that happen!"

"No, I can see why that would upset you," Levi said, as he watched Monty sliding one of his great aunt's porcelain lambs toward the edge of a cabinet with one fluffy paw – though he stopped when he realized he was being looked at.

"Yes. Monty's been my best friend for years and years now," Margot said, gazing at the cat fondly as he tried to appear insouciant in the face of his plans of destruction having been interrupted. "He's always been there for me, no matter how many failures I've had or how discouraged I've been."

"Then… you really do need to find this flower and go back to the magical world," Levi said quietly, gazing at her with his blue, *blue* eyes.

Margot looked up at him, a tight feeling in her throat. *Yes, I really do* – she knew that was the right answer, and the answer she *should* be giving him right now. But somehow, she couldn't force the words past her lips.

If I go back, I really won't see Levi again, she thought as she let her eyes drift over him, over the blackness of his hair and his beautifully chiseled features, over the broadness of his chest and shoulders. *But... it's not like I can ask him to give up his whole life and come with me back to the magical world either. And if I don't go back, can I live with knowing how much I've disappointed everyone? And not going back would mean giving up Monty as well, and the dream I've worked so hard for for so many years, of becoming a full-fledged witch...*

"I – I guess I do," she eventually managed to stutter out, though she knew she sounded less than convinced of this. But right now, her heart just wasn't in it. She wasn't sure why she felt such a connection to Levi – who was, after all, a man she'd only just met – but she did.

"Then I'll help you."

Margot looked at him, blinking, surprised at the determination in his voice. He looked just as determined as he sounded – his mouth, with its full lips that offset the hard cut of his features, was pressed into a line, his eyes lit with purpose.

"I don't know how exactly I can be of much use to you, but any way I can help you, I will. You shouldn't go out onto the mountain alone, in any case – you'll need some help. And I don't know if you'll get it from the authorities here. After all, they have a responsibility not to allow people onto the closed tracks during winter, and they'd only be doing their

ZOE CHANT

jobs preventing you from going. But I think this is a special case, if it's really what you need to do."

Margot could feel her eyes growing wider with every word Levi spoke.

He might not have turned out to be a wizard-errant after all, but clearly he was just as gallant as the ones from the stories of old, who were always willing to assist anyone with any magical quest they undertook, no matter the difficulty or danger.

Did I really find a man who's just like the ones from the tales I grew up with when I was a girl?

Margot had always dreamed of that kind of thing – the wizards and knights from the storybooks of her childhood. But she'd never really thought anyone like that could really actually *exist*.

"Really?" she asked, her fists clenched together on her lap. "You really don't mind helping me?"

"Really," Levi said, with a firm nod.

"Oh, *thank you!*"

Before she really knew what she was doing, she'd bounded to her feet and thrown her arms around Levi's shoulders.

She hadn't meant to – it was just that she'd been so demoralized before coming here, and despite the joy of everything around her and how excited she'd been by learning about Christmas, about *everything* about the non-magical world, she'd quickly begun to realize just how impossible a task it was she'd set for herself. To have someone like Levi offering his assistance – well, it was a little hard *not* to be overwhelmed by joy, and the impulsive need to – to –

Um.

It was only a second after she'd flung her arms around him that Margot realized just how close Levi was to her – his

80

body was pressed against hers, firm and warm, the broad plane of his chest rising and falling with his breath. His *warm* breath, which was currently ghosting over her face, making the strands of her hair that had escaped their braid over the course of the day tickle against her skin.

And then there was the way he smelled – soft and masculine all at once.

And his lips were *right there,* so close to her, slightly parted, as if he were just on the verge of gathering her up in his strong, muscled arms and kissing her –

"Margot," Levi whispered, his voice husky, as she felt his large hands come up, resting gently against her waist.

Margot felt a hot shiver pass through her at the sound of his voice, and all at once, she realized she *wanted* him to kiss her – more, possibly, than she'd ever wanted anything before in her life.

Involuntarily, her eyes flickered down to his parted lips.

Is he going to kiss me? Please – let him kiss me –

She closed her eyes, waiting – only for Levi to take a step away from her, his hands falling from her waist, his long, dark eyelashes flickering as he blinked.

"Margot, we should get some sleep if we're going to head out early tomorrow," he said in a strangled voice, as he moved, rapidly, toward the door. "The bedroom is just through there." He gestured vaguely at a door on the other side of the room. "I'll just be downstairs if you need anything. Have a good night. Sleep well. See you in the morning."

And then, he disappeared through the door that led down to the stairs, closing it softly behind him, and leaving Margot staring in his wake.

CHAPTER 6

*I*diot. You stupid, stupid idiot.

Levi groaned as he pressed the heels of his hands into his eyes.

To say he'd had better nights of sleep would have been a distinct understatement. He wasn't sure he'd slept a wink – and it was all his own fault.

He'd so nearly given in last night – he'd wanted to kiss Margot so badly, the heat within him almost unbearable. She'd been so close to him, her soft pink lips so close to his own, her breasts pressed against his chest, her arms around his shoulders. It had taken every ounce of self-control he had to force himself to step away from her and leave her where she was in the living room of his great aunt's apartment.

You already know it wouldn't work out, he berated himself. *I can't offer anything a woman like her deserves. And she told you herself that she'll be going back to the magical world as soon as she finds this flower she needs. You saw how determined she was. She said she needs this. The only thing I can do is try to help her.*

Even if it meant she went back to the magical world and he never saw her again, Levi knew he could feel satisfied

CHIMERAS AND CHRISTMAS CAKES

with himself, knowing that he'd helped Margot achieve her dreams. If that was the one service he could perform for his mate, then he knew he could live happily, knowing *she* was happy.

He didn't know if Margot could tell how close he'd been to kissing her yesterday evening. All the other chimeras he knew had mate bonds with other chimeras, or at least other shifters, like his Great Aunt Aida's belated bond with her dragon man.

Levi didn't know if a human would feel the connection they had with each other the same way a shifter would, or even if Margot, even as a witch, would know much about mate bonds. Shifters tended to be a little cagey about that with non-shifters.

But it doesn't matter anyway, Levi told himself as he stood up, groaning a little as his back protested. He'd spent the night curled into a pretzel shape on one of the armchairs Aida had had scattered in seemingly random corners of the shop, in amongst all the chaos of the bookshelves. It definitely hadn't been designed for someone of his height to even sit in, let alone attempt to sleep in.

Sighing, he supposed he'd better go see if Margot was awake. He didn't have the faintest clue how he was going to help her find the flower she needed to prove herself as a witch, and he knew that it would almost certainly be prohibited for people to be roaming around the wilderness of the mountains at this time of year. Girdwood Springs was surrounded by a national park, and most of it was completely untamed.

If I could shift, this wouldn't be an issue, Levi thought grimly as he mounted the stairs. If he could shift, he could simply spread his eagle's wings and soar through the air, taking Margot wherever she needed to go. He would have been able to find this snow flower in no time.

83

ZOE CHANT

But that doesn't matter, Levi thought, as renewed purpose flowed through him. Whether he could shift or not, he'd help Margot. He wouldn't let anything stand in his way. She'd get what she needed to prove herself as a witch, and he'd do everything in his power to help her.

Reaching the top of the stairs, he knocked gently on the door. It *was* early after all, and if Margot was still sleeping he didn't want to startle her.

No answer.

He knocked again, before calling, "Margot?" through the wood of the door.

Still no answer.

Perhaps she was a sound sleeper, or perhaps she'd closed the door to the bedroom, Levi thought.

Grimacing, he realized he'd probably have to go inside. He hadn't seen any bags with Margot, and she hadn't mentioned that they'd need to go collect her luggage from anywhere. But he'd just have to hope she had sleepwear with her. Somewhere.

"Margot, I'm coming in," he called again, but still there was only silence from beyond the door.

He *really* hoped she hadn't been so horrified by his behavior yesterday that she'd fled in the night, Levi thought, as he opened the door.

But apparently that wasn't the issue at all – nor was it that Margot was still sleeping. He could detect sounds and smells from the kitchen from the moment the door creaked open.

The smell of… *something,* anyway, though it took him a moment to place it as – as –

Burning!

Racing through the living room, dodging around piles of books as he went, Levi found himself standing in the kitchen doorway, looking at Margot – who was wearing a *very* short nightgown, showing off a pair of extremely

84

CHIMERAS AND CHRISTMAS CAKES

shapely legs. Her head was buried in a book – some romantic bodice-ripper if the cover and title, *The Duke of Passion*, were anything to go by – holding it in one hand, while her other hand was gesturing vaguely toward a pan on the stove, which was where the burning smell was coming from, a spoon slowly revolving above it as if by magic.

Or, Levi thought as he stood in the doorway, *literally by magic.*

"Something's burning!" Levi said, as, tearing his eyes away from the sight of Margot's legs, he dashed across the room.

"Oh!" Margot looked up, her cheeks pink, as she practically flung the book away from her, sending it flying over the breakfast counter and out into the living room, presumably from whence it came. "Oh my goodness!"

Before Levi could do anything, the pot that had been on the stove was suddenly levitated from the hotplate and dumped out into the sink, where the contents sizzled for a moment, the smoke dying slowly away.

"Oh, dear," Margot said, looking forlornly down at it. "I am so sorry. I'd only meant to make us some breakfast, but I got caught up in… in reading a book, and I guess I just…"

She looked truly miserable, and Levi wanted to reach for her, to tell her it was okay – it didn't matter, it was only some… well, whatever had been in the pot. It was definitely unrecognizable now.

"Don't worry about it," he said. "I'm just glad you're okay. Nothing's on fire, so no harm done."

Margot still looked a little desolate. "I guess I really *am* bad at cooking," she murmured. "I'd just wanted to thank you for your hospitality."

"Must have been a pretty engrossing book," Levi said, glancing over his shoulder to where she'd flung it. "Happens to the best of us."

Margot colored a little. "Um. Yes. It was. Very *very* engrossing."

"And I guess you weren't kidding about the burning things," Levi said with a small laugh, hoping she'd see the funny side of his words – he'd never been very good at amusing banter.

To his relief, Margot's lips finally twitched into a smile. "Yes. I suppose I should have known better. But perhaps I can make some coffee? I think it would be quite difficult to set *that* on fire, at least."

Levi laughed softly. "You have a point there. And maybe let me take care of the… the…" He peered over the rim of the sink. No, he really had no idea what Margot might have been trying to make.

"It was supposed to be scrambled eggs," Margot said, frustrated. "But obviously that is not how they turned out."

"They look pretty scrambled to me," Levi said, as he went to the fridge to find more eggs. The remark earned him an outraged little yell, and a light tap on the back of his head with the wooden spoon Margot had been magically stirring the pot with. "Okay! I deserved that. I'm sorry."

Despite everything, Levi felt his mood lightening. If Margot had noticed anything about how he'd felt yesterday, she'd clearly chosen to politely overlook it. And it didn't change anything about the fact that he'd still do whatever it took to make sure she succeeded in whatever she needed to do.

She's still my mate, even if I can never claim her the way I want to.

Still, it made him ache as they bustled around each other in the kitchen, Margot taking care of the coffee while he washed out the pan and started over again with the scrambled eggs.

It was as if they'd already known each other for years, and

CHIMERAS AND CHRISTMAS CAKES

knew exactly how to move around each other in the cramped space of the kitchen.

You could have this every day, if you'd only tell her... Levi thought wistfully – but he knew it wasn't true. How could he ask Margot to give up everything she clearly cared so deeply about, for him? A chimera who couldn't even shift?

"The coffee is prepared!" Margot announced with a flourish of a teaspoon. "Do you have it with cream? Or sugar?"

"No, just black is fine," Levi said, glancing up from where the eggs were almost ready. "Take a seat at the counter and I'll be there in a moment."

Thankfully, Levi belatedly realized as he walked to the counter a moment later with the plated eggs – which were no gourmet presentation but they looked edible, at least – Margot had chosen to sit on the living room side of the counter rather than the kitchen side. He wasn't sure he'd be able to keep his eyes off the sight of her bare legs otherwise.

"So," he said, as he placed the eggs down in front of her, and lifted his coffee. "Do you want to tell me more about this snow flower?"

"I wish I could," Margot said, as she lifted a forkful of eggs to her mouth. "Oh, goodness," she said as she chewed. "This is quite delicious!"

They ate in silence for a few moments. Levi hadn't realized quite how hungry he was, but then, he supposed, he'd dashed off to sleep on the armchair last night after only having had his very late lunch of goulash and Christmas cake yesterday.

"My apologies, I forgot what I was saying for a moment," Margot said as she finished off the last of her eggs. "I meant to say, I wish I *could* say more about the *flos nivis.* But so much of the knowledge about it has been completely lost. I

only know it grows here on these mountains, and it blooms only during the coldest days of winter."

"Well, seems like you've arrived at the right time for that," Levi said, as he glanced out of the kitchen window to where there was snow piled high on the sill. "It's been record low temperatures all this week. If your flower is going to be blooming, it's definitely doing it now."

"Then we should hurry!" Margot said, a new light entering her eyes. "I'm so glad I was finally able to get something right!"

Levi tapped at his phone, bringing up his weather app. "Well, according to this, the temperature was the coldest it's been all year last night," he said thoughtfully. "So today seems like our best chance."

"Then we should set out at once!" Margot stood up, a determined gleam in her eyes. "I'm sure that together, we'll have no trouble finding the *flos nivis*. I feel like I could do anything, as long as you're by my side."

Levi wasn't sure he felt quite so confident about it, but he *was* determined to help Margot. "You did bring some cold weather clothing, didn't you?" he asked, as he too stood up. "It'll be even colder up on the mountain than it is in town. And we should definitely bring some snacks and supplies. It's amazing how much energy walking in snow conditions uses up."

"All taken care of," Margot said, and, reaching down she lifted up the tote bag she'd been carrying yesterday, patting it with a smile.

Levi eyed it dubiously. "It's… all in there, is it?"

"But of course! All stored in the pocket dimension in my bag," Margot laughed. "Oh… but of course, I keep forgetting. I guess in the non-magical world you have to carry everything you need around with you."

"Uh, yeah, that's… usually how we do things around

here," Levi said, eyes still on the – completely normal-looking – tote. "My stuff is all in my suitcase in the bedroom. I'll need to go get changed if we're going up into the mountains."

He neglected to mention that it was all still in his suitcase because he hadn't even bothered to unpack it and put it in Aida's free wardrobe space, since he'd been so determined to make this the shortest possible trip: arrive, sort and get rid of the bookshop's stock, put the place up for sale and then leave.

He actually hadn't even cared if whatever real estate agent he appointed to handle the sale got a good price for the place or even if they swindled him blind, since he'd never expected or wanted to have to deal with the sale in the first place. But watching Margot as she wound her way expertly through the piles of books his great aunt had left everywhere, as if she'd been living here for years instead of only a few hours, looking as if she was right at home with the homey, worn furnishings, made an ache start up in his chest that he quickly decided he'd need to ignore.

And it seemed Margot hadn't been lying about her tote bag containing everything she needed, either. Right now, she was reaching inside of it and pulling out an amazing array of winter clothing, from snow jackets to hiking boots to mittens to scarves.

"Do you think this will be enough?" she asked, gesturing to the massive pile of clothes she'd heaped on the sofa.

"Uh, sure. It should be," Levi said – and he was pretty sure she'd pulled out enough to last several days in the snow, let alone what he hoped would only be a few hours. "But I better go get ready myself. We don't want to leave it too late."

"No indeed!" Margot gave him a brilliant, sparkling smile, her green eyes dancing with light, and Levi felt his heart miss a beat. "The early bird catches the slug!" She paused. "Is that the right way of saying it?"

ZOE CHANT

Levi smiled. "Close enough."

"Hmm. I should ask Monty if he wants to come, I suppose," Margot said, glancing over her shoulder and into the living room. "Oh – there he is."

Levi looked past her to where he could see an enormous fluffy black ball asleep on the sofa, in amongst all the books. As he watched, Monty half opened his large yellow eyes, just far enough that Levi could see them glitter with what was a clear signal to leave him where he was.

"Well," Margot laughed. "I suppose that answers that question." She turned to him, eyes shining. "Shall we get ready to go?"

Of course, the hiking trails that Levi thought would have been incredibly beautiful in spring, fall and summer were all closed, with signs up saying that access to them was prohibited. They passed the park ranger's cabin, barely visible beneath its mantle of snow.

Levi felt a twinge of guilt as they snuck past it – he hoped some diligent park ranger wouldn't get in any trouble due to their trespassing, since really this was all on them.

"Are you cold?" Margot asked, her breath misting out from above her several layers of scarves, and glancing up at him. She'd definitely brought more than enough clothes – she now resembled an ambulant snowman more than anything else, so padded up with winter gear she was.

"Oh no, not really," Levi assured her. "I might not be able to shift, but I do have some of my shifter abilities, and a pretty high tolerance for cold is one of them."

Most shifters ran hot, after all, and they healed fast from injuries as well. Levi couldn't do either as well as a chimera

90

CHIMERAS AND CHRISTMAS CAKES

who could actually shift, but he still was able to cope with both better than a regular human.

"Only I have a spell that will surround us with a little ball of warm air, if you *do* happen to start feeling the cold," Margot said. "I promise, I know how to do that one. You will *not* be set on fire. Not even a little bit."

Levi opened his mouth, then closed it again. He wasn't sure what to say to that – it wasn't that he didn't trust Margot's spell-casting abilities, *but...*

"I'm fine," he said.

They trudged up the beginning of the trail, still just visible in the snow.

"You don't happen to have a spell that helps you find the *flos nivis*, do you?" he asked, as the snow became deeper. It was fresh and fluffy, and soon he was sinking in it up to his ankles.

"No, I'm afraid not," Margot said. "But I can tell you a few things about it. The flower itself is white, with a bluish tinge. Sometimes the buds can look pink. And it's an evergreen tree, so it will still have its leaves even at this time of year. Also, unlike a pine or a fir, it doesn't have needles – its leaves are a distinct star-shape. And if it gets old enough, it can grow into quite a mighty tree!"

Levi nodded. He supposed that, at least, gave them something to look out for, and it would be pretty difficult to mistake it for any of the other evergreen trees they were trudging past. Still, given the size of the mountain, it still felt a little like looking for a needle in a haystack.

The snow got deeper the farther they went up the path, and the farther down in his chest Levi's heart sank. He was pretty sure a tree as unusual as the snow flower sounded would be pretty remarkable – so the fact he'd never heard of anything like it before probably meant they weren't going to stumble across it while walking along one of the obviously

91

ZOE CHANT

well-worn hiking trails. He'd looked through a few books Great Aunt Aida had had in the bookshop about local flora, and none of them had mentioned anything that sounded like what Margot had described either.

"I wonder if it may be a little deeper in the forest," Margot wondered aloud, clearly having had the same thought.

"That might be true, but I don't know how I feel straying too far from the path," Levi said, even as his sense of duty to his fated mate rebelled – really, their mate bond dictated he should do whatever Margot requested of him. But it also meant keeping her safe, and traipsing through the forest in the middle of winter didn't seem a great way to do that. "These woods are pretty thick, and you'd be surprised how quickly you can completely lose your way."

"Oh… yes, I understand completely," Margot said, nodding. "I'm always losing track of where I'm headed. It's why I learned how to cast a trail marker spell so quickly, so I wouldn't get lost quite so frequently."

"A trail marker spell?"

Margot nodded. "It's quite simple once you know how. It does exactly what it sounds like – marks your trail for you! So if you take a wrong turn or some such thing, you can easily find your way back."

"Well…" Levi said, frowning. He still wasn't quite sure it was a good idea, but nor were they going to find the snow flower like this either. "If you're really sure it works, could you cast it now, so that if we leave the path we can find our way back to it if the weather turns bad?"

"Oh, yes, of course!" Margot nodded vigorously. "Don't worry – I've used it hundreds of times and it's never been wrong. I'm very experienced. You see –"

Once again, she made the curling motion with her fingers he'd seen her make when she'd been casting the spell on the cakes back at Aida's apartment. A warm, glowing ball of

92

magic grew in her palm before she released it – but this time, instead of the light dying away to nothing after a moment or two, it stayed where it was, like a glowing lantern hovering a few feet above the ground.

"I can see how that would be useful," Levi said, impressed. It was clear that despite her conviction that she was a complete failure, there were many spells that Margot could cast expertly.

He supposed he hadn't tried the cake yet to see if it had remained completely fresh overnight, but she'd certainly seemed to know what she was doing then – and as for the eggs this morning, that hadn't been Margot's magic that had caused that. That had seemed all down to just how very engrossing *The Duke of Passion* had been.

"It'll stay here until I recall it," Margot explained, as they left the path. After a few steps, she cast another glowing ball of light, and left it hovering in place. "We can follow them back to the trail."

They continued on, the deep snow making their progress slow, but steady. Margot paused to cast balls of light as they went, and sure enough, when Levi glanced behind him, he saw a trail of them marking the way back to the path, and safety.

But it didn't change the fact that looking for the snow flower wasn't getting any easier. No matter how much he looked around him, Levi couldn't see anything that fitted the description Margot had given him.

"It seems like it should stand out amongst all these fir trees, shouldn't it?" Margot asked, a little apprehensively. "It *is* terribly inconvenient that it only flowers in winter. If it were spring, we wouldn't have to be walking through so much cold snow like this! Or... I suppose, I could have been wrong all along, and this place just isn't the Mountain of Sources after all."

ZOE CHANT

"We'll find it, Margot," Levi said, what he hoped was reassuringly – he really didn't have a lot of practice at being reassuring. But he thought it had worked, judging from the brilliant smile Margot flashed him.

Even though he was a shifter, Levi still found he was feeling the cold. It was already freezing in town, but here on the mountain it was colder still – and seemed to be getting even colder, even though it was mid-morning.

As they walked, they passed a ramshackle old cabin that was obviously left over from when this had been hunting grounds.

Levi only knew a little of Girdwood Springs's history, mainly gleaned from when he'd been flicking through books on the subject before he prepared to toss them into a box marked 'FREE' and set outside on the curb.

But he did know all of this land had once been privately owned by the Girdwood family, and they'd left it in trust to be used only as parklands, in perpetuity.

In a way, he supposed, it was comforting to know such a beautiful place would be safe forever.

"You said they grow into quite large trees, didn't you?" Levi asked.

"That's right," Margot replied, nodding. "But they get really big only once they get older –"

She cut herself off as a howling wind cut suddenly through the trees, chilling them both to the bone – Levi could feel it even through his snow jacket and sweater, and the natural heat of his shifter body. He could tell Margot was feeling it too, if the way she suddenly huddled down into her very many layers of clothing was anything to go by.

Could it be –?

Levi didn't want to believe it, but grimly, he realized it was true.

A snap storm.

The temperature was plummeting, and Levi could hear the tree trunks groaning as they too were suddenly chilled, their sap hardening within them. And that wasn't all – he could smell snow, fresh snow. A moment later, and large, icy flakes of it began to descend from the sky, faster and in larger amounts than should have seemed possible in such a short amount of time. The wind picked up again, sending the hard snow flurrying against his face, chilling it to the bone.

"Quick!" Levi yelled above the sound of the howling wind. He wrapped an arm protectively around Margot's shoulders, pulling her against him. "Let's get back to the trail!"

But he already knew they wouldn't have time to get back to the trail and then follow it back into town. The storm was already upon them, fast and furious.

The cabin, Levi thought, as he pulled Margot's shivering body even closer against him. Just as she had said, he could still see the trail marking spell glowing even through the snowfall. He hoped he could still find the cabin itself – they'd passed right by it, so the trail marking spell should be able to guide them that way. But he knew that it was easy to miss things even a few feet away from you in such conditions.

Thankfully, however, he was just able to make out the side of the sturdy cabin, illuminated in the glow of the trail marker. Gasping as the cold air closed around them like a fist, he guided Margot to it.

Either the door had never had a lock on it, or it had rusted away over the years since anyone had last used this place, because it opened with only a few quick tugs. Quickly, Levi ushered Margot inside, and then, together, they heaved the door closed again against the wind, the snow spiraling all around them.

Levi let out a sigh of relief once the door was finally closed against the storm, but they still weren't exactly out of

ZOE CHANT

their predicament – the storm might have been shut out, but it wasn't any warmer in here than it was outside. He was still shivering, and he could see Margot was too, despite her layers of clothing, her breath misting the air in front of her face.

"You said… you said you had a spell that could envelop us in a ball of warm air?" Levi asked. He hadn't been *entirely* sold on the idea before, but now, he was willing to take the risk.

Margot nodded, her teeth chattering. "I – I c-c-can c-cast it, if you l-l-like?"

There was no time to even consider the memory of what Margot had told him about her accidentally blowing the roof off the herbology department's greenhouse or setting anyone's beard on fire. They both needed to warm up – now.

"Go for it."

Margot clearly didn't need to be told twice. Magic glowed in her palms, and then Levi felt as if he'd – somehow – walked into a balmy spring day, warm air wafting around him in a way that was extremely pleasant. He found that he was feeling comfortable again in no time..

"I guess I don't need this anymore," he said, as he pulled his winter cap off his head – in fact, wrapped as he was in all this winter gear, he was now starting to sweat a little. He shed his jacket and sweater, hanging them up to drip dry on a hook by the door.

Margot too was rapidly shedding all the layers she'd encased herself in, letting out a *woo* of relief as she shook the rapidly melting snow out of her long blonde hair.

It was amazing how comfortable he felt here, Levi thought as he wandered around the cabin. It was small, but that didn't matter – Margot's spell had made it warm and cozy.

But, he thought, frowning as he went to the cupboards

that lined the walls, it was clearly many, *many* years since it had seen any use. There were no supplies here – not even incredibly out-of-date canned food, or moldy bread, or *anything at all.*

No bed or anything either, Levi thought as he glanced around. The whole cabin was completely and utterly bare. And who knew how long it'd take for the heavy snowfall to pass?

"Goodness, what an adventure!"

He turned in time to see Margot gazing around them with large eyes. She didn't seem especially fazed at all – but maybe she just hadn't realized yet that they'd be stuck here for an indeterminate amount of time with no food and nowhere comfortable to sleep, even if, at least, she'd made it warm enough that there was no chance of them freezing to death.

"Well, I don't know about you, but I am *quite* hungry," Margot announced, as she strolled around the room. "Would you like something to eat?"

Levi shook his head. "I already checked, Margot. We have absolutely nothing to eat here. We might be here for hours, and we ate all our snacks earlier."

Margot turned to him, her eyes wide with surprise. "But of course we do!"

"I looked in the cupboards – they're totally bare," Levi argued, frowning. "And I'm not sure we can gnaw on the wooden walls."

Margot laughed. "Oh – what a silly suggestion. No, we shouldn't need to do *that.* I have absolutely everything we might need right here!"

She lifted her tote bag from her shoulder. It just looked like an ordinary tote as far as Levi could tell. How could it have everything they needed inside it?

But then, the memory of what she'd told him before

ZOE CHANT

they'd left came rushing back. Something about her not needing to carry luggage because she had a – a pocket dimension? – that she carried around inside her bag with her.

Still, how much could it possibly contain? Levi thought, as he eyed the bag dubiously.

"But before food, let's get some light in here," Margot muttered, as she rummaged around in her bag. "I don't know about you, but I just can't eat in this gloomy light."

Levi realized that Margot had absolutely not been joking when she'd said that they had everything they needed in her magic bag.

She pulled out an entire array of candles, big and small, and arranged them around the cabin, before lighting them all with a quick flick of her finger. Immediately, the once-gloomy cabin was bathed in flickering golden light that slid through Margot's hair, turning it to spun gold, and illuminated the flush of her cheeks in the warm air.

Levi swallowed. He'd already known how attracted he was to Margot. But now, as she busied herself laying out a soft rug that she had also – somehow – pulled from the depths of her tote, he was finding her almost irresistible.

But I can't, he thought desperately, even as he felt heat gathering within him. *How can I tell her she's my mate, when I couldn't even help her do this one thing that she needs from me?*

Despite everything, they hadn't found the snow flower before the storm had closed over them. And by the time it passed by, the snow would be even thicker on the ground than it was already. The conditions would make it almost impossible to travel anywhere across the mountain on foot.

And I can't shift, he thought miserably. *If only I could, all of this would be so easy.*

Within him, he felt his chimera give a quick twitch of its tail.

98

CHIMERAS AND CHRISTMAS CAKES

It would be, wouldn't it? it said with a lazy yawn.

Levi felt a sudden fury rise up within him. It was his chimera's fault he couldn't be the mate Margot needed.

If it would reveal itself, then none of this would be happening. He could fly them across the mountainside in the blink of an eye, alighting here and there to search, before soaring off again to inspect another location.

Instead, here he was, relying on Margot herself to – uh –

Pull an entire picnic basket out of her tote bag?!

It wasn't that he minded relying on Margot – that was what the mate bond was, after all. They were supposed to help each other, be there for each other. It was more that he hadn't been able to offer Margot literally *anything.*

"There," Margot said, with an air of satisfaction as she opened her picnic hamper to reveal a full set of plates and cutlery strapped into the lid, and, inside the basket itself, what looked to be an incredibly hearty meal, which quickly revealed itself to be roasted chicken drumsticks, potato salad, corn on the cob, and green beans.

As he watched, Levi felt his stomach rumble – he really hadn't realized just how hungry he was.

"Wow. This all looks absolutely incredible," Levi said, as he came and sat down with Margot on the fluffy rug she'd laid out, surrounded by the flickering light of the candles.

"Oh – I didn't cook it, I'm afraid," Margot said, biting her lip. "It was cooked by my cousin – she's a real expert. And she's friends with a unicorn shifter, who gives her all her produce."

"Well, that pretty much guarantees it'll be delicious," Levi said, as he reached for a plate and began serving up Margot a generous helping of potato salad. But that must have meant that Margot knew about unicorns and the power they had to give any plant life, and, more than that, to make them lusher and greener than any human hand could, and to grow fruits

99

ZOE CHANT

and vegetables more delicious than any others. "Did you notice, then, that the ingredients of the Christmas cakes we ate were grown by a unicorn?"

"Oh!" Margot said, her eyes widening. "I *thought* I recognized that taste. Well, well, well. I can't tell when someone's a shifter, of course, but you must have known that that nice Sylvie was a unicorn right away."

"Not her," Levi said, as he began piling his own plate high, as Margot tore into her chicken drumstick with gusto. "Perhaps it's her supplier. She may not even know."

"Or," Margot said, once she'd swallowed and wiped her mouth with the back of her hand, "her mate is a unicorn shifter."

Levi froze, a forkful of potato salad halfway to his mouth.

"You – you know about mate bonds?" he asked, after he'd managed to unfreeze himself.

"Oh… not very much, of course," Margot said. "Only that they exist, really. Well, of course *you* would know how cagey shifters can get about things like that!"

Levi nodded slowly, as he finally remembered to eat his potato salad. Margot was right – the recipe itself was delicious, rich and creamy, but these were *definitely* potatoes that had been tended by a unicorn.

He supposed that did answer his question about whether Margot knew about mate bonds – but she didn't seem any the wiser as to their own connection.

That, at least, should make it easier to give her up, Levi thought as he chewed on a – again, delicious, the skin crispy and spicy – chicken drumstick. He knew now at least that he wouldn't be condemning Margot to a life of feeling incomplete, like half of her soul was missing. She'd probably just think of him – hopefully fondly – every now and then, as someone who'd tried to help her when she was in a pinch.

"Oh, but that reminds me!" Margot cried suddenly, as she

CHIMERAS AND CHRISTMAS CAKES

set her now empty plate aside – she'd polished off her food in record time. "I brought cake!"

Sure enough, when she reached into her tote, the next thing she pulled out was the box of cake Sylvie had given her at the market stall. And sure enough, the cakes looked just as delicious as they had then. Margot's spell had clearly kept them completely fresh.

"Which one do you want to try first?" Margot asked, her eyes sparkling in the candlelight.

"Well, I have to admit, I don't have much of a sweet tooth. This angel cake, with the vanilla cake and whipped cream would be my first choice," Levi said.

"As for me, I'm going to try the cherry pie," Margot said, reaching into the box and pulling out the sliver of pie, with its sugared lattice and glistening, dark red cherries. "And here's your angel cake."

The angel cake tasted just as good as it looked, the cake moist but light, the whipped cream frothy with just a hint of sugar, and something that Levi identified after a moment as lemon rind and violets.

Even knowing the ingredients had come from a unicorn, the cake was unbelievably delicious – Sylvie was clearly a genius baker, with or without any help.

"That is incredible," Levi murmured, as he licked a scrap of cream from his thumb. "You *have* to try a bite, Margot."

But Margot was clearly in raptures about her cherry pie. Her eyes were closed, her mouth chewing slowly, her lower lip glistening with just a hint of cherry syrup. Her cherry pie was obviously just as delicious as his angel cake.

And, looking at her now, it was taking every ounce of Levi's self-control not to lean in and kiss her, right on her perfect mouth.

"Oh... wow," Margot said, when she finally opened her

ZOE CHANT

eyes again. "That was *heaven.* Here – let me get you a little bit!"

So saying, Margot sliced off a little bit of her pie with her fork, and then, to Levi's horror leaned over, as if she intended to feed it to him.

She was *way* too close, and Levi knew if she came any closer, he'd lose his composure and do something he knew would only cause both of them pain.

But as Margot leaned in, her warm, cherry-scented breath brushing over his face, Levi found he couldn't tell her to stop – nor could he stop himself, either, from raising his hand and cupping his palm to her flushed cheek as she drew nearer.

Margot blinked, stopping, the fork still hovering in front of his lips.

"Levi?" she asked, her voice a little breathless, her eyes wide.

As quickly as Levi had raised his hand, he dropped it again, grimacing.

"I'm sorry, Margot," he said, shaking his head as he pulled away. "I shouldn't have done that –"

"But why not?" Margot burst out, interrupting him. "I've been wanting you to do that since – since –" She blinked, a little frown of her own crossing her lips. "Well, I actually don't remember. But almost as soon as I met you, I'm sure. I thought you were going to – to kiss me last night, but then…"

She trailed off, a blush creeping up her cheeks. She put the fork with its morsel of cherry pie aside, and then buried her face in her hands.

"Oh boy, I really have embarrassed myself now, haven't I?" she moaned. "I'm *so* sorry – I completely misread things, I guess. Can you please just forget I said that, so we can go back to enjoying our cake?"

Levi stared at her. *She'd been wanting me to kiss her?*

102

CHIMERAS AND CHRISTMAS CAKES

Perhaps that wasn't so surprising – the mate bond *did* work that way. Perhaps Margot didn't know what it was, but she could still feel its effects.

Still, seeing how mortified she was, Levi couldn't help himself from reaching out and drawing her hands away from her face, holding them between his own.

"Margot, believe me, I *wish* I could kiss you," he said, his voice husky.

"Then... why don't you?" Margot asked in a small voice. "I promise, I'd really like that very much!"

Levi swallowed. He could feel the truth pressing up against his lips, and he realized he couldn't do anything but tell it.

"Because... because you're my mate, Margot. We share that bond, just like you've heard about."

Margot stared at him, her green eyes wide. "We're *mates?*"

Levi nodded. "Yes. But Margot... I'm not someone it's good to share a mate bond with."

Shaking her head, Margot only kept staring at him. "I don't understand. Why not?"

"For the reason I told you earlier," Levi said, pain creeping up his throat. "I can't shift, Margot. I can't do any of the things a shifter *should* be able to do for his mate. It happens sometimes in chimera shifters – you said yourself how much they love to keep themselves to themselves, and how reclusive and mercurial they can be. Mine just won't show itself, no matter how hard I try to coax it to the surface. I don't think I'll ever be able to. And a shifter who can't shift is..." He trailed off, shaking his head. He couldn't quite bring himself to finish the sentence.

"What?" Margot's eyes were suddenly blazing. "Only the kindest, sweetest, most wonderful person I've ever met?" she asked, as she pulled her hands free of his grip and raised them to his face. "The person who went completely out of his

103

ZOE CHANT

way to help me find the *flos nivis*, even though he only just met me and had never heard of it until just then? Who took me to see the Christmas marvels, even though he wasn't a wizard-errant at all? Who gave me somewhere to stay when I didn't have anywhere? And who – for some reason – can see Monty, when no one else here can?"

"Margot…" Levi said, his heart in anguish.

"Do you think I care about whether or not you can shift?" she asked, without taking the slightest bit of notice of him interrupting her. "When I can see who you are in your heart?"

Levi closed his eyes, wanting to block out her beautiful, sincere expression.

But it was no good. He knew he couldn't resist her any longer.

In the next moment, he'd swept her up in his arms, pressing their lips together – and after a moment, he felt Margot's arms wrap around his shoulders, pulling him even closer still.

"Margot," he murmured when he could finally bring himself to pull away, taking a moment to appreciate her flushed, breathless state, her disarrayed hair, before he pulled her in again for another heated kiss.

CHAPTER 7

From the moment Margot drifted back into consciousness, she could feel a smile twitching at the corner of her lips.

And, she thought, rolling over onto her side so she could see Levi's still-sleeping face, she didn't believe anyone could blame her for that.

She curled up against Levi's side, warm and happy, both of them covered up by the cozy blanket they'd fallen asleep under last night. A delicious, satiated ache filled her body – she didn't think she'd ever woken up feeling quite this *content* before, ever, in her life.

My mate. Levi is my fated mate.

It was amazing to her how easily the thought drifted into her head. She'd never in a thousand years ever suspected she would be a shifter's mate, even though she'd met several shifters down through the years, and she'd known about the mate bonds they could share.

It just didn't seem possible a shifter could ever share that with me.

ZOE CHANT

Especially not someone like Levi.

She'd known from the moment she met him that there was something about him – something that had called to her.

Perhaps it had been the mate bond all along, but Margot didn't think that was the only reason. Despite his occasional gruffness, it was clear that Levi had a kind heart and a generous spirit. She didn't care even a little bit that he couldn't shift – what did that matter, when he'd helped her so much, even though it had been pretty clear he didn't much care for Christmas himself?

And then there's the fact he's so handsome, and sweet, and he clearly is fond of Monty too...

Margot pursed her lips a little at the thought of Monty. It was possible, of course, that he was still curled up on Levi's sofa, not having moved an inch since yesterday. But there was also the possibility he'd gotten bored and hurled every porcelain item in Levi's great aunt's house to the ground, before wandering off to go spectrally bother someone else in town.

Well, I'll just have to hope that's not the case, Margot thought, as Levi's thick, dark eyelashes fluttered, and then he woke.

"Okay," he said, when he turned to look at her, his blue eyes still a little hazy from sleep. "I'm really glad to know that what happened last night wasn't just some incredible dream." He frowned a little. "Unless it *was* a dream, and you have no idea what I'm talking about right now, or this is a dream within a dream –"

Leaning forward, Margot cut off the flow of his words by pressing her lips against his.

"Does that answer your questions?" she asked mischievously, when she finally pulled back.

"Uh, yeah," Levi said, and Margot felt quite smug at the slight breathlessness in his voice – it was a fitting, if small,

106

CHIMERAS AND CHRISTMAS CAKES

payback for how breathless he'd made *her* last night. "Pretty much."

He sat up, the blanket falling away from the broad plane of his chest, and it was all Margot could do not to pounce on him and re-enact the previous evening – except for the frown that crossed Levi's face in the next moment.

"Levi?" she asked, reaching over to cup his cheek with her palm. "Is there something wrong?"

"No..." Levi said, before shaking his head. "At least... I don't think so."

"Then what is it?" she asked, her eyebrows drawing together.

"I don't really know," Levi replied after a moment. "It was just that... for a moment, I thought..." But then he trailed off, shaking his head. "But maybe I was wrong."

Margot wanted to question him further, but she also didn't want to pry too much – mate bond or no mate bond, she knew she'd chattered at him enough yesterday, and made him reveal things that clearly caused him pain.

Still...

She wanted him to know he could tell her anything, and she'd still accept him. Ever since last night, it was as if she could feel the magical bond that flowed between them – sturdy and golden and glowing, which nothing could ever break apart.

But even as she thought that, she became aware of a horrendous growling noise filling the cabin – and then became aware that it was her stomach.

Or rather, *both* of their stomachs.

"Okay, wow," she laughed. "I guess we worked up quite an appetite."

"You can say that again," Levi said, a flash of heat entering his eyes, and Margot couldn't stop the warm shiver that passed through her.

ZOE CHANT

Okay! No! Food first! Then... whatever else, she told herself firmly. She honestly felt if she gave in to her more primal urges now, they'd probably never get out of this cabin.

Not that that would be so bad, she thought, as she rummaged around in her tote bag for the food they had left over from last night. Chicken drumsticks and potato salad might not have been the most conventional of breakfasts, but right now, Margot would take it.

And so would Levi, it seemed, from the way he tucked into his own plate of food with gusto.

Together, they ate in happy silence, the cabin filled with the sound of their munching, until finally they both sat back, contented and full.

"This cousin of yours is quite the cook," Levi said. "I'd really like to meet her one of these days to thank her – she really saved our bacon."

"Well, of course you can," Margot said with a smile. "I really hope you'll be able to meet *all* my family – we're pretty close, after all! And if you're my mate, then of course they'll be absolutely dying to meet you too. I don't think anyone else in my family has ever had a mate bond with a shifter before, even though we know a few."

As she spoke, she noticed that Levi's expression was growing more and more somber.

"Margot, you know, though, that I'm not really like other shifters," he said.

At first, Margot just blinked at him, not sure what he meant. Then, of course, she realized.

"Oh, but Levi – do you really think I, or any of them, would care about that?" she burst out before she could stop herself, shoving her foot right down her throat as per usual. "No – all they'll care about is how kind you are, and how much you helped me. Once they get to know you, I'm sure it won't even enter their heads."

108

CHIMERAS AND CHRISTMAS CAKES

"Perhaps not," Levi said quietly. "But they do seem like they have pretty high expectations."

"They do," Margot admitted. "But of *me*. It's because my parents are both such powerful magic users – naturally, it's kind of disappointing to them that it doesn't come as naturally to me as it does to them. They really want a child who can follow in their footsteps, and become a great magical researcher. And I just don't think I'm really cut out for that."

"Well, I don't think that's true," Levi said with a smile. "You figured out this place might be the place to find the snow flower – it sounds like that took a lot of work and determination. Not to mention cross-referencing a lot of material to narrow it down. That's no mean feat, Margot. You shouldn't undersell yourself."

"I… I suppose so," Margot stuttered, surprise filling her. She'd never really looked at it that way – she'd always just loved messing around in libraries, poring over old books and annotating them, taking notes and collecting information. It had seemed quite easy to her – almost second nature. It was practical magic and spells she was useless at – and that was what she needed to pass her course.

But… maybe I'm not so useless after all? she thought, swallowing. She'd always kept the amount of time she spent in libraries and dusty book towers to herself – she was sure if she mentioned it, Professor Imari would just tell her that if she'd devote as much time to studying magic, she'd surely have graduated by now.

"And my parents would *love* you," Levi continued. "Well, not that they don't love me, either, but I guess they're just… concerned. All my siblings have big families, but all of them learned to shift early, and in chimera society, proving you can shift is a huge benefit when you're finding your mate, or looking for a partner. Chimeras who can't shift… well. They have a harder time. I know some chimera shifters who never

ZOE CHANT

learned to shift – and they never were able to start their own families either. I just assumed that would be the case for me too, no matter how much I wanted a family or a partner in my life."

Margot nodded, even as her heart was bursting with sadness for Levi, and the pain and loneliness she could hear in his voice – but also with love.

Well, he'll never have to feel that way again. I'll make sure of it.

"You've definitely found that now," she murmured softly, as she leaned forward, pressing her palm to Levi's cheek. "As long as you don't mind spending your life with someone who once blew off the herbology department's greenhouse roof, and set her professor's beard on fire. And some other things too, but I'll stop right there in case you start to reconsider this whole thing."

Levi laughed, soft and husky. "No chance of that. I already knew all of that anyway, and I still knew you were the only person I could ever imagine having – or wanting – as my mate." He looked at her, his blue eyes burning. "And… you're sure you're okay with –"

He stopped again, frowning.

"Levi? What is it?" Margot asked, concern rippling through her. "Is everything okay?"

Levi shook his head, his hand pressed to his chest. Margot's concern grew into alarm, and she sprang up, her hands on Levi's shoulders.

"Levi?!"

But instead of answering her, Levi leaped up from the little love nest they'd made for themselves last night, striding to the door of the cabin.

"Levi!"

Thankfully, when Levi flung open the door of the cabin, it looked like the snowstorm had blown over during the night – snow flooded in through the door, white and fluffy and

crisp, but it wasn't falling from the sky anymore, and Margot could see sunshine glittering through the trees.

But still, alarmed, Margot jumped up, taking a moment to wrap the blanket they'd been lying beneath around her.

Is Levi not cold, going out there butt naked like that?!

She appreciated the view, for sure, but right now, Margot didn't understand at all what was going on, and she didn't think striding out into the freezing cold morning air the day after a snowstorm was normal behavior, even for a chimera shifter!

When she reached the door, Levi had taken a few strides through the snow, and was now standing knee-deep in it a few feet from the cabin.

"Levi?" she called again from where she stood in the doorway.

Levi blinked, turning to look at her. "Margot…" he said, before shaking his head, as if awakening from a dream. "Margot, I think something is happening."

"Um… yes, you just walked out into the snow," Margot replied, confused. "Is, uh, that what you meant?"

"No, I think I – Margot, I think I feel my chimera. I think it's awake. And I think it wants to come out."

Margot felt her mouth popping open in surprise. "Your chimera?!"

Levi nodded. A look of confusion crossed his face – but beneath the confusion, she could see determination.

"I think so. It's never… never felt this way before. I can feel it moving. Looking around. Like it suddenly wants to know what's going on outside of its dreams."

Margot felt hopefulness surging up inside her. *Could this really mean…?*

"It's still cautious though," Levi said after a moment. "I think it's still going to need some convincing –"

ZOE CHANT

He cut himself off suddenly, blinking again, his fists clenched at his side.

Margot was momentarily frightened, but then she saw Levi's expression harden even more into determination.

Is he –?

And yes, sure enough – she saw it.

She'd seen a shifter shifting before – some of them had been her former classmates at university after all, before they'd graduated and left her behind. But still, she was filled with a sense of absolute wonder as she watched now as a shimmer ran over Levi's body, and then he began to – to *grow*.

Margot held her breath, knowing her eyes were practically bulging out of their sockets. She might have seen shifters before, but she'd never seen a *chimera.*

And he was more magnificent than she ever could have imagined.

Large, white eagle's wings sprouted from Levi's back, so mighty they almost reached the lower levels of the forest canopy above when he stretched them out fully, flexing them as if they were stiff or tired.

A shining tail of delicate, silvery scales whipped out behind him, curving and glistening in the early morning sunlight.

But most magnificent of all was the noble lion's head and body – golden fur covered him, a full, shaggy mane covering his head and shoulders. Amber eyes turned their gaze to her as she stood in the doorway, frozen in amazement.

Margot could admit that if a lion she'd – somehow – randomly encountered had looked at her, she would have either screamed or fainted on the spot out of sheer terror.

But she felt none of that now. The only thing she felt pulsing through her was joy – and love.

112

CHIMERAS AND CHRISTMAS CAKES

"Levi, you shifted!" she cried out – stating the obvious, of course, but right now, she just couldn't help it. She didn't even feel the freezing cold snow against the bare soles of her feet as she dashed across the snow to where he stood, standing proudly in the small clearing that surrounded the cabin.

"Can I – I mean, is it okay to –?

Margot honestly wasn't completely sure about shifter etiquette – was it okay for her to run her fingers through his rippling golden mane, or touch the delicate feathers of his wings?

But Levi let out a low rumbling sound – closer to a purr than a growl – as if to let her know that she had his permission... or that, in fact, he'd like it very much.

Margot lowered her hand to his golden fur, marveling at how warm he was, and how soft the fur was. She could feel his muscles shifting beneath the surface too, as she ran her fingers up to where his wings sprouted from just behind his shoulders, his golden fur seamlessly becoming pure white feathers.

"Wow," she breathed, not sure what else to say. She wasn't frightened at all. Somehow, she knew this was still *Levi* – and that Levi would never, ever hurt her, no matter what form he took.

"Levi, this is incredible!" she laughed, as, as she petted him, a little crooning noise of contentment began booming in his chest. "But why do you think it happened now?"

Levi could, she realized, hardly give her an answer while he had a lion's head. But that raised another question, she supposed – now that he'd shifted into his chimera form, could he shift *back?*

The chimera was looking around, blinking, as if it had just awoken from a long, deep sleep – which, Margot

113

supposed, it had. But it was probably seeing the world fully for the first time. She supposed she should give it a moment to get its bearings.

Laughing, she skipped back a few steps to stand on the well-worn porch of the cabin, casting a quick warming spell on her feet, which she had, belatedly, realized were freezing cold.

She watched, joyful, as the chimera moved slowly around the clearing, first sniffing at the ground and then gazing up at the sky. Its paws sank into the snow as it went, but it still seemed remarkably light on its feet for such a large beast, moving with grace and elegance.

Magnificent, Margot thought as she watched him. *That's the only word for him. Magnificent!*

She was content to watch for as long as the chimera wanted to explore, but before long, it turned back to her, striding over to where she stood. She supposed she was about to find out whether, having mastered becoming a shifter at last, Levi could now master becoming his human form again.

But she needn't have worried.

After a pause, during which she imagined some internal negotiations were happening inside Levi's head, his body began shrinking, once again becoming the man she knew – and loved.

"Oh, Levi! I'm so happy for you!"

Without thinking, she flung herself forward against his chest, wrapping her arms around his shoulders. After a moment, she felt his strong, warm arms come up to envelop her, pulling her close to his chest.

Their mouths met in a kiss, and Margot let her eyes slide shut, savoring the sensation of his lips against hers, the warmth of his body, the embrace of his arms.

"This is so wonderful," Margot said breathlessly when

they finally managed to break apart. "Do you think… do you think this is because it's Christmas? I read that it's a time of year when special things happen…"

"Well, I'm not sure about that," Levi said with a small smile. "But something special definitely happened to me last night."

Margot laughed, feeling a blush creeping up her cheeks – but she couldn't say she disagreed.

Quite beyond special, really…

"And maybe…" Levi continued, before trailing off. Margot cocked her head, waiting for him to go on.

"Maybe it wasn't just that," Levi finally said after a moment of thought. "I don't know if this makes any sense, but maybe it was finally accepting that I could be a worthy mate for you, even if I couldn't shift. Just feeling that no matter what, I wanted to be with you. That you were my *mate*, and that telling you was the right thing to do."

"That sounds like it could be true," Margot said, nodding. "Maybe accepting the mate bond was what made the chimera finally want to show itself. If you knew from the first moment we met, then it *did* take you a little while, I guess," she laughed.

Levi looked at her ruefully. "I was an idiot for not telling you right away."

But Margot only shook her head. "Well, I can see how it might be a difficult thing to spring on someone! And back then, I thought you were a wizard-errant, and I wasn't exactly letting you get a word in edgewise. So there's that as well."

Laughing, Levi tucked a loose strand of hair behind her ear. "Well, I admit, I was pretty confused back when we first met," he said. "But I always knew you were my mate. I'm so glad I finally got the courage to tell you."

"Me too," Margot said, nodding. "And not just because it

ZOE CHANT

means you can shift now… well, maybe that's why, anyway. But because if you hadn't, I never would have known. But I don't think I ever would have forgotten you, either."

A shiver passed through her at the thought that she might never have discovered the bond they shared, and she would have gone back to the magical world none the wiser, with only the memory of his amazing blue eyes and the kindness he'd shown her.

But that reminds me...

In the excitement of discovering what she and Levi were to each other and Levi's newfound ability to shift, Margot had almost – *almost* – forgotten why she was here in the first place.

The flos nivis.

Her stomach clenched as she thought of it. Finding it would mean bringing it back to the magical world. And going back to the magical world meant –

Would Levi want to come with me? Can I ask him to leave his family and everything he has here to come live with me there?

But even as she thought it, Margot was filled with a different kind of confusion.

The non-magical world was *completely* different from what she'd been led to believe growing up. It wasn't that it was thought of as *dangerous* per se, but she'd definitely been told that it wasn't very welcoming, and that magic users would never be accepted there.

Perhaps she wouldn't be able to use her magic as openly as she did back home, Margot thought, as she gazed around at the unutterable beauty of the mountain landscape around her, but she felt a sad tug in her chest at the thought of leaving so soon. Everything she'd encountered here had been *fascinating,* from the snow to the decorations to the Christmas cake to the people themselves. And she really wanted to know more.

But I can't give up on my quest to find the flos nivis *either.*

She'd come so far, after all – she didn't want to give up now. Not when she was so close.

I'll deal with those problems later, she told herself firmly. *Find the* flos nivis *first, worry about everything else later.*

"I think I can help you find the flower you need better now as well," Levi said, as if he'd been reading her mind. "Now that I can fly, we can cover much more ground, much more quickly."

With a skip in her heartbeat, Margot realized he was right. "But will we be able to see it if we're flying high above?" she asked.

"Don't worry about that," Levi reassured her. "While I was wandering around in chimera form just now, I realized just how much *better* my senses are when I'm a chimera. I thought they were pretty good when I was in this form – better than a normal human's senses, that's for sure – but now I realize how much I was missing out on. Everything just seems so much more… vivid. I could hear birds singing that I can't make out at all now, and even the sounds of animals moving through the snow from miles away. And my eyesight is better too – I'm sure I could see a tree like the one you describe if we keep to just above the forest canopy."

"We?" Margot blinked at him. "You mean… I'd come with you? How? I can't –"

She suddenly realized what Levi meant, and her mouth snapped shut as she stared at him.

He smiled – an absolutely *wicked* smile, like she'd never seen on his face before. It *definitely* sent a warm shiver right though the pit of her stomach.

"I would want to be sure I had the right flower," he said. "So naturally, I'd carry you on my back – there'd be no point in me flying all around, only to bring you back the wrong thing. So we'd definitely be saving time this way."

ZOE CHANT

"But – but – I can't even ride a – a –" Margot spluttered to a halt, as she realized she didn't know *what* she couldn't ride, given she'd never ridden anything in her entire life.

She'd read about children receiving things called *bicycles* for Christmas as part of her research, but they didn't have those in the magical world – if they needed to get somewhere, they either used a teleporting spell, or they just sat in a chair and magicked it to movement to carry them, while they sat on board and read a book to pass the time.

But something alive? Even if it's Levi?!

But even as she thought it, Margot could also feel a thrill of excitement building within her. She'd never been that good at self-levitation spells, so she'd never experienced flying before.

Wouldn't it be exciting to try it?

"I'd never let you fall, Margot," Levi said, putting a hand on her shoulder. "You'd be completely safe."

"Oh! It's not that at all," Margot assured him. She knew she'd be safe with him, no matter what. "I just hadn't thought about it! But… but now that you mention it, I can't wait to try."

A grin spread across her face as she said it. She really, really couldn't. And she could see from the answering smile on Levi's face that he couldn't either – he was just as excited as she was.

"Let's go pack up the cabin," he said, "and then, let's go flying."

***

Maybe, Margot thought, as the air rushed past her, sending her hair streaming out behind her, now that Levi had learned

118

CHIMERAS AND CHRISTMAS CAKES

how to shift into his chimera form, flying simply came naturally to him – an instinct.

Certainly, he'd seemed to pick it up right away: he'd done one test flight by himself first, breaking through the trees with only a couple of mighty sweeps of his wings, his shape a dark silhouette against the clear, bright blue of the sky when she'd gazed up to follow his movements.

Her heart had leaped for joy as she'd watched him soaring above, wings outstretched, tail expertly keeping him balanced in the air. It was lucky, she supposed, that they were out here on the mountain during winter – it was highly unlikely anyone would spot the soaring shape of a chimera out here!

By the time Levi had landed again in a cold spray of snow, Margot had been itching to clamber up on his back and fly with him. Any doubts or fears she'd had had melted away as she'd watched him.

And now, protected from the freezing mountain winds by her warming spell, Margot was having every bit as much fun as she'd thought she would.

The world was laid out below her in blues and greens and whites and blacks, the snow-covered mountains rising all around them, the dark trees of the forest below, the unbroken blue of the sky above.

As they soared, Margot could feel a laugh bubbling up within her. She just couldn't help it – all of this was so... so *fun!* It was almost easy to forget that she needed to keep her eyes peeled for the *flos nivis*. But she thought she could be forgiven a little marveling at the way she and Levi were gliding through the beauty of the mountain landscape, with his strong wings, beating just behind her where she was straddling his shoulders, keeping them safe and airborne.

I'd have worked harder at learning levitation if I'd known

ZOE CHANT

flying was like this, Margot thought as Levi brought them around in a wide arc, dropping a little closer to the tops of the tallest trees. *But then, maybe I never would have met Levi, and never would have gotten to experience... well,* this!

But as much fun as she was having, she knew she had a job to do. She had to resist the urge to simply snuggle up in Levi's beautiful golden mane and forget everything else in the world except him, and the unparalleled view of the mountains and forest.

Levi had told her that his eyes in his chimera form were pretty sharp, but she knew it would be better if they were both keeping an eye out for anything that could be the *flos nivis.*

She hoped it'd be easy to spot – it was a bright green, whereas most of the trees here were either dark green firs, or they had lost their leaves for winter. Still, it seemed a long shot.

That was, until she saw a sudden flash of green from below, a different color to its surroundings, growing in amongst a group of bare-branched trees.

"There!" Margot cried out, pointing below – but she knew from the way Levi had suddenly slowed that he'd seen it too.

As fast as they were going, Levi had to circle back quite a way, but it was obvious his chimera had excellent homing instincts. When he folded his wings to guide them down to earth, it was only a few feet away from the tree they'd seen, the bright spray of its leaves obvious amongst the dark bare branches.

Margot's breath caught in her throat as she slid down from Levi's back, sinking up to her shins in snow. Next to her, Levi shifted back into his human form – fully clothed, to Margot's mild surprise, though she'd seen him shift *into* the

120

CHIMERAS AND CHRISTMAS CAKES

chimera while he'd been dressed after she'd revoked the trail spell and they'd finished cleaning up the cabin to leave it exactly as they'd found it, so she wasn't quite sure why she was so surprised. She supposed at least that saved them a lot of social embarrassment!

"Is that it?" Levi asked, as together they trudged toward the tree, speaking the words Margot hadn't quite been able to bring herself to say, as her heart hammered in her ears.

"I – I think so," she said, as she approached it. The tree was actually little more than a sapling – they'd been lucky to see it at all.

But it had the same star-shaped leaves as she'd seen in the illustrations in her tome of botanic wonders, and here it was, magically green and lush even in the dead of winter, when most other trees like it had long since shed all their leaves.

But...

"But it's not flowering," Margot said, worry misting over her former joy, as she circled the tree.

And sure enough, there wasn't a single flower to be seen anywhere on the tree – not even a tightly furled bud, waiting for colder weather to bloom.

"Are you sure this is the right kind of tree?" Levi asked, as he lifted a hand to touch one of its brilliant green leaves.

"I – I can check," Margot said, rummaging in her tote for *Botanical Wonders* – the book that contained all the information anyone still had about the *flos nivis*. Finding it, she opened the massive book, flipping to the correct page.

"See – look here," she said, pointing to an ancient illustration of the leaves. "It's the same leaf shape, isn't it? And the same color too. And look at the bark – it has these silvery patterns, just the same as in the book. I think this really might be the *flos nivis,* but..."

She trailed off, biting her lip.

ZOE CHANT

It didn't matter how *sure* she was that this was the right tree. There were no flowers on it, nothing that even slightly resembled the white and blue petals that were painted on the page of her book.

Desperately, she pored over the tiny, spidery handwriting the book was written in, trying to find more information, while Levi looked over her shoulder.

"It… it *does* say here that only mature trees will flower, no matter what time of year it is," she said. "But it doesn't say how to tell if the tree is mature or not. It *does* mention that very old trees can grow to be extremely tall and mighty, but not how they look before they've fully matured."

"This tree looks pretty small," Levi observed – and indeed, it was only a little taller than he was. Levi might have been tall for a person, but for a tree, it wasn't very high at all. "Perhaps this one simply hasn't reached maturity yet?"

"I suppose not," Margot murmured, as she tucked her book away in her tote again. "You mentioned the temperatures over the last few days have been at record lows, so I imagine if it was going to be flowering, it'd be doing it now."

"Especially after the storm last night," Levi agreed. "I can't imagine any better conditions for a flower called the snow flower to be blooming in."

Disappointment made Margot's heart sink. They'd found the *flos nivis!* But it wasn't in flower, and it didn't seem like it would be old enough to do so, perhaps for many years.

Her feelings must have been clear on her face, because Levi pulled her into a hug, enveloping her in his arms. "Don't worry – now that I can fly you anywhere you need to go, we can find another one, one that's old enough to have the flower you need. It's really only the flower that you can use?"

"Yes," Margot said, her voice a little muffled as she pressed herself against Levi's warm, solid body, allowing herself to be soothed by his closeness. "The tome was very

122

CHIMERAS AND CHRISTMAS CAKES

clear on that point. Only the flowers contain magical properties – the rest of the tree is just… well, a tree."

"Then we'll definitely find you that flower," Levi said, his voice determined.

***

But despite all their determination, it simply seemed that today was not their lucky day, Margot thought, as, with every passing moment, her hope diminished that they'd find the *flos nivis.*

They'd flown in every direction they could, Levi's strong chimera body never tiring, his wings carrying them far and wide over the mountains where Margot had read the *flos nivis* grew. But they never spotted a flash of green like they had before – no matter how hard they searched, it seemed the tree was nowhere to be found, or else the trees simply weren't old enough to have grown high enough to be seen from the air, meaning they definitely weren't old enough to flower, either.

Margot's heart sank. She'd had so much hope, but now, that hope seemed destined to be dashed.

But at least all of this means that Levi was finally able to change into his chimera form, she told herself, as she pressed her cheek against the shaggy hair of his mane. *That has made all of this worthwhile.*

And it had. Despite her disappointment that her own quest had ended in failure, she simply couldn't be too downhearted. After all, she'd discovered that Levi was her mate, and that bond had meant Levi was now the chimera he'd always wished he could be.

It truly wouldn't have mattered to Margot whether he

123

ZOE CHANT

could shift or not, but it was more what it *meant* that made her happy: Levi had accepted that he was worthy of her, worthy of *everything*. And that had meant his chimera had finally felt comfortable enough to emerge into the world.

So I can't be too sad, she told herself, even as the anxiety of almost certainly having to return to the magical world empty-handed grew inside her.

What *was* certain was that they wouldn't be able to stay out here for much longer – there were storm clouds gathering over the mountains, and it was clear they were in for another big dump of snow. No matter how strong and brave Levi was, even a chimera couldn't battle a snowstorm.

"Perhaps we should head back," Margot called to him, burying her hands in his mane. "I don't want to get caught up in all those dark clouds!"

Levi let out a low crooning sound of regretful agreement, before he began turning them in a wide, slow circle, heading back to the town of Girdwood Springs. As they approached, Margot could see it glittering in the swiftly dimming light, like a beautiful little beacon nestled amongst the mountains. She liked to think at least some of the Christmas lights she'd seen on her day at the markets were making up some of that warming glow, as if guiding them home.

Levi descended a little way from the beginning of the hiking trails, nearby to the closed ranger's hut they'd seen the day before. Given that the parklands were closed, Margot had assumed no one would be around to see a giant chimera descending from the sky above, but still, she breathed a sigh of relief once Levi was back in human form, and they hurried to the park exit just as the first large flakes of snow were beginning to fall.

Stores on the main street of Girdwood Springs were just beginning to pack up for the day as they made their way back to Thorne's Antique Booksellers – Margot watched a little

124

CHIMERAS AND CHRISTMAS CAKES

wistfully as the red and green tablecloths of the cafes were folded away, the sparkling tinsel taken down for the evening, the tiny glowing lights flickering off.

She wondered if she'd at least be able to treat herself to one more day of Christmas before she had to go back to the magical world and admit she'd failed to find the snow flower – she felt, given everything, she deserved to do at least *something* to cheer herself up.

Even if I am a complete failure now, she thought sadly. This really had been her last chance. But she hadn't been able to find what she needed.

I guess I'll have to break the news to Monty, she thought, as Levi unlocked the front door. *I wonder if he'll mind. I guess at least this way he'll get to be reassigned as a familiar to a real witch.*

She suppressed a sob. She'd miss Monty so much – and, she thought, in his own way he'd miss her too. She really did think all his teasing was because he was fond of her. But now, she'd failed him too.

Her heart sank, and she had to blink back tears as she walked.

"I'm sorry, Levi," Margot blurted out, as soon as the door of the bookshop was closed behind them, and she'd been enveloped in its comforting scent of old paper, well-read books, old leather bindings and aged wood.

Levi turned to look at her, a puzzled expression on his face. "What on earth would you have to be sorry about?"

Shaking her head, Margot flopped down onto one of the worn armchairs that seemed to sit in random places around the shop; it let out a little sigh as she dropped her weight into it that sounded as sad as she felt. "I feel like... well, that all of this has just been... a... a wild hen chase," she said. "Is that the right way to say it?"

"It's close enough," Levi said with a smile, as he came to

ZOE CHANT

stand in front of her. "And I'm still not really following what you mean."

"I mean I dragged you all over those mountains, and not a trace of the *flos nivis* was to be found!" Margot said, dropping her head into her hands. "And... aside from that, you now have to deal with a failed witch for your mate! I definitely won't be graduating now – I really don't have anything else to offer the magical world. This was my last chance. I don't know how I'm going to show my face there again."

"You're not a failure," Levi said firmly, coming to kneel in front of her and cupping her face with his hand. "Not in any sense of the word. You're my *mate*. And you've done more for me than I could ever possibly imagine. I never would have discovered I could shift if it wasn't for you. I probably would have just finished packing up this bookstore like a grump, tossed out all the books, and gone back home to live the rest of my life the same way I lived the first twenty-seven years: bitter and alone."

He paused, shaking his head, pain briefly flashing into his eyes.

"I was so angry my chimera didn't seem to want to show itself that it affected every other part of my life. But you made me realize – with or without my chimera, that's not how I want to live anymore. I had no idea telling you that you were my mate would finally coax my chimera out – I'd resolved never to tell you. I'd just help you because that's what I *should* be doing. So even before I knew how it'd change things for me, you were making me want to be a better person than I had been."

Margot swallowed. Her heart had glowed with more and more love with every word Levi had spoken. And, despite her sadness, she knew it was all true. There was no way to doubt it: Levi's eyes were alight with sincerity. And she knew

126

he'd never say these things just to make her feel better – he meant every word.

"You're my *mate*, Margot," Levi said. "And that means more to me than anything else in the world. Nothing about meeting you has been a waste of time. It's the best thing that's ever happened to me, whether it led to me being able to shift or not. The only thing that matters is you."

"Levi –" Margot murmured, before she rushed forward, throwing her arms around him. Her heart was beating swiftly within her, filling her with the golden warmth of his love.

His lips found hers, and they kissed – just like every other kiss they'd shared, Margot could feel the heat behind it, but also, the strength of their bond.

We really are fated mates, she thought, a little dizzily, as her lips parted.

She never wanted the kiss to end – despite her low mood, despite the fact she knew she might have to return having totally failed, she could at least see a future for herself now: a future with Levi by her side, their mate bond only growing stronger with every year they spent together.

Maybe, she thought, a little breathlessly when they finally managed to pull away from each other, *maybe he'd even let me help him sort out his great aunt's bookshop...*

There had to be a treasure trove of knowledge about the non-magical world in here, after all! It would take years to go through it all.

I think I'd enjoy something like that, Margot thought, her lip twitching irresistibly into a smile as she looked down at Levi's face.

"Well," Levi said, his voice a little husky, "I don't know about you, but after all that flying, I have to say I'm pretty hungry."

ZOE CHANT

"Me too." Margot stood up, pulling Levi up with her. "But perhaps I –"

She stopped talking abruptly, shock and surprise halting the words as they came out of her mouth. She stared.

"Margot?" Levi asked, concern in his voice, before he followed the direction of her stare, and stopped in his tracks.

"Was… was that there before?" Margot whispered, barely daring even to blink, in case what she was seeing before her very eyes would disappear in an instant.

"I can pretty categorically say it wasn't," Levi said.

And Margot herself was pretty categorically sure she could say he was right. There was no way either of them could have missed this – the large, bluish-white bloom of the flower that now sprouted from one of the massive, dark wooden beams that crossed the ceiling of the bookshop.

"If I didn't know any better," Levi muttered after a moment, "I'd say that looks exactly like –"

"The *flos nivis*," Margot finished for him. And indeed, there was pretty much no mistaking it. The flower looked exactly like the illustration in her book, with its large, lily-like petals, white in the middle and becoming a delicate pale blue at the edges. A few leaves had even sprouted alongside the flower – and they were the same brilliant green star-shapes that they'd seen earlier today on the immature tree they'd found on the mountain.

"But… but how can this be?" Margot asked, her eyes wide as she circled below the flower. "Is it even *real?* I don't under-stand how a flower could just – could just –"

She could barely bring herself to say it. How could it be possible that the very thing they'd been searching for all this time had just grown out of the wooden beam of the bookstore?!

"I don't know, Margot," Levi said, shaking his head. "In fact, I have absolutely no idea whatsoever." Then, a

thoughtful frown crossed his face. "But I think I may know of someone who can tell us – or rather, someone who knows how to *find* someone who can tell us. But we'll have to hurry if we're going to catch them."

Margot felt a thousand questions bubbling to the surface of her mind, but in the end, she pushed them back down, silently following Levi as he grabbed her hand, and then dashed with her to the door.

CHAPTER 8

"Yep," the man Sylvie the baker had introduced to them as her husband – and mate – Gale said, as he circled below the flower growing out of Levi's Great Aunt Aida's bookshop's ceiling. "That is *definitely* a snow flower."

Levi had *known* whoever was supplying Sylvie with fruits, nuts and spices for her bakery had to be a unicorn – he'd known it from the very first bite he'd taken of her Christmas cake.

He just hadn't expected it'd be so easy to find him. Levi had been envisioning a wild goose chase – or hen chase, as Margot might say – to track down Sylvie's supplier, with him having to make up some ridiculous cover story as to why he even wanted to know. But in the end, everything had been quite simple. Gale had even been right there in the bakery as they arrived, just at the very moment Sylvie was flipping the *OPEN* sign to *CLOSED*.

But she'd very kindly let them in anyway, and Levi had been able to sense the presence of a unicorn from the moment he'd stepped over the threshold.

130

CHIMERAS AND CHRISTMAS CAKES

A unicorn would be able to tell them whether this was what they'd been looking for, Levi knew. Unicorns had a natural affinity for plants after all, and their magical powers were, famously, to be able to grow anything at all – and even, in some cases, bring plants that had died back to life.

Levi wondered if the presence of a unicorn had had anything to do with the flower suddenly blooming above them now. He had to admit, he was a little surprised at the presence of a unicorn here at all. But from the very brief history Gale and Sylvie had given them as the four of them had walked from Sylvie's bakery back to the bookshop, it seemed he'd only come here for a holiday, and had decided to stay on after discovering Sylvie was his mate.

And, Gale had said, with a wink at Sylvie, *because Girdwood Springs has the best cake I've ever eaten – who could leave after tasting that?*

"It seems like the wooden beams this shop is made out of – or partially made out of, anyway – are from felled snow flower trees," Gale the unicorn said, as he reached up to press a fingertip against the dark wood. "But it's *old* – very old. How long has this shop been here, anyway?"

"I'm not really sure," Levi said. "I only just took it over – and my Great Aunt Aida only owned it for about fifteen years, and I'm guessing it was here well before that."

"It certainly was," Sylvie said, nodding. "I remember it standing here when I was just a kid, and I grew up in Girdwood Springs. You might be better off consulting someone who knows a lot about the history of the town, like Kira, the park ranger here. Or you might even find some info in some of the books you have here in the shop. Some of them look like they might have been here a while too!"

"Oh – but did the beam really just... burst into bloom like this?" Margot asked, her green eyes wide as she stared up at the flower. "How can it be? We searched *everywhere*! And...

131

ZOE CHANT

snow flowers are so rare, why would anyone have built a building out of them? Even if it's a very, *very* beautiful building."

"I guess if the place really is as old as all that, people may not have known what they were cutting down," Gale said. "After all, it's not as if it's well-known to humans that snow flowers have magical properties – not even shifters or magic-users know all that much about it."

"Yes, so much knowledge about it has been completely lost," Margot murmured. "But… if I cut this flower down, it'll die eventually, no matter how many ageless spells we cast on it. I can keep food fresh for a pretty long time, but a living organism is a lot more complicated than that. I can't stop a person or even a plant from aging indefinitely. I don't think even a very powerful witch or wizard can do that. I don't think I want to kill something so rare, just so I don't fail to graduate."

Just as Gale and Sylvie had explained their own history, Margot and Levi had done likewise – and to Levi's mild surprise, neither of them had seemed all that perturbed by the presence of a witch amongst them.

Just as long as you're not... well, Sylvie had said. *Maybe that's Henry and Luna's story to tell. But all I'll say is, as long as you're not here to curse anyone and make a total hash of it in the process, you're good.*

Margot had reassured them both that she'd never, *never* curse anyone, and Levi found himself burning with curiosity about just who Henry and Luna were, and what they had to do with curses and witches.

Oh, they're just our resident hellhound and his mate, a travel writer, Sylvie had said. *But they're off on assignment right now. When they get back, I'm sure they'd be very happy to tell you all about the last time they ran into a witch. And a wizard. Star-crossed lovers doesn't even* begin *to cover it.*

132

CHIMERAS AND CHRISTMAS CAKES

Levi had quickly begun to realize that Girdwood Springs wasn't exactly your average mountain town, or a place that was a stranger to shifters – sure, most of the people in town didn't know that there were shifters living here, but those who *were* in the know were in the know, and they were very happy to guard their secrets, and welcomed them to town just as they would anyone else.

And for the first time, he'd also begun to wonder – was there some kind of life he could build for himself outside of his chimera village after all?

You would have known that long ago, if you'd ever bothered to venture outside of it, his chimera spoke up suddenly, surprising Levi. He was still getting used to hearing its voice and its opinions inside his own head – though given that it had been less than a day since it had started speaking up regularly, he supposed that was to be expected.

That's mighty rich, coming from someone who's spent the last twenty-seven years asleep, he shot back – and, from the way it huffed and turned its back, Levi knew he'd scored a hit.

"Well, that's a good point about preserving the flower," Gale said thoughtfully as he gazed up at the beautiful white flower on the ceiling. "I'm not really sure why it's blooming now, and I can't say for sure it'll ever do it again if we pick this one. But then again – I *am* a unicorn, and I've been told I have a way with plants."

"You mean… it might be possible to take this flower without hurting it?" Margot asked, her eyes full of hope.

"Not this flower specifically," Gale said, "especially if you need to take it back with you to study. No, I mean I might be able to pick the flower, but leave this beam itself sprouting so that in the future it'll grow more flowers. It's a long shot, but I might even be able to take a bit of the wood from the beam – as long as Levi doesn't mind me damaging it a little – and seeing what I can do to coax some more life out of it yet."

133

ZOE CHANT

It sounded *way* too miraculous for Levi – raising a tree from the dead! – but then again, he really didn't know that much about the full extent of a unicorn's powers. It was entirely possible Gale could do exactly what he was suggesting.

"Of course I don't mind," he said. "Scrape away as much wood as you need. If you can't get results from one piece, then come back and try another."

"Thank you," Gale said sincerely. "I'm interested to see what I can do – and preserving such a rare tree is definitely a worthwhile project for me. Perhaps if I'm successful, we can repopulate the mountain with it."

"We did see one immature tree while we were searching," Margot piped up. "But it wasn't ready to flower yet. So it's not completely gone – but it really was only the one."

"Once it's springtime, I should go check it out myself," Gale mused. "Or get Kieran – oh, he's a griffin, Sylvie mentioned you met his mate, Natasha, she runs the fanciest B&B you're ever likely to set foot in – to go have a look. He knows these mountains like the back of his hand. Or claw, I guess."

More shifters! Levi thought, shaking his head. Was there any kind of shifter that *hadn't* set up home here in Girdwood Springs? Next Gale and Sylvie would be telling him a manticore was the local bank manager, or a wyvern ran yoga classes in the park.

"In any case, I think I can take this flower for your studies, while preserving the rest," Gale said, taking a pair of sharp-looking secateurs from his back pocket. "Ah – you see here, if I just snip this bit –"

With a sharp *click!* Gale had snipped the flower away from the section that had grown from the snow flower beam, leaving behind the bright green leaves and a few small, tightly furled buds that were visible now that the flower

wasn't hiding them. They were tinged slightly pink, just as
Margot had described.

"Here you go," Gale said, handing the flower to Margot.

"Oh, *thank you*," Margot said, her voice overflowing with
gratitude, as a warm glow of magic emanated from her hands
and enveloped the bloom. "That'll keep it fresh for a little
while," she explained.

"Hmm," Gale said thoughtfully as he looked at the
flower in Margot's hands. "You mentioned you needed to
bring back something really spectacular in order to graduate from your magical university as a full-fledged witch,
right?"

Margot nodded fervently. "Oh, yes. And now that I've
found – with help from all of you, of course! – the *flos nivis*,
I'll finally be able to say I've contributed something of real
value to the magical world. People will be able to study it for
years to come! Magical botany will be very much advanced
with this discovery!"

"Well," Gale said, exchanging a knowing look with Sylvie,
"maybe this is old hat in the magical world, but would a
curse-breaking mushroom be helpful to you at all? You could
bring two things back instead of just the one."

Levi watched as Margot's eyes grew as round as saucers.
"The *aurum lacunosa*?" she asked breathlessly. "Are you saying
that grows here too?"

"It sure does," Sylvie said with a smile. "In fact, I baked
one once. *That* was a challenge I'll never forget."

"But they're deadly poisonous!" Margot burst out, her
eyes still wide. "How ever did you do it?"

"Well, I…" Sylvie began, before she shook her head. "But
then again, maybe that's not my story to tell either. You'd
better ask Caleb – he's the one who had the curse that
needed breaking. A centuries-old dragon feud, or something
along those lines. Oh, yeah – he's a dragon too. And no

ZOE CHANT

longer under a bad luck curse, thanks to that yellow mushroom."

"Well, that would be most, *most* useful!" Margot said, her excitement almost palpable. "We *do* still have samples for the *aurum lacunosa,* but it became rare – very, very rare! – during the Witching War of… well, maybe I don't need to go into the whole history of that." She cleared her throat. "Suffice it to say, there were *a lot* of curses that needed breaking after that entire hullabaloo."

Levi shook his head. If the Witching War had actually been anything like what it sounded like, then he could well imagine that.

"Well, in that case, we can ask Caleb and Kira to show you to the cave where they found it growing. Between a dragon and a chimera, you should be able to make it out there once this snow has passed."

"I really, truly can't thank any of you enough for all the help you've been to me," Margot said, her voice fervent, her eyes looking a little damp and misty. "If it wasn't for you – *all* of you – I never would have been able to succeed in my quest. I don't know how I shall ever repay this debt to you all."

"Oh, believe me, you don't owe us *anything,*" Sylvie said warmly, reaching out to pat Margot's shoulder. "I'm just glad we were able to make this Christmas a good one for you – and you've given Gale a new project! He's been helping me out with the bakery garden and orchard since his garden center is closed at this time of year, so he doesn't have much to do. This will definitely keep him occupied for a while."

"Hey, you make it sound like you don't appreciate having me getting under your feet while you're trying to work," Gale laughed. "But no, seriously – this is definitely fascinating. A snow flower beam, bursting into bloom – I definitely have to find out more about this."

CHIMERAS AND CHRISTMAS CAKES

"Well, it's really Levi's shop," Margot pointed out, turning to him with eyes full of love – love that made Levi's heart skip a beat. "Or, I should say, his Great Aunt Aida's."

"Yes, I ran into Aida Thorne once or twice," Sylvie said, nodding. "But I have to admit, I mostly read, uh, contemporary books, romances and things, so I wasn't in here much. And she was a little bit... well, reclusive, I suppose you could say."

"That sounds like Great Aunt Aida," Levi said. "Not that I really had a chance to get to know her well before she left our village to come and run this bookshop."

"Where did she get to?" Sylvie asked, before raising a hand to her mouth, her face suddenly pensive. "Oh... I hope it wasn't bad news."

"Not at all – the opposite in fact," Levi said, shaking his head with a smile. "She met her mate – a filthy rich dragon shifter, by the sounds of it – while she was in Florida, and they're off on a world tour to celebrate their love." He laughed. "She sent us a note telling us she was leaving us the shop so we could do what we liked with it, lock, stock and barrel."

Levi's heart caught in his throat as he suddenly remembered that what he'd been planning to do with it was put all the books out on the street for free, and sell the place no matter how low the price.

But could he do that now that he'd promised Gale that he'd let him study the snow flower from here? Who knew what would happen to the shop if he sold it on now – it could be bought by someone who intended to tear it down, and destroy one of the few remaining snow flowers in the world, and whatever magic that had caused it to bloom.

And... do I really want to sell it, anyway?

At first, the bookshop had seemed like nothing but a hassle to him – something he had to go deal with before he

137

ZOE CHANT

came home to deal with yet another miserable Christmas, surrounded by all the things he knew he'd never have: joy, love, a family of his own.

But now, he saw it all quite differently.

The bookshop was the first place he'd ever laid eyes on Margot. It was where he'd first realized the mate bond they shared, and where they'd laughed together over the eggs she'd burned. It was where the snow flower she needed so badly had first bloomed, and provided her with her ticket to graduation as a full-fledged witch.

But that in itself came with a complication. As much as he now wasn't sure at all about leaving the shop with all of these memories behind, wouldn't he have to, if he was going to go with Margot and live with her in the magical world?

To Levi, it wasn't much of a question that he'd support Margot and go wherever she went. And she'd worked so hard for this – there was no way he could ask her to stay here with him to run a rickety old bookshop, or come and stay with him in his chimera village.

"Did… did you still think you might sell this place?" Margot asked hesitantly, as if she'd read his conflicted thoughts on his face. "Do you think you'd mind letting Gale do his research for a while before you do?"

Levi swallowed. "Yes, of course. But I think it's going to be really hard for me to sell it after everything that's happened here. And I admit… Girdwood Springs has turned out to be a little different to what I thought it was too."

Sylvie laughed softly. "You'd be surprised how often people say that."

Levi could believe it. He'd thought when he'd arrived that it was just a little mountain town that was *way* too obsessed with Christmas, which had done nothing but depress him. But now… well, he still thought maybe it *was* a little obsessed with Christmas. But he was finding that was bothering him

138

CHIMERAS AND CHRISTMAS CAKES

less and less – now that he actually had some positive memories to associate with it.

And the people here have been nothing but kind and welcoming, he thought. *And it's clearly the kind of place shifters can live in peace.*

Chimeras were so reclusive that after a while they tended to mistrust the world outside their villages, and not many chimeras lived outside of them. Aida had been an exception – but hadn't Levi always admired her just a little bit, for running off to find her own happiness?

Impulsively, Levi nodded. He'd made up his mind.

"I'm not going to sell it," he said decisively. "But I'll have to find someone in town to go through all this stock and sort it out and catalogue it properly, and then run the place for me. So I'd be really happy to listen to any suggestions you may have for who'd enjoy doing something like that." He nodded to Sylvie and Gale. "I'd definitely trust anyone you recommend."

"Oh… do you mean, then, that you don't want to run this place yourself at all?" Margot asked, blinking.

"It's not that I don't want to," Levi told her. "In fact, in some ways it could be pretty fun, I guess. But if I'm going to go back with you to the magical world, then I won't be here to do it."

Margot blinked again, in a rapid flutter of her long, golden eyelashes. "Well," she said, before stopping, biting her lip. "Well," she started again. "What if… what if *I* said I'd like to run the bookshop. And catalogue everything in it. And help you organize it all. Would – would that be something you'd be interested in doing?"

Levi stared at her in surprise. Could Margot really mean what she said?

"But what about your graduation as a witch?" he asked. "I thought you'd planned to go back to the magical world and

139

ZOE CHANT

research the snow flower?"

"I did," Margot said, dropping her eyes. "Well – what I mean is, I planned to present the snow flower – and now, the *aurum lacunosa* too! – to the magical world. But I'm not nearly skilled enough in magical botany to really do that kind of research on it, to unlock its secrets and make sure they're better documented this time. I'd leave that to witches and wizards with *far* more skill than I. My contribution was only going to be bringing it back." She raised her eyes to the leaves and buds still sprouting from the beam above their heads. "But… I think I'd *love* to be the custodian of this rare plant, in such an unlikely place. And I'd definitely love to help run this bookshop – with you. I've been having such fun here – I feel like I've learned so much, but there's still so much left for me to learn."

"Well, all I can say to that is, you'd both be very, very welcome here," Sylvie said with a warm smile. "And that means you'll both be here for Christmas, too – and you'll get to see which of the new-fashioned Christmas cakes won the poll."

Levi and Margot both laughed – and Levi felt his heart soaring within him.

Our mate wants to stay here with us, he thought, as he looked down at Margot's brightly smiling face, her eyes seeming to shine like emeralds.

Of course she does, his chimera snorted. *I don't know how you ever doubted it to begin with.*

CHAPTER 9

"*D*o you feel like you're really ready for this?" Levi asked.

Margot squared her shoulders and then nodded, anxious but determined.

"I'm as ready as I'll ever be. At least now I'll have an answer one way or the other, even if it's bad news."

He pulled her into a hug, and she relaxed against him ever so slightly, some of the tension running out of her body as she sighed.

It had been two days since the encounter with Gale and Sylvie, though it felt like only a matter of minutes – locating the *aurum lacunosa* in the middle of a snow-covered forest and bringing it back safely had been a challenge, and then there had been the matter of notifying Margot's university so that they could send Professor Imari out to verify her findings. Throw in the fact that they'd been trying to tidy up the bookstore and the apartment above to make them a little less hard to navigate, as well as meeting various inhabitants of the town, and they'd barely had a moment to themselves.

Levi ran his fingers gently through her hair, and she

almost made an embarrassing sound at how nice it felt, the gentle energy of the mate bond and the soft touch of his fingers relaxing her tense muscles.

He murmured, "How could it be bad news? Not only did you locate the *flos nivis*, but you're giving them the location of that magical mushroom as well. If anything, they should be bumping your grade up even higher. These are pretty monumental discoveries for the magical world, from what you've told me."

Margot looked up at him, staring into his beautiful eyes and almost getting lost for a moment before she remembered what she was going to say.

"Oh, so I should get a C-minus instead of a D?" she laughed, happy enough about the turn things had taken over the past few days that she felt she could genuinely poke fun at herself.

After a moment, however, her mood fell a little, uncertainty once more pushing itself to the forefront of her mind. "I don't know, though. We were only able to locate the *aurum lacunosa* after Gale so kindly gave us all that information and Caleb showed us where to find it – before then, I didn't even know that it was growing in this area. If anything, *they* should be the ones getting the credit for it."

Levi's smile in return was so reassuring that she found herself starting to lighten up again before he even spoke.

"I wouldn't worry about that – out here in the human world, they call it 'networking'. It's seen as a good thing," he said.

"Networking?" Margot mouthed the word to herself again, trying to puzzle it out.

He nodded. "It means that you're good at meeting the right people and making friends with them, so they can help you at the right time," he explained. "Humans see it as a skill

CHIMERAS AND CHRISTMAS CAKES

by itself, just like magic." He paused. "That's my understanding, anyway."

"Well, I hope Professor Imari also appreciates this 'networking'," Margot said hesitantly. "In any case, I will still credit Gale and Sylvie for their assistance, as well as Kira and Caleb for their aid in finding the correct location. I could not have done it without them."

"Fair enough," Levi agreed. "But just remember that you couldn't have done it without *you*, either. You're the one that made it all happen, Margot. You're the one who, through research, managed to discover that Girdwood Spring was the most likely place for the snow flower to be growing." He caught her gaze and held it with his own, and it was breathtaking in its intensity. She shivered.

"It's one of the things I love the most about you," he continued. "You always want to do the right thing by others, even if it means potentially hurting your own chances. Just make sure that you don't talk yourself down – you deserve everything good that comes of this."

She melted against him once more, closing her eyes, simply happy to feel the protection of his strong arms around her and listen to the slow, steady beat of his heart. No matter what, everything was going to be okay. If Levi believed in her, then she could believe in herself, too.

She wasn't sure how long she stayed wrapped up in his arms, simply enjoying his warm presence, but eventually she pulled back with a sigh.

"They'll be here any minute," she said. "I guess we'd better make sure that everything is in place."

Not that there was anything much more to do – they'd already cleared a path through the store so that everyone could make their way easily to the beam that had sprouted the snow flower, and then tidied up the area beneath it and arranged

ZOE CHANT

some chairs so everyone could sit. Cups were patiently awaiting the pouring of hot tea, and there were still plenty of Sylvie's perfectly-preserved cakes to go around, despite her and Levi's best efforts over the past couple of days to eat them all up.

Monty had helped, in his own way, knocking books off of shelves – *So that the shelves will be less encumbered with the weight of these silly books, and therefore easier to move,* as he had so helpfully explained – as well as swishing his tail about and sending giant plumes of dust into the air.

If you don't appreciate my dusting, he had sneered, *then I can stop at any time, and I will save my efforts for those who value them.*

While it was typical Monty behavior, Margot had thought she'd detected a hint of apprehension beneath it all, and so she hadn't scolded him too hard for drowning Levi in a sea of dust. After all, today wasn't just deciding her fate – it was deciding his, too. And while he would never admit it, she was pretty sure that he liked being her familiar, terrible at magic though she was.

She herself was definitely apprehensive about it, though she'd been trying to keep her fears at the back of her mind. Levi's confident explanations of why she would attain a passing grade, as well as his general caring, calm presence, had done an awful lot to keep those worried thoughts at bay, and she was more grateful than she could possibly express. She really did not think she could bear to lose Monty.

A sudden fluttering at the edge of her consciousness alerted her to the imminent arrival of her parents and Professor Imari – and, if the sudden lifting of Levi's head was anything to go by, his elevated chimera's senses had picked up on it, too. The chimera was still a source of wonder to her, and she was ever so excited to spend more time in its company and learn more about it!

In the meantime, however…

CHIMERAS AND CHRISTMAS CAKES

She took a deep breath and stood up a little straighter, before breathing out and heading down the stairs, taking care to at least keep a somewhat sedate pace. The last thing she needed right now was to fall down the stairs and trip face-first into the deadly mushroom sample! That was definitely D-minus material at best, and she really did not want to have to call upon her mother's skills in healing magic to rescue her from a faceful of fatal fungus.

Stairs successfully navigated, she exited the shop, Levi close behind her, and went around to the back of the building.

There, dusting snow off their shoulders and standing up from a green chaise longue that had definitely not been there earlier, were her mother, her father, and Professor Imari.

"When you said they were going to fly here..." Levi murmured, sounding somewhat perturbed.

"Don't worry, they would have cast a spell of invisibility. No one would have seen a couch sailing over the town," Margot whispered back, before raising her voice. "Mother! Father! I'm so happy to see you!" She managed to force her face into a mostly natural smile for Professor Imari too, bowing to him as befit his rank. "Professor Imari, I am happy to see you also."

Professor Imari nodded to her – though she couldn't help but notice his beard was still looking a little ragged from their last encounter. She gulped – but it seemed that for now at least, he'd decided to let bygones be bygones, flaming beards or not.

"And I am happy to see you too, Margot," Professor Imari said, returning her bow with a dignified nod. "I hear that you have made quite the astonishing discovery."

"Well, I don't know about *that*," Margot said automatically, before, remembering the faith that Levi had shown in

145

ZOE CHANT

her, she amended, "but I do think that it will be of interest to you."

Her parents, generally the type to act formally when in company, surprised her by both coming to her for a hug at the same time; startled, it took her a moment before she thought to hug them back, wrapping her arms around them both and closing her eyes.

I suppose that this is the longest I've ever been away from home, she thought, still somewhat dazed. *And they're probably thrilled that I've finally managed to do something worthwhile, and perhaps will no longer bring shame upon them.*

It was an unfair thought, and she quashed it quickly, tightening her arms around them. She knew that her parents loved her unconditionally.

"It's so good to see you Margot," her mother said when they pulled back, and Margot could see the concern in her eyes. "You haven't encountered anything too frightful here, have you? Have you been safe? I've been so worried while you've been gone."

"Oh, no, Mother, there was no need for that!" Margot burst out. "I know what you warned me about, but really, everything's been fine – better than fine! I've had the most wonderful time –"

"Well, perhaps we can hear more about it once we have completed the examination," Professor Imari broke in, just a *little* peevishly, and Margot wondered whether, in fact, those *by*s really were as *gone* as they'd seemed.

But before she showed them through to where the *flos nivis* was blooming, she knew there was one more thing she had to do. Turning, she linked her arm through Levi's, drawing him forward from where he'd been standing a little behind her.

"I'll show you the *flos nivis* in just a moment, Professor," she said. "But first, allow me to introduce Levi Thorne – he

146

CHIMERAS AND CHRISTMAS CAKES

helped me locate the flower, as well as providing me with accommodations, and other invaluable assistance."

"Well, it's certainly very good to meet you, Levi Thorne," her mother said, bowing to Levi as if he were a foreign dignitary.

"We're certainly grateful for any help you've given our daughter," her father added, with his own bow. "We owe you a debt."

"Oh… not at all," Levi said, lowering his eyebrows from where they'd risen on his forehead – but then, Margot supposed, he just wasn't used to magical world formalities.

And she supposed that it was a bit awkward for him, given that he was meeting her parents for the first time *and* they had no idea that he and Margot were mates, but that was probably a conversation best saved for another time. There was already enough going on today without bringing *that* into the equation – and this was supposed to be a formal examination event, after all.

Although maybe they'd give me a passing grade just to congratulate me for finding such a spectacular man.

"He's a chimera shifter and familiar with magic users," Margot said, "so you can talk freely around him. There are also some other shifters in this town, including some who assisted with the location and identification of the *flos nivis*, but most of the townspeople are human."

Professor Imari nodded. "You have created a network of contacts within a short timeframe," he said approvingly. "That is a fine skill for a magic user to cultivate."

She detected the slightest hint of a smile at the corner of Levi's mouth, and had to restrain a smile of her own. She supposed that Professor Imari, enchanted with human culture as he was, would be *au fait* with the human concept of 'networking'.

In any case, she wanted to get this over and done with as

ZOE CHANT

quickly as possible – even with the calming presence of the mate bond, her stomach was still tying itself up in knots. Now that everyone was here, it had suddenly become much more real.

Margot smiled tightly. "If you would all please follow me inside, I can show you the flower that I believe to be the *flos nivis*."

"Please, lead the way," Professor Imari said, and the five of them traipsed through the snow to the front of the shop. Margot knew that the others would normally levitate themselves over any such obstacles, but they were being discreet in case any regular humans happened to be nearby. She wondered how they were faring, having to use their physical muscles instead of their magical ones! One upside of being so bad at magic, she supposed, was that she was much more practiced at doing the hard physical slog than many people she knew.

"Oh, this place is *charming*," her mother said as they entered, and her father nodded approvingly as he gazed around.

"I could definitely spend some time looking through these books," her father said, examining a shelf. "Some of them appear to be quite ancient, and possibly self-published at that. Some of the most innovative writings have come from those who could not find someone to publish them, but who wrote out their life's work anyway, in the hope that someone else would read it in later years."

Margot's mother turned to face them. "Do you own this store, Levi? It's quite impressive."

Levi's face twitched into an unreadable expression, as he obviously tried to work out how much to say. "I inherited it just recently, so I'm still trying to work out exactly what to do with all of it," he said eventually. "I had no idea that it was potentially made from a rare magical wood, I can tell you

148

CHIMERAS AND CHRISTMAS CAKES

that much." He gestured toward the back of the store. "If you'd like to head this way, Margot can show you the site of her discovery."

Margot followed the rest of the group, grateful to Levi for turning the tide of the conversation back toward the *flos nivis*. The anticipation was killing her!

"Oh, hello Monty," said her father as they reached the area where the beam was located, and Monty was waiting for them. Her father leaned down, giving him a scratch behind the ear, before pausing for moment, before glancing toward Levi. "Ah…"

"It's okay," Margot said. "He can see Monty."

Her parents exchanged a confused glance, but then, apparently, waved it off as something that would be best left until later.

Margot invited everyone to sit and then poured some cups of tea, lifting the pot telekinetically and managing not to spill any despite her nerves – it was a mere trifle as far as magic went, but she thought it best to demonstrate that she at least had the basics down pat.

Professor Imari sipped his tea, sighing in satisfaction, before getting down to business. "So, Margot," he said with a patient smile. "Please tell us all about this discovery of yours. We're all extremely excited to hear about it."

Standing slowly, Margot took a slow breath in and out. *This is it.*

"Well," she said, the tremble in her voice barely perceptible, "as you are aware, for my research project I've endeavored to discover the location of the *flos nivis*, renowned throughout the ages for its many and varied magical properties. After having spent many weeks deep in research, I narrowed down its most likely location to the Mountain of Sources – which, I believe, is located here in Girdwood Springs."

149

ZOE CHANT

Professor Imari's eyebrows shot up his forehead, resembling nothing so much as two furry caterpillars arching their backs. "This here is the Mountain of Sources?"

"Just over there a little," Margot said, indicating with her hand. "What I believe to be the actual Mountain is a couple of hours' walk south of here... or about ten minutes via chimera."

Professor Imari shook his head in astonishment. "The location of the Mountain of Sources has been lost for generations. If you *have* managed to rediscover it, that would be quite the feather in your cap. Further proof would be required, however."

Margot exhaled a shaky breath. *So far, so good.*

She chanced a glance over at her parents. They looked excited, interested. Even hopeful.

If I could live up to that hope, it would be a marvelous thing.

She plowed on.

"While we were able to locate a tree that appeared to be the *flos nivis* during a spell of extreme cold weather, it was too young to yet be flowering."

The disappointment was plain on her parents' faces – not disappointment *in* her, but disappointment *for* her. She hoped that it wouldn't remain there long.

Professor Imari regarded her thoughtfully. "If indeed it is a *flos nivis*, then it may provide us with the flower's remarkable properties in time; however, by all accounts it is a very slow tree to grow. It could be generations before it can prove useful to us."

Margot nodded. She knew that, while an interesting discovery on its own, it was not necessarily enough for her to earn her qualifications... especially if she couldn't identify it beyond a doubt.

"Are you certain that this tree was the *flos nivis?*" Professor Imari continued.

CHIMERAS AND CHRISTMAS CAKES

"Certainly it met all of the other criteria," Margot replied. "The color and shape of the foliage, as well as the bark and the general shape of the tree, were an exact match to all of the accounts. But I am aware that without the presence of the flower, it may not be enough for absolute confirmation."

She looked over at Levi for a moment. The love and encouragement in his eyes was enough to keep her going.

"However," she said, "if you would like to direct your eyes upward for a moment…"

Confused, the Professor and her parents stared at her for a moment, before following her pointed finger. She heard several gasps.

"Could it be…?" whispered the professor. Rising from his chair, he levitated up toward the beam for a closer look, quickly followed by her parents.

Margot looked up as well, her heart in her throat. Above her, three snow flower buds were in the process of unfurling. Two of them were only slightly open, but the third one was large and glorious, its blue-edged petals almost seeming luminous in the gloom.

With evident difficulty, Professor Imari tore his gaze away from the flower for long enough to look down at her, bewilderment evident on his face. "The *flos nivis* is growing out of your friend's *bookshop?!*"

"It would appear so," Margot said, still feeling a little bewildered about it herself. "As best as we can tell, the local populace must have used the wood of the *flos nivis* back when it was more abundant, unaware of its magical properties."

"Fascinating," the professor murmured, turning back to the flowers, studying them intently. "Levi, did you say your name was?" he asked, still staring at the flowers. "Do you know whether the previous owner of this store was aware of its… rather *unique* properties?"

Levi shrugged. "I honestly couldn't say. She never

151

ZOE CHANT

mentioned it, but then again, she pretty much kept herself to herself."

"A unicorn shifter has also moved into this town in recent years," Margot added, "so it may be that his presence has also influenced its sudden growth."

"A unicorn shifter!" Professor Imari exclaimed, shaking his head. "This town is full of surprises."

"He's going to assist me in researching it further," Margot added, barely daring to let the feeling of hope grow inside her. "He also gave me this, to provide to you."

Hands shaking, she reached into her tote and slowly, carefully, pulled out a gently glowing orb.

Holding it out in outstretched hands, she watched as the three witches and wizards descended to the ground to inspect it.

Inside the orb, protected from the ravages of time, was the original *flos nivis* flower that Gale had so carefully cut for her.

"Here," she said, holding out the orb. Professor Imari's eyes glimmered in its pale golden light. "This is the first flower that bloomed. I have protected it with an ageless spell, but you may wish to bolster it, since as you know, living organisms are tricky things to keep from aging."

Even as she spoke, she could feel the orb's power increase as Professor Imari strengthened it, taking it carefully from her hands.

"You have outdone yourself, Margot," he said, barely taking his eyes off the flower within the orb. Margot could hardly say she blamed him – she'd had several days to get used to it, and she still found it entrancing. "I think it's safe to say that you have most definitely passed."

"What?!" Margot exclaimed, barely daring to believe what she thought she'd heard. He'd just said it so casually! "Do you really mean that?"

152

CHIMERAS AND CHRISTMAS CAKES

"Of course I mean it," Professor Imari said. "This will revolutionize the way we practice magic."

Margot stood there, vaguely aware that her mouth was hanging open, but utterly unable to do anything about it.

I've passed? Me? I'm a witch?! A real, proper, full-fledged witch?!

With a smile, Professor Imari waved his hand, and Margot suddenly found herself enclosed in a robe of deep navy blue, a tall, pointed hat appearing upon her head.

In wonder, she raised her hand to touch its wide brim, scarcely daring to believe it was real, before running her hands over the gold trim of the dark blue gown that lay over her shoulders.

I passed! I'm a witch!!

"You are now the recipient of the Diploma of Magic," Professor Imari declared, and an ornate scroll popped into her hand. Feebly, she grabbed at it before it could hit the floor, her fingers slack in shock.

Strong hands wrapped gently around hers, keeping the scroll intact, and she looked up – to see Levi smiling at her. It was a bigger, more unguarded smile than she had ever seen from him, and she couldn't help but smile back.

"This is real, right?" she whispered.

His smile broadened even further, if that was possible.

"It sure is," he said, and the next thing she knew, his arms were around her, holding her up.

She clung to him, eyes brimming over with happy tears.

"Thank you," she murmured. *"Thank you."*

"Make sure to thank yourself as well," Levi replied. "You deserve it."

She could've held on to him forever, but after a long moment he pulled back, and it was only with disappointment that she managed to release her hold on him. After a second, though, she realized why he'd given her space, as the next

153

ZOE CHANT

thing she knew, she was being attacked from all sides – both of her parents were hugging her fiercely, barely leaving her with enough air to breathe.

Or maybe she just couldn't breathe because she was so deliriously happy.

I'm a witch. I did it.

She was vaguely aware amongst all of this that Monty was rubbing up against her legs. It was probably the closest he would ever get to actually expressing relief and gratitude, but she was more than happy to take it.

I would pet you right now, but it's a bit impossible, she thought to him.

Perhaps later you can give me some fish, since you're feeling so generous, he replied.

All the months – *years*, really – of tension and uncertainty suddenly fell away, and Margot felt almost hollow. The stress had taken up so much space within her that, she suddenly realized, there hadn't been a whole lot of room for much else. She'd been so focused on becoming a witch, even though she knew she wasn't very good at it and wouldn't be able to work successfully at it, that she hadn't thought much about what she *wanted* to do.

She had Monty, now. She had Levi. She had the satisfaction of locating the *flos nivis* and passing her degree. But where to now?

"We're so proud of you, my sweetpea," her dad said, only slightly releasing his vise-like hug.

"Very, very proud," her mom echoed, pushing Margot's hair back from her face and cupping her cheek, tears glistening in her eyes.

"Thank you, both of you," she said honestly. "You both believed in me and helped me so much, and I couldn't have done it without you. I know it can't be easy, having a child who's so bad at magic."

CHIMERAS AND CHRISTMAS CAKES

Her parents looked aghast. "Don't say that!" her mother exclaimed. "It was only hard in that it was hard to see you hurting so much when it didn't come naturally to you. But it's never been hard to have you as our daughter."

Her father nodded in agreement. "Of course we would never think that, Margot."

"Thank you," Margot said again, meaning it, feeling her throat closing up, her eyes growing damp. She blinked, trying to hold back her tears. As horrible and stressful as things had been, she knew she should always be grateful for having had such supportive parents.

"This discovery really will revolutionize magic," her mother went on. "We can't wait for you to come back and continue your studies! So many doors will open for you now."

Margot took a deep breath. She hadn't had much opportunity to think about these things consciously over the past few days, but on a more unconscious level, she'd realized that she knew exactly what it was that she had to do with her life.

"Actually," she said haltingly, "I... I think I want to stay out here in the non-magical world for a while."

It would have been funny, in any other situation, how round her parents' eyes went.

"B-but darling," her mom said after a short, shocked silence, "why on earth would you want to do that? Becoming a witch is all you ever wanted, and you can't do that out here."

"I – I *thought* it was what I wanted," Margot said slowly, picking her words carefully. "But I think I just wanted the idea of not failing at it. Of not disappointing you both."

Her parents looked bewildered. "Disappointing us?" her father said. "You could never disappoint us."

Margot shook her head. "I know how much it meant to you both that I graduate. Especially given your own standing

155

within the community." Her voice dropped to a near-whisper in shame. "How could you be taken seriously, if your own daughter couldn't even pass her basic studies? And you were so supportive of me, always helping, always encouraging – I didn't want to let you down."

"Is that what you think?!" her mother asked, horrified. "We only supported and encouraged you because we thought it was what you wanted! You always seemed so determined."

"But that was for you –" Margot began, before she cut herself off, fighting the urge to slap herself on the forehead.

Had they really all just been entirely misinterpreting each other this whole time?! Had her parents really only fretted about her poor grades and gotten her tutors and spent so much time trying to help her because they'd thought it was what *she* wanted, while all the time she'd only been pouring so much effort and stress into it because she wanted to please *them*?

She'd always been so terrified of disappointing them – and she'd thought they'd *wanted* her to do well in her studies. But it seemed like they'd been misunderstanding each other the whole time. Perhaps they'd been just as terrified of disappointing her by not being supportive of something she seemed to want as she was of disappointing them.

Her father sighed, just a hint of good-natured exasperation in the sound. "Clearly we all need to work on our communication skills."

"Clearly," Margot murmured, shaking her head. If only they'd all spoken their minds *years* ago.

"But… are you sure you won't come back?" her mother asked. "You clearly have an aptitude for the research side of things. You managed to re-discover the location of the Mountain of Sources after all these years. You could make all kinds of wonderful discoveries."

"I'm sure I could," Margot said firmly – the words didn't

CHIMERAS AND CHRISTMAS CAKES

come naturally to her, but she wanted to try to start putting into practice the self-confidence that Levi had been assuring her she deserved to have. "But right now, I have other things I want to do."

Should I tell them now? she wondered, before deciding, *Well, what the heck. I might as well.* Best to clear up any misconceptions now, if they were going to try to communicate more clearly.

Steeling herself, she pressed on. "I've decided that I'd like to tidy up this bookstore and run it with Levi," she said, raising her chin determinedly. "I would like to do so anyway, but, also… Mother, Father, I have to tell you that Levi is my mate. As I mentioned, he's a chimera shifter and… he realized that we share that bond. And for now at least, I feel that I want to stay here. With him."

Her parents took it remarkably well, really – there were some raised eyebrows and surprised mutterings, and they exchanged a quick glance. But then, apparently, they came to an accord.

Once again, her father smiled and hugged her again, followed by her mother.

Three hugs in one day! Margot thought, a little dazed.

"If that's *actually* what would make you happy, sweetpea, then of course you have to do it," her father said, looking at her with slightly misty eyes. "I can't say I'm not surprised. But as you know, some of our best friends have mate bonds with shifters, and we've never seen them anything other than deliriously happy with each other. And I know we've only just met, but this Levi seems like a good sort. And I'm glad you finally have found the thing you *really* want to do."

"Just as long as you promise to come visit from time to time?" her mother asked, putting her hands on Margot's shoulders, her own eyes looking a little damp.

"Of course," Margot promised. "And you'll have to come

ZOE CHANT

visit me, too. There are so many wondrous things out here that I'd like to show you!"

Her parents looked a little dubious – they *had* lived their lives within the magical realm, after all, so it would probably take them a bit of time to get used to it – but they nodded.

Margot practically felt weak with relief. All of this had gone better than she had ever dared believe.

But, she realized, there was one more person to thank.

She turned to Professor Imari.

"Thank you for giving me this chance, and for believing in me," she said sincerely. "You didn't have to do that. Especially since I, uh, set your beard on fire."

Professor Imari smiled. "You have always had talent and dedication, Margot. It's just that your skills lie in a slightly different area. There is no shame in that."

Margot smiled. As unpleasant and stressful as her studies had been, she thought that perhaps they had helped to make her the person she was today and bring her to this wonderful point in her life.

And if things hadn't happened just the way they had, then she never would have met Levi, she thought, as she turned to him with shining eyes. He'd been standing back, letting her have her moment of glory – but now, he came to stand by her side, warm and solid and comforting.

Still, she was glad to finally be graduating, and not having to worry about… well, *any* of the things she'd spent the last six years worrying about. The idea that she could live her day-to-day life without having this constant fear of failure hanging over her head was going to take some getting used to.

"Oh, one more thing," she said, suddenly remembering, and she reached into her tote. "Here – it's a bonus. We found this up on the mountain as well, with some help from the locals – Kira,

158

a human park ranger, and Caleb, a dragon shifter. I wasn't entirely sure that I could trust my own abilities with containment spells in this instance, so I have used something that Levi tells me is called 'Tupperware' to seal its deadliness away."

She handed the container to Professor Imari, who took it, his brows pinching together in confusion.

"What is this…?" he asked, before understanding dawned on his face. "Is this… is this the *aurum lacunosa*?! The curse-breaking mushroom?"

Behind her, her parents gasped. A pink glow quickly appeared around the Tupperware, encasing the deadly fungus in the container within several layers of protection.

"You really have outdone yourself," Professor Imari breathed, lifting the mushroom to stare at it with great intensity. "I do think that you may have located the Mountain of Sources. The chances of both these plants being at the same location otherwise would be so small as to be negligible."

I did it, then? I located the Mountain of Sources?!

Margot was almost dizzy with relief, the proud smiles of everyone else in the room making her feel deliriously happy. She practically collapsed down onto one of the chairs, smiling gratefully when everyone else followed suit, as if they had all been planning on sitting down.

"How about some cake to celebrate?" she said with a shaky but relieved smile, removing the ageless spell from Sylvie's spread.

"No more from you," Levi said, hopping back up to slice and serve the cake, and pour more tea. "You just take a break."

And so she did, relaxing back into the chair and listening to the chatter around her, watching Professor Imari gazing in wonder at her discoveries, her mother and father leaning

over to Levi to start getting to know him better – and he them.

Everything is perfect, she thought happily. *I never could have imagined that things would work out this well. Perhaps this is my own Christmas miracle.*

EPILOGUE

*S*ylvie burst in through the door of the diner with a precarious tower of boxes in her arms, snowflakes falling off her hair and tumbling onto the ground. A heavenly smell followed her in, and Margot took a moment to inhale deeply.

"All done, finally!" Sylvie exclaimed, as she dumped the boxes on the nearest table. "All the customers have picked up their orders for tomorrow, and everything the rest of us need is right here."

"You're an absolute gem, Sylvie," said Natasha as she checked over the boxes, looking for the one with her name on it. It was enormous, but Margot knew that its contents were also for the guests at her B&B. Not that she would have blamed her if she'd wanted the whole lot for herself!

Well, for herself, and her mate, Kieran. There were many shifters and their mates in Girdwood Springs, it seemed, and Margot was still getting to know them all.

For now, though, she was concentrating on the excitement of trying her first-ever hot dog. She didn't know what they were and had no idea what to expect, but Levi had been

ZOE CHANT

singing their praises all day. He had also assured her that they were not, in fact, actual dogs, which had been a relief.

In any case, there *was* an actual dog here – a scrawny, outrageously silly-looking dog that went by the name of Fillmore, who was currently yapping and darting about, trying to catch the invisible cat that *he* could apparently see, but the others couldn't. It seemed that it was simply the mate bond that rendered Monty visible to Levi, rather than the fact that he was a shifter, and so Monty remained invisible to the others in the room unless he chose to reveal himself.

He *had*, however, apparently chosen to make himself visible to Fillmore, for the sole purpose of driving the little dog insane – though insane with fun, Margot was relieved to say.

Fillmore was bounding around, trying desperately to catch Monty's tail, which Monty was flicking about just out of his reach from atop a bar stool.

Margot didn't think that the others were quite used to her familiar yet – Levi had definitely gotten some strange looks when he'd started talking to Monty and offered him a piece of chicken! Monty, being Monty, had refused to make himself visible in order to save poor Levi the embarrassment of having to explain, but Levi had dealt with it rather well in the end.

She was proud of him. He still wasn't exactly particularly *social*, but he had definitely loosened up a lot since she first met him. Being able to fully experience life as a chimera shifter had made him so much happier.

And, she liked to think, meeting *her* had contributed toward his happiness as well. Certainly it had contributed toward hers.

"Three hot dogs, coming up!" said Henry, the hellhound shifter behind the counter, as he slid two plates toward them. Alarmed, Margot caught hers, worried that it would

CHIMERAS AND CHRISTMAS CAKES

just continue sliding down the counter and end up on the floor. She definitely didn't want Henry's hard work to go to waste!

She looked down at her meal, trying to work out how she felt about it. It definitely *smelled* good, all kinds of hot meat and bread and oil smells, and she *did* recognize some of the elements, such as the onions and the pickles. And she was always up for something new, even if it *was* Christmas Eve and this definitely *wasn't* Christmas food.

Confused, she looked around for some cutlery to eat it with, wondering if she should ask Henry for some. But then she heard Levi's gentle laugh beside her.

"Like this," he said, picking up one of his hot dogs in his hands and taking a large bite from the end. He started chewing and his eyes slid closed in bliss, the happy sound he made sounding almost obscene.

"Oh," Margot said in understanding, picking up her own hot dog and taking a careful bite. Ketchup and mustard squirted out the other end as she bit down, but she didn't even care, because Levi had been right – these *were* amazing, the meat hot and juicy in her mouth, the salty flavors bursting on her tongue.

"Mmph," she said, taking another bite before she had quite finished the first one. It was just so good!

She only managed to stop because she wanted to try one of the 'fries' that was on the side of the plate – she'd heard that they were excellent as well. And it was definitely true – the first one she popped into her mouth was quickly followed by another, then three more, then a fistful. The hot, salty crunchiness was just addictive, and she had to force herself to take a break for a minute so that she could let her food settle.

"Good, aren't they?" Levi said with a smile.

Margot nodded enthusiastically, jamming some fries

ZOE CHANT

inside the hot dog bun so that she could enjoy all the flavors at once.

"If you order some more," she said, "I can put them in my bag for later. That way, we don't have to leave the house over the next few days if we don't want to."

She'd meant it in a *mostly* innocent fashion, but Levi's eyes gleamed. "That's the best idea I've heard all day," he said, and he called over Henry to put in an order of truly gargantuan proportions.

Further down the counter, Henry's mate, Luna, had a look on her face like she was surprised but trying very hard not to show it.

Luckily, Levi seemed to know exactly what was going on and how to deal with it. "Magical storage," he clarified. "They'll come out just as good as they went in."

Luna seemed to take the explanation in stride, looking confused for a moment before nodding in understanding. "Sounds useful – I'd love to have something that did that."

"I could make you one, if you like," Margot offered. She would have done so anyway, but it was also Christmas, after all – and if she'd learned anything, it was that Christmas was a time when generosity was particularly welcomed.

Luna blinked, before her face broke out in a smile. "Well, if you're really offering, then I'm not going to say no! I would absolutely love that, thank you. I'd love to be able to carry some especially delicious or hard-to-find food around for a few days to try it again – or just make sure I've always got a snack on hand! But is there anything I can get for you in return?"

"It would be my pleasure," Margot beamed. "And you don't have to get me anything – just being here and enjoying Christmas Eve with all of you is present enough. Besides, your dog is keeping my familiar entertained, as much as he

would never admit it, so that counts as a present in my book."

They watched as Fillmore continued to leap around, seemingly chasing nothing. Margot knew that Monty could go up high or leave the building if he wanted, so the fact that he was indulging Fillmore was a positive sign that he was enjoying his company.

"So, how's the bookstore going?" Luna asked. "I can't wait to come in and have a look once it's done."

"It's going really great," said Margot, beaming. "Well… sometimes I get distracted while doing stocktake and I pick up a book to see what it's about, and I end up reading the whole thing. But other than that, it's really good."

"We're going to try to keep most of the character of the place, while just cleaning up and modernizing a couple of things," Levi added. "Getting lost in a bookstore is one thing, but getting taken out by a collapsing bookshelf or choking on the dust is another."

"We really have no idea how to run a bookstore," Margot admitted. "But Levi is showing me how to use this 'internet' of yours, and also my parents have a lot of knowledge of libraries, so at least they can provide some information in terms of how to arrange things so that people can find them."

Levi nodded. "Half the people in this room run businesses, so we've been getting advice from them as well. And I've been in touch with Great Aunt Aida, so I might be able to check in with her if I need to… provided she can find the time to get back to us."

Levi's Great Aunt Aida, it turned out, had also learned how to shift recently, with her ornery chimera apparently becoming more mellow now that it had met its mate. A couple of postcards had shown up in the past week, and Levi had marveled at how happy she seemed. Of course, he'd

ZOE CHANT

explained, he'd been just a kid when she left, so he hadn't really understood then why she'd done it.

But finding your mate and learning how to shift, no matter what age you are when it happens... let's just say I think I can understand how she feels, Levi had explained.

It felt like everything was just coming together perfectly. Margot could hardly believe how unhappy she'd been a few short weeks ago, and how wonderful everything was now. She finished off the last of her hotdog, licking the ketchup and mustard off her fingers.

Sylvie slid onto the stool next to Levi, passing over a box that was presumably full of cake. "And this is for the two of you! Merry Christmas!"

"Sylvie, you shouldn't have," Levi groaned good-naturedly. "We still haven't finished the last lot you gave us!"

"You must almost be done with them by now, though," Sylvie grinned. "Besides, I have it on good authority that they'll keep for a long time."

"That is true," Levi admitted. "Thank you, Sylvie. And Merry Christmas." The Christmas well-wishes sounded genuine, rather than having been drawn out of him on pain of some terrible torture, and it warmed Margot's heart to see Levi enjoying Christmas.

Suddenly, she remembered something she'd been curious about.

"Oh!" she cried, sitting up straighter on her bar stool. "Sylvie! Which Christmas cake won the poll?"

Sylvie rolled her eyes dramatically. "Would you believe it was a three-way tie?"

"Honestly? I would," said Luna. "They were all amazing. I had to close my eyes and pick one randomly in the end."

"Well, you still did a better job than Margot here," Sylvie said, her eyes narrowed in mock anger. "She circled all three options."

166

CHIMERAS AND CHRISTMAS CAKES

"Is that not how things work here?" asked Margot, doing her best to radiate innocence.

"You know it's not," laughed Sylvie. "But that's okay. The only reason I put it up for a vote was because I couldn't decide, so I guess it makes sense that no one else could decide, either."

"Well, I voted for the chocolate, so you'd better have rewarded me for my decisiveness," Levi said, gesturing at the box.

Sylvie's eyes sparkled with mischief. "I guess you'll just have to find out."

"I guess so."

The evening passed in laughter and fun, Henry stuffing Margot's tote full of delicious-smelling food while the older lady who ran the diner, Eula, was out of the room – apparently she was the only person here who was unaware of shifters or magic, though Margot got the impression that she had probably caught on that there was *something* going on with everyone, and knew more than she let on. *Everyone here has their secrets,* she'd said to Margot with a knowing smile. *Even me.*

Margot was having such a delightful time, and part of her wished that this night could stretch on forever... but the other part of her *really* wanted to head back to the home she shared with Levi, so they could be back in time to celebrate when the clock ticked over to midnight. It would be her first Christmas, and she wanted to spend it with Levi.

She looked up to catch Levi's eye, and he nodded, understanding her at once.

"I think it's time we headed off," he announced, standing up and pulling on his coat. Margot followed suit, lifting her tote, now full of enough food to probably last them a year, let alone a few days.

"Thank you, everyone – I truly mean it," she said, smiling

167

ZOE CHANT

and waving to everyone. "These past few days have been wonderful, and I cannot wait to see you all again. I hope you all have a very merry Christmas!"

The others responded in kind, calling out well-wishes, and Margot turned to where Monty was curled up, quite visible now, with Fillmore, the two of them snuggling together on a rug in the corner of the room. Monty had gotten quite the amount of attention once he'd stopped being invisible, and it had absolutely gone to his head.

"Come on now," she said, and Monty opened one yellow eye, before closing it again. She sighed. "Or don't. You know the way home. But you'll miss out on your Christmas treat. I guess I'll have to eat that fish all by myself."

I was just about to get up anyway, Monty told her tetchily as he dragged himself to his feet, arching his back and stretching like he didn't have a care in the world.

Of course you were, she replied soothingly.

"Good night," she called out as the three of them left, a little flurry of snow entering the diner as they exited.

It was perfectly wonderful to wander the fairy-lit late-night street, snowflakes drifting dreamily down from the clouds, Monty chugging his way through snowbanks like they were no impediment whatsoever. She leaned against Levi's side, simply enjoying his warmth while everything else was so cold. She knew that she could cast a warming spell if she needed to, but it was so much nicer like this.

She couldn't wait for tomorrow! They were going to cook a turkey with all the trimmings – she even knew what they were, now – and she was so looking forward to making roast potatoes, and glazed parsnips, and all other kinds of wonderful things. She couldn't guarantee that they'd be *good*, but they'd be made with Levi, and that was all that mattered.

They reached the bookstore both too quickly and not quickly enough – she would've been happy to stay out in the

CHIMERAS AND CHRISTMAS CAKES

snow forever, but also Levi had promised to make her eggnog, and she *did* really want to try that!

Stomping the snow off her boots before unlacing them and taking them off, she headed inside, enjoying the relative warmth even as she missed the snow.

Well, I shall be seeing you in the morning for my promised fish, Monty said, as he bounded away into the shelves, to where Levi and Margot had set up a cozy little cat bed for him, and where he seemed to prefer to spend the cold winter evenings. *Do not disappoint me!*

As Margot shook her head fondly, Levi bent down – and when he rose, he'd picked up a letter that had clearly been delivered earlier in the day and had been lying just inside the entryway. As he turned it over and read who it was from, Margot saw his eyebrows rise slightly in surprise.

"What is it?" she asked.

"It's from my family," he said after a moment, hesitating before opening up the envelope.

Inside, there was a card with a jaunty Santa on the front and text that read *WISHING YOU HAPPY HO-HO-HOLI-DAYS!* She didn't quite understand it, but presumably it made some kind of sense to those in the know.

Levi opened the card with a mild expression of trepidation, but as he read, his face relaxed.

"What did they say?" she asked, when he'd closed the card again. "If it's something you wish to speak of, of course."

"No, it's okay," said Levi with a small smile. "My family were just saying that they're happy for the two of us, and are wishing us well for the holidays."

His expression turned thoughtful. "I feel like I have a different perspective on Christmas, now – like I could enjoy spending it with my family." He quickly continued, "But I want to spend this one just with you in our home, of course. But maybe in the future, we could spend a Christmas with

169

my family? If you like?" He sounded almost tentative, but there was nothing Margot thought she would enjoy more than a big family Christmas… except for a small, intimate Christmas with Levi right now, of course.

"I would love nothing more," she said reassuringly.

"Maybe we could go there for New Year's Eve," he mused. "Chimeras aren't quite so obsessive about that, so at least it wouldn't be a huge party – just a nice opportunity to meet everyone and have a good time."

"That sounds wonderful," she said, already excited at the possibility. "But you will have to obtain some party poppers! And a pair of novelty glasses with the year on them!"

Levi laughed. "I can definitely do that. But enough talk about my family – let's just enjoy each other's company tonight."

"Yes, let's," she agreed.

They headed toward the staircase, wending their way through the now somewhat less crowded bookshelves, and paused to admire the snow flowers that sprung forth from the ceiling beam. There were five of them now, in full bloom on this cold, cold night, their petals almost sparkling with a crystalline brilliance that reminded Margot of frost.

"They would be beautiful anyway," she murmured, "but they will always hold a special place in my heart because of how they brought us together."

Levi nodded. "I don't want to even think about what kind of miserable night I'd be having if you hadn't walked into my life. I love you, Margot. My mate."

"My mate," she replied dreamily, leaning into his warmth once more.

They admired the flowers for a few moments longer, before continuing up the stairs.

"You just sit yourself down," Levi said, "and I'll make you some eggnog. My family's recipe is fairly simple, but that just

CHIMERAS AND CHRISTMAS CAKES

means that it's harder to screw it up. I like to think it still comes out tasting pretty good."

"I'm sure it'll be perfect," said Margot truthfully, as she got a small fire going in the fireplace – using kindling and matches, not magic! – and then settled down on the battered old couch. It wasn't fancy, but it was comfortable, and it was perfectly positioned for watching the snowflakes whirling outside the window.

She reached into her tote and pulled out the original box of cakes that Sylvie had given her, now mostly empty, and opened it up. One of the remaining cakes was the traditional Christmas cake that Sylvie had given her. She'd been saving it up until the time was right – and she felt that that time was now.

Pulling out two plates and some knives, she laid the cakes out, slicing herself a piece of the Christmas cake. It was loaded with fruit, and it smelt absolutely divine.

At that moment Levi returned, carrying two steaming cups of eggnog, the sweet, gently spiced scent carrying across the room.

"This smells lovely," she said, as she gratefully accepted the warm cup. She took a careful sip, and it was perfect – not overly heavy or cloying, with just the right amount of sweetness and spice… and, of course, a dash of alcohol, which warmed her up from the inside out.

"Mmm," she said, closing her eyes for a moment in happiness. "This really is wonderful, thank you. I'm so glad I got to drink nog with you at Christmas."

"My pleasure," said Levi, sounding almost a little embarrassed at the praise.

She reached for the slice of Christmas cake – it seemed like something that would go well with the eggnog.

At the first bite, she knew that she had been correct. The cake, like the others, was a rich, spiced perfection – the